Footballer

My Story

www.**transworldbooks**.co.uk

Footballer
My Story

Kelly Smith
with Lance Hardy

BANTAM PRESS

LONDON · TORONTO · SYDNEY · AUCKLAND · JOHANNESBURG

TRANSWORLD PUBLISHERS
61–63 Uxbridge Road, London W5 5SA
A Random House Group Company
www.transworldbooks.co.uk

First published in Great Britain
in 2012 by Bantam Press
an imprint of Transworld Publishers

A CIP catalogue record for this book
is available from the British Library.

ISBNs 9780593069332 (cased)
9780593070222 (tpb)

Addresses for Random House Group Ltd companies outside the UK
can be found at: www.randomhouse.co.uk
The Random House Group Ltd Reg. No. 954009

The Random House Group Limited supports the Forest Stewardship Council
(FSC®), the leading international forest-certification organization. Our books
carrying the FSC label are printed on FSC®-certified paper. FSC is the only
forest-certification scheme endorsed by the leading environmental
organizations, including Greenpeace. Our paper procurement policy
can be found at www.randomhouse.co.uk/environment

Typeset in 11.5/16pt Sabon by
Falcon Oast Graphic Art Ltd.
Printed and bound in Great Britain by
Clays Ltd, Bungay, Suffolk

2 4 6 8 10 9 7 5 3 1

MIX
Paper from
responsible sources
FSC
www.fsc.org   FSC® C016897

Contents

1	Harvester Hangover	1
2	Girls and Boys	5
3	Arsenal, England and the USA	18
4	She's Leaving Home	28
5	Success in a Number 6 Shirt	38
6	1999 And All That	45
7	The American Dream	52
8	Highs and Lows in Philadelphia	63
9	Numbing the Pain	73
10	Rock Bottom	85
11	A Gunner Again	95
12	Football's Coming Home	102
13	The Invincibles	115
14	Kiss This	125
15	Jonathan Ross, Take That and the Queen	142
16	Pelé, Ronaldo and Torres	152
17	Boston Calling	160
18	The Year of Truth	173
19	So Near Yet So Far	190
20	Journey to Germany	203

21	Penalty Shoot-Out Heartbreak	223
22	Hope	237
23	Arsenal Part III	251
24	A Stupid Mistake	260
25	London 2012	266

Kelly Smith's England Career Statistics	279
Acknowledgements	283
Picture Acknowledgements	285
Index	287

Footballer

My Story

1

Harvester Hangover

WATFORD TO LOUGHBOROUGH IS A PRETTY STRAIGHTFORWARD car journey. It is less than a hundred miles in distance and it's M1 all the way. It should take two hours at the most on a good day.

But today is not a good day. Today is a day I have been dreading for a while. Today is the day I meet up with the England medical staff to assess my recovery from a third serious injury in less than three years. I am worn out and I am worried.

Next year England will host Women's Euro 2005. It is the biggest women's football event ever to be staged in the country and our national coach, Hope Powell, has the best squad the country has ever had. And I am supposedly its star player.

But, at the moment, I can't play football. I can hardly walk. And I can only drive an automatic car, because that does not require me to use both my feet.

The broken leg I suffered six months ago, playing for New Jersey Wildcats against Delaware, is by far the worst injury of my career. So bad, in fact, it could be the end of my career.

It was caused by a reckless challenge from a stupid player who shouldn't even have been on the field. It still haunts me how dirty, vicious and unnecessary it was. I can't accept that. I can't understand that.

I don't know the girl's name and I don't want to know the girl's name. And hardly anybody knows how I have coped with it all. The answer is half a bottle of vodka every night until I just can't function any more. My father knows – that's why he flew over to America to bring me home last month. But elsewhere it remains a secret.

Vodka numbs the pain. Vodka numbs everything. I drink it to feel better within myself, to make me a happier person. After a severe anterior cruciate ligament injury, meniscus damage to my knee and now a serious leg break, plus the fact that the Women's United Soccer Association league in the USA has suddenly folded, I find I need vodka a lot right now.

Lately I have asked myself: What's the point? You have dreams all your life and you work hard to achieve them. Then, one morning, you wake up and it's all gone. I can't comprehend that. I get emotional about it. I think that's because I never really got to show my true potential out in the States – because of all my bad luck with injuries. And what am I supposed to do with my life now? There has been talk of a professional league in England but it hasn't happened yet.

I was born to be a footballer and I still want to be a footballer. I remain confident in my own ability and I still have self-belief. I know the player that I was, I know the potential that I have, and I know the level that I want to reach. But I am finding it so hard mentally to keep going because there is a fear that I am going to get crocked again. And I am struggling to handle that.

I hate not playing football. It is all I have ever wanted to do. Vodka makes me feel better about things. It makes me feel like I am in control. It makes me confident.

I turn off the M1 at junction 23 and head towards Loughborough. This is a town famous for sporting excellence; Lord Sebastian Coe studied and trained here. It is all too much for me to handle. I need to calm myself down. I see a sign for a Harvester pub and I don't need to think about what to do next. I park the car, walk into the bar and order myself a couple of vodkas, and then a couple more. I set about drinking myself into oblivion.

After a while – maybe a few hours – I suddenly decide I am ready to face the England camp after all. So I get back on the road and a few miles later I am there. I am late, but I don't seem to care. Right now, I have a 'fuck it' mentality. It has taken a long time for me to get here, but here I am.

Lois Fidler, an old friend of mine, is one of the few people in my life who knows about my drinking habits. When I see her I find I can't really speak to her properly. Lois immediately recognizes that I am completely out of it so she hides me away in a dorm room to recover. But I have brought a bottle of vodka with me so I continue drinking in there.

Lois informs the medics that I am drunk. So they come to see me. They won't let me out of the room because I am intoxicated and obviously it's not a good thing for people to see me like that. But the secret is out. Hope comes in and has a right go at me.

It is from this point in my life that I will have to accept that I have a problem regarding alcohol. I will soon see that it is a serious issue when a player turns up at camp pissed out of their face. For now, I am told I need to get treatment. So an appointment is arranged for me at the Priory. There's a long road ahead, but afterwards it may be possible for me to one day achieve the dreams I have had all my life – to be the footballer I have always wanted to be.

2

Girls and Boys

I WAS BORN KELLY JAYNE SMITH AT WATFORD GENERAL Hospital on 29 October 1978. *Grease* was the big hit movie of the year, and 'Summer Nights' was number one in the pop charts when I arrived in the world, despite it being a cold autumn day in Hertfordshire.

I was the first child of my devoted and loving parents Bernard and Carol. My brother Glen came along two years later and that's it, that's my family. I lived in the Garston area of Watford until my late teens, when I moved to the United States to play football. So I am a good old Garston girl through and through.

The first address I lived at in Garston was on Fourth Avenue. I went to Lea Farm Junior School, which was just down the street from us, literally five hundred yards away. So it was an easy walk to school every day as a youngster. Later we moved around the corner to Kilby Close. My parents still live in that same house, number 73, today.

Apparently, as soon as I could walk I had a ball at my feet. Mum and Dad tell me I learned to do both at around the same time. On a family holiday in the early 1980s I was seen trudging around the back garden of this house with a plastic ball, shuffling it along the ground with both feet as I toddled along.

As a girl at primary school I was on my own where football was concerned. Most of the girls spent playtime skipping, and playing tag or kiss-chase. But I was never with the girls at playtime. I was always with the boys, playing football.

We played wall ball and other games together. I forget the exact name of this one game – we called it 'King of the Square' or something – but it was all about one-touch football. We also had jumpers for goalposts and played small-sided matches against each other.

There was a big wall at the end of our playground which was very good practice for hitting the ball when you only had one chance to do it. You couldn't take more than one touch so it was just about knocking the ball and then someone else would come in and knock it after you. You had to try to hit the ball as hard as you could, and if the ball went over the wall you were out.

Sometimes we would get some chalk and draw a triangle, a circle or a square on the wall and try and hit the ball into those target areas. As more of a challenge to myself, I would keep score of how many circles and squares I hit. It was more of a competition against the boys that way.

So without knowing it, I was actually working on my skill set from a very young age. That's probably why I am so technical today, because I was always in the playground, in the park or in the back garden playing these sorts of games. I really do think that kick-started my development. I don't think kids these days start off playing those games any more, which is wrong in my view. They seem to play five-a-side a lot but don't practise their skills enough.

I felt this was what I wanted to do from very early on in my life, and I knew I was good at it. The game came naturally to me at a young age. It wasn't something I needed to work on. It was a gift. And gender was never an issue at that age. I never felt unwelcome. I did wish that there were other girls playing because then I wouldn't be the only one. But, sadly, nobody was interested. I suppose it wasn't the done thing back then.

But then, I wasn't seen as a girl by the boys at Lea Farm, I was just Kelly. I was just one of the lads. I was always pretty much one of the first players to be picked too. When we stood in line my name was called out early, so that obviously helped me. I fitted in really easily with them and I played in the school team with them. It was cool.

I can clearly remember playing for the school and thinking that the football pitch was absolutely massive – maybe because we were all so small. Playing on those pitches was constant running and hard work for me. Obviously I had to be quick to beat the boys and get past them. And I did that. But once I had beaten them I still had half of a field to dribble down before I could try and score a goal against what seemed to be a little lad standing in a huge goalmouth. It's funny looking back that the one thing I remember more than anything else from those early days playing football is the size of the pitch.

I played football regularly after school with my friend across the road, Graham Head. He played for Garston Boys

Football Club, and one Sunday morning I went down there to watch him play. Out of the blue Dick Bousefield, who ran the team, asked me if I wanted to play for them. I was made up, it all seemed so exciting. I came home and told my dad that I was in the team. The first team kit I ever played in was the blue and black striped shirts and black shorts of Garston Boys.

That is when football first began to feel a little more serious. I was now wearing a proper kit and playing every Sunday morning against the best of the boys in my area.

I looked like a tomboy back then as I had short hair. Not too many people from the other teams knew that I was a girl. I was just a boy playing in a boys' team, and it carried on like that for a while.

Every Sunday morning without fail I would wake up feeling excited. I was always up early because I knew I was going to be playing football. I can clearly remember dew on the grass and every detail associated with those mornings, on this big football pitch, doing what I loved.

I was always a midfielder or a striker. And at that age I stood out because I was really good with the ball at my feet and dribbling around players, which some of the boys in the team couldn't do. They just weren't as good as me technically so I got noticed a little bit. It was just a lot easier for me to control the ball at my feet than it was for them, and I remember dribbling a lot and scoring a lot of goals for them.

The natural talent was there, but I never stopped training. At home, I had now moved on to kicking the ball up above my head, controlling it and bringing it down. I would also put cones out in a row and do some tight dribbling in and around them. I would practise with a golf ball as well, because it was a lot smaller, and working with it improved my touch. I would play with balls of different sizes and different weights and it all helped to develop my touch.

Garston Boys played eleven-a-side, but it wasn't competitive, just friendlies. I think they got on the phone and arranged their own fixtures as they went along. We played ten teams or so, home and away, from September until the end of the year, then come January new fixtures would be arranged until May.

I remember a game against a side called Evergreen when my dad was standing at the side of the pitch with a man he used to go to school with called Barry Frankham, who was a physio at Barnet at one time. Barry asked him, 'Is your boy out there, Bernard?' And my dad just shook his head, said no, and told him his daughter was. When Barry found out which one I was, he called out to his son, 'Hey Kevin, that's a girl running rings around you!' That's an example of the sort of thing that used to happen in those days.

But I hit my first real problem in football when Garston Boys came to play the teams again in the second half of the season. Suddenly nobody would give us a game if I was playing. As I said, I did dominate a lot of the matches and people were obviously aware of that now. Although, to be honest, I think Dad and I were at first maybe a little bit oblivious to how the skills I had at that stage could stand out on the pitch.

Dick came up to my dad and told him that they had to let me go because they couldn't get any teams to play them. Dad was told that because the games were friendlies there was nothing anybody could do, so that was that.

I was devastated. But when I told the boys at my school what had happened they quickly arranged for me to have a trial at a football club they all played for called Herons. I went along, got selected and played for them for a bit before a similar thing happened down there.

I knew football would continue to be my main sport, though. I lived and breathed it.

I enjoyed other sports too. At the Francis Combe School, which I attended from the age of eleven, I particularly loved Physical Education lessons. I wanted to be active all the time, not just with PE and football but hockey, netball, athletics and rounders as well.

I wasn't so hot on maths. I hated maths. I used to bunk off maths.

We used to have a maths lesson lasting an hour and a half every Monday morning, which I absolutely hated. So I would avoid it at all costs. My Aunt Beryl, my dad's sister, lived around the corner on Coates Way, about fifteen minutes' walk from school. I would leave home as normal but take the key to my aunt's house with me and stop there for a bit during maths. My aunt would already be at work so she never knew about it. I don't think any of my family knew about it! I would just sit there, have some biscuits and watch whatever was on the television, *This Morning* or whatever. I would make it look as though I hadn't been there, of course. I would make sure I put the biscuits back exactly right. If I had a blackcurrant juice I would wipe the cup so there were no stains on it and put it back in the cupboard. I would eventually take myself off to school and bowl up to my next lesson. I would just say I'd had a dentist appointment or something. Nothing ever happened about it.

I was crap at maths. I really struggled with it. I didn't understand why you had to know algebra and x = 1 and all stupid stuff like that. It just did not sit well with my brain. So that was my biggest challenge at school. I didn't mind English and most other subjects. But PE was always my favourite. I just liked being around the PE staff because they were cool people to hang out with. I also knew I was good at sport so I thrived on it.

Football was the game I continued to excel at, but I was also good at netball and I had county trials in that sport while I was at Francis Combe. I liked netball because it was quite similar to football in many respects (apart from using your hands obviously), such as speed of play. It was a fast-paced game with quick one-touch movement but I played goal defence so I was mainly stopping the shots from the opposition rather than scoring goals. If football had not existed it is possible I would have focused on netball because I did enjoy playing it. I hated wearing the skirt though. That wasn't me. I would much rather wear a pair of shorts.

Football was always the winner for me. I was always play-ing football in the house or in the back garden, often with my brother. We had a soft foam ball and we would use the couches for goalposts and play one-on-one. When we broke ornaments and stuff that game got banished, so we used a balloon instead. It was always Glen and me going against each other. It was good fun.

Indoors or outdoors, I always felt very comfortable with a

ball at my feet. I would juggle a hacky sack and knock balls against the garage shed; I would play keepy-uppy by myself and do dribbles in the garden, around the swing, pretending I was on a football field.

Keepy-uppy became a bit of an obsession with me. I used to love counting them all up to see if I could beat my existing record. I would set myself targets too: when I got to fifty, my next goal would be to get to fifty-five. I seemed to spend all my spare time out in the back garden constantly playing with a ball, juggling it or heading it, trying to reach ever higher numbers.

My interest in watching professional football didn't come through Dad but his friend, Russ Crowson. He was the person who took me to my first match, and that was at Highbury. He was an Arsenal fan and I went along with him. I became an Arsenal fan pretty much through that.

It was the early 1990s and Arsenal were on their way to winning the league title again with a great side that included Tony Adams, David O'Leary, Lee Dixon, Nigel Winterburn, Alan Smith, Paul Merson and Paul Davis. I always loved watching Ian Wright too. He joined the Gunners a little later. I liked him so much because of the way he played the game. He wasn't perhaps the most talented footballer but his energy and buzz, and that smile on his face, were just fantastic. He loved to celebrate goals and he always played with such enthusiasm. You could tell that he loved the game, that he was passionate about it. He was the main player for Arsenal for a long time, scoring all the goals.

Wright was my hero, but the player I really wanted to be like was Ryan Giggs. I moulded myself on him. He was left-footed, I was left-footed. He was a winger, I was a winger. He was a good, fast dribbler, I was a good, fast dribbler. He could beat players, I could beat players. He could pick out a cross, and so could I. I saw similarities between him and me, and from the age of thirteen or fourteen I started to try to be more like him.

The Premier League had just started and Manchester United were dominant. I religiously videotaped *Match of the Day* and specifically looked out for Giggs. He would do a move, a turn or a cross during a game and I would literally rewind the tape for hours and practise the same moves with a ball at my feet in my parents' front room. I did that constantly, every day, every week. Time and time again. Mum and Dad would be busy doing their thing – maybe Mum was doing the ironing, maybe Dad was at work – and I would come home from school, put the video on and do that.

There was one boy I remember playing against when I was young who later went on to play against Ryan Giggs. Paul Robinson, who played for St Michael's School at the time, is the same age as me and he played left-back for Watford and West Bromwich Albion before moving on to Bolton Wanderers. He has also been on loan at Leeds United. He now has over five hundred senior appearances to his name, including 227 in the Premier League.

A few years ago the England women's team trained at Bolton before an international match, and as I was getting off the bus I saw Paul and we had a catch-up. He has done really well for himself and carved out a good professional career, which is great. But he is the only boy I played against in my schooldays who made it professionally. There were a couple of other lads who probably could have done but they gave up a long time ago and are now pursuing different careers.

I never gave up, even though after getting kicked off both the Garston Boys and Herons teams I'd decided not to play with or against boys any more. It just didn't feel right. Parents of boys from other teams didn't like the fact that I was a girl, so I couldn't play. I was so upset by that because people were effectively saying that I couldn't do something that I absolutely loved; even worse, they were actively stopping me from doing it.

Looking back, I suppose it was a bit embarrassing for some parents because I was a girl scoring goals in a boys' match. It was a problem for them to see a girl like me dominating a game featuring their sons. The whole thing soured so quickly. It went from 'Who is this wonder kid?' to 'Get her off the team!' There was uproar. I was even shouted at by adults on the touchline at matches and all sorts. It was all very sad and an awful experience for a youngster to go through.

As I had decided that what I wanted to do with my life was play football, Dad approached Watford Ladies. They had no facilities for girls' football but they remained the best option for me at that time. They had a five-a-side team and they played in a league, so I played with them – me, still a girl, and four grown women. They were big women too, aged somewhere between eighteen and thirty I would guess.

I remember going to Ipswich for a five-a-side tournament and they decided to put me in goal so that I wouldn't get hurt! That was their decision, not mine. I wanted to play out on the pitch, but I suppose they were right, I would have got killed. We got to the final and lost 1–0. It was the only goal I conceded that day. I was pleased with my performances and quite domineering in my own little way, protecting my goal. But all the time all I wanted to do was get out on that pitch and show these women what I could do. It's a funny memory because I was so small compared to all the other Watford ladies.

There were boys' teams and there were women's teams but there were no girls' teams on the scene until a lady called Jackie Burns, wife of manager Norman Burns, called my dad one night and told him about Pinner Park. Norman was running a girls' team there and he wanted me to join them. My dad and I were apprehensive about it. We didn't know anything about them. But Debbie Garvey, who had just joined Watford Ladies and was a similar age to me, did know about them.

In the end, both Debbie and I moved to Pinner Park. We were both playing five-a-side for Watford Ladies at the time so that created some animosity between the two teams. Watford didn't like the idea that Pinner Park had taken two young girls from them, despite us being out of our depth over there really. There were simply no facilities for youth football there. At Pinner Park I could play with and against girls of my own age, which suited me much better.

We regularly got to the final of a five-a-side competition which was organized by the Metropolitan Police and held at Wembley Arena every year. That was a very big thing. The former England goalkeeper Ray Clemence presented the trophies. We won that tournament three or four times on the trot. We had a fantastic team, with girls from all over London playing for us. Nobody could touch us.

Pinner Park had progressed to playing eleven-a-side football as well, in the Greater London league. So we played regularly in both five-a-side and eleven-a-side competitions and we became one of the best teams around. Arsenal would have a team in those events as well. Deep down, I always hoped that I would get spotted by Arsenal. But I never heard anything from them and I wasn't the type of person to do anything about it on my own.

I spent about four or five years at Pinner Park in all. It was a good solid grounding for me. Eventually the side amalgamated with Wembley Ladies after Norman moved over to join them. So, essentially, Pinner Park became Wembley Ladies Reserves.

John Jones, who managed Wembley Ladies, wanted me in the first team more or less straight away. But I was still only fifteen years old and just about to sit my GCSE exams at school. We spoke to Norman about it all. He advised me to stay in the reserves for a little while, so that is what I did. As soon as my exams were out of the way and I was heading towards further education, I joined up with the first team at Wembley.

It wasn't the sort of life my heroes like Ian Wright were having but it was as good as it could get for a woman who wanted to be a footballer. The Football Association had finally assumed responsibility for the administration and organization of the women's national league – it was renamed the FA Women's Premier League in 1994 – and the cup competitions. The new league set-up comprised three levels with ten teams in each one. Wembley Ladies were in the top division, so that was good.

But women's football remained an amateur sport in England, and that meant, in essence, that I played it in my spare time, fitting it in around my studies. I had no choice. The game was not what I had hoped or imagined it could be when I was a young girl. There was certainly no money in it.

In fact we had to pay to play the game. At the start of each season I had to hand over a fee, for referees, pitches and so on. It may have had 'Premier League' in its title but it certainly didn't feel Premier League to me.

3

Arsenal, England and the USA

I CAN REMEMBER TELLING THE CAREERS OFFICER WHO CAME TO our school that I might try for the army. This was mainly because I didn't know what else to do for a living. I had always wanted to be a professional footballer in a women's professional league, but as there was no such thing at that time I couldn't see how my dream could come true. One thing was clear: a professional league for women wasn't going to happen in England any time soon. I don't think I was ever serious about the army, I just thought to myself: 'What else can I do?' I considered training to be a firefighter and a policewoman as well. There was also the Physical Education route, which had always interested me.

So from the age of sixteen I went to West Herts College in Watford and studied for a BTEC National Diploma in Sports Science. Football looked like it was going to be no more than a pastime for me. But in my heart there was always that hope of one day being a professional footballer.

Then, during my second year at college, I was spotted playing in the Watford Football Festival – an annual tournament featuring teams from the USA, Denmark,

Germany and Sweden. I was representing Pinner Park that day and we got to play an American team in the final. During the match a guy called Terry Undercoffer got talking to my dad on the touchline and told him that this player for Pinner was a really special talent and that she could probably get a scholarship to go to the States.

That player from Pinner was me.

After the match I met up with Terry and he sold the whole dream package to me: scholarship, education, housing and, of course, football. He told me that I could play football every day!

This was my dream. I was stunned. Obviously I was very interested but I didn't want to leave England at such a young age. I also wanted to finish my BTEC diploma and make sure I had that under my belt before I went anywhere in the world.

But a scholarship like this to the USA did not come around every day. In my eyes it was an opportunity to be a professional athlete because I would be playing football every day, which is all I really wanted to do. The alternative was to stay at home and train on Tuesday and Thursday evenings with my club side. Ultimately, that wasn't enough for me. I wanted to be on a ball each and every day. I needed to be on a ball each and every day.

Three American colleges showed an interest in me: Seton Hall, in New Jersey; Rutgers, in New Jersey; and George Mason, in Virginia. I spoke with all three coaches and I felt most comfortable with the head coach at Seton Hall.

Betty Ann Kempf was good friends with Terry. He had passed my contact details along to her and that is why she'd become interested in me. Terry was obviously scouting for Betty Ann at the Watford Football Festival and had put my name forward.

I was flown out to view the campus and I met up with a few people who would help me out along the way, such as academic advisers. I stayed with a few of the girls in the dorm for a long weekend and they showed me round the place. I got to see a game with them too and it felt pretty much like it was the right choice for me from the off. The other two options, Rutgers and George Mason, just faded from my view.

But within this dream offer was a dilemma: I wanted to go and do it but I didn't want to leave home. I remember wishing more than anything that I could have this opportunity in England, but it just wasn't possible for a woman to be a professional footballer in my home country.

I was a timid character, and to leave home at such a young age was a massive thing for me to do. But I had to do it because I wanted to pursue my dreams. So I took the opportunity with both hands, held on to it and never let it go. However, I remained determined to get my BTEC qualification before leaving. I was anxious about insisting on this to Betty Ann, but I had to. I couldn't risk cutting off my studies and going over to the States and it not work out for me. I needed to have something to fall back on. I needed a Plan B, just in case. They agreed to my terms and I got my head down and studied hard.

What an incredible turnaround. That was the start for me. My dreams in football had always been to play professionally, to play for Arsenal and to play for England. If you class Seton Hall as a professional arrangement, as I do, I managed to achieve all three of them before I turned twenty.

I'd also spent two successful seasons at Wembley Ladies after leaving school. I made my senior debut for them against Doncaster Belles in an FA Cup game in the 1993/94 season. The Belles really were the team to beat at that time with vastly experienced England internationals playing for them such as Gillian Coultard and Karen Walker. No team could get anywhere near them, and as a result nobody gave us a prayer against them. But we held them at home in a cracking game that finished 3–3 and I scored my first senior goal in that match. Sadly, we lost the replay and they went on to win the cup for the third time in five years.

The following year I won my first full England cap, just three days after my seventeenth birthday, in a European Championship qualification match against Italy at Roker Park, home of Sunderland AFC. I had been playing well for Wembley so it was pleasing to be recognized in this way, but I was still pretty young to be selected. Ted Copeland was the coach who gave me my first England cap.

There is a funny story attached to my England debut. Norman Burns always believed I would play for England one day and he promised my dad that when it happened he was going to be there to see it with him. It just so happened that my first call-up was a good five hours' drive up north for him. Obviously he didn't want to travel all that way and not see me play so he called someone – I'm not sure whether it was the coach or a member of staff – and told them that he was my uncle and he wanted to know if I was playing or not, because he wanted to be there to see it if I was. Incredibly, they told him I was due to start. So Norman actually knew before I did! He made the trip all the way up to the north-east with my dad. It was a cold night in early November and we drew 1–1, but they were both ecstatic.

Carolina Morace was playing up front for the Italians and she was impressive. I started the match on the left wing, running up and down and trying to get crosses in for the forwards. Marieanne Spacey and Karen Walker were up front that night. My future England coach Hope Powell played in that match too. It was a good experience for me, and it was great to win a cap.

A few weeks later I scored my first goal for my country in a 5–0 home win against Croatia, at The Valley, home of Charlton Athletic. At that time, the England women's team still had to play in England men's shirts – but that didn't matter to me when I was hitting the back of the net.

Playing and scoring for England was great, but I had become disillusioned at Wembley. As I grew older and I grew in confidence, I found I always wanted the ball – and I didn't always get the ball. The training there was also based on fitness rather than contact with the ball, and that frustrated me a lot. The coach, John Jones, always put a lot of emphasis on physical fitness in his coaching sessions. He focused on fitness work much more than ball work. I wanted to play on the ball as much as possible. I thought he had his priorities the wrong way round.

After one particular game I made a decision, and it was final. I told my dad that I had had enough at Wembley and I didn't want to play for them any more. It didn't go down too well but I wanted out. And I couldn't have found a better place to go.

I signed for Arsenal Ladies the following week, and I opened my heart to team coach Vic Akers about everything, telling him that I had been hoping and praying that this would one day happen to me. Wherever I had played, I remember always thinking to myself: 'I hope there's a scout from Arsenal here today.' Vic told me in no uncertain terms that he would never have come in for me in this way. He knew all about me, of course, but he explained that Arsenal Ladies always waited for players to come to them, not the other way round. I was a very shy person so that wasn't going to happen. I would never have gone for a trial at Arsenal under my own steam. So I suppose it had been a stand-off between the two of us: he wasn't going to come for me and I wasn't going to go to him.

Vic would always mention my name to Norman Burns when he saw me play, both at Pinner Park and Wembley Ladies. I never knew about it at the time of course, but he'd subtly let it be known to Norman that he would be interested in me going to Arsenal Ladies if it suited me. So when Norman heard from my dad that I was unhappy at Wembley and looking to leave, he gave Vic the nod straight away.

I am really glad he did. Vic has been absolutely fantastic for me and my career. He has done wonders for Arsenal too. And, of course, it was another dream come true to play for them.

I am an Arsenal fan; my affinity has always been with them. I had supported them as a kid and I just wanted to wear their strip and play for them. I had the first yellow JVC kit with the blue shorts. That strip was my pride and joy. I'd always wanted to wear that kit and to be called an Arsenal player.

When I signed for Arsenal, Vic was brilliant. He showed me the marble hall at Highbury with the bronze bust of the club's legendary manager Herbert Chapman and then he took me out on to the pitch. I was in my element. It was so surreal for me to be in that stadium that day, looking around the empty stands. Vic took me upstairs and I saw all the trophies from the glory days. I went into the changing rooms too and saw all the bathtubs the greats had used. For me, having supported them from such a young age, it was a truly amazing experience. Vic even gave me a pair of Ian Wright's boots as a gesture afterwards – what a great way for him to sell the club to me! After all this, how could I possibly say no?

I signed my Arsenal contract in the club boardroom. It was near the end of 1996 and I remember the room was full of Christmas cards. My dad was looking all over the place to see if the club had received one from Watford FC – he eventually found that they had!

We went outside to watch the first team train, and as we walked down the tunnel we came face to face with Martin Keown. He was coming in from the opposite direction and looked absolutely massive. I think the top of his leg must have been the thickness of my waist. We sat in the stands and watched the training session in full. Arsène Wenger had not been at the club very long (that's how long ago it was), and I watched him intently that day. He stood on the touchline talking to Pat Rice, his coach. It was great to see all that going on right in front of my eyes.

Vic was really sweet throughout. He was so made up with me signing for him that he got it mentioned in the Arsenal match-day programme soon afterwards. And I was so made up I thought all my Christmases had come together at once.

I am proud to say that I helped Arsenal Ladies win the Premier League title at the end of that season, scoring two goals and providing an assist for the third in a 3–0 win over Liverpool which secured the championship for us. We were allowed to play that final game of the season at Highbury too, which was a massive treat for all of us and the ultimate for me.

But then it was time to say goodbye. Vic and I both knew that once my studies were completed, my move to the USA was assured. So I bid farewell and headed west. Vic was disappointed, but he was also really good about it all. He told me that if it didn't work out for me I was more than welcome to come straight back to Arsenal.

I'd had a great season with Arsenal and it was a hard decision for me to go to New Jersey: after all, I was now living part of my dream by playing for them. My England career was progressing nicely too. I was now firmly established in the team and I had scored a few goals. By the summer of 1997 I had four to my name from fourteen appearances. All of my strikes had come in our European Championship qualification campaign: two against Croatia, one against Italy and one against Portugal.

The match against Italy was played in Calabria, a beautiful spot in the southern part of the country that forms the toe of the Italian boot. Sadly, this match turned out to be a costly

2–1 defeat for us. Italy won the group and England finished behind them in second place.

We missed out on a place in the 1997 Women's European Championship, held jointly in Norway and Sweden, after losing to Spain 3–2 on aggregate in a two-legged play-off. We lost 2–1 away in Montilla, near Cordoba, and could only draw 1–1 at Prenton Park in the return leg.

Italy, the country I had made my international debut against, were a decent side. They finished as runners-up in the tournament, losing 2–0 in the final to Germany. And Morace, the striker who had impressed me so much at Roker Park on my debut, scored both their goals as they knocked out co-hosts Norway at the group stage. She went on to be the top goalscorer in the finals, with five goals. Spain got to the semi-finals there as well. So, all in all, we had come up against two of the better teams in Europe during our failed attempt to qualify for that competition. It had been my first international campaign. I had played in eight games and enjoyed the experience. But we didn't get to go to the party at the end. I would have to wait a few more years before I reached my first international tournament with England.

There was no written agreement with Seton Hall, just a verbal one, so I could have withdrawn and stayed at Arsenal. But, as I said, Arsenal and England wasn't the whole dream. Deep down, I knew I owed it to myself to go. I didn't have a job when I was at Arsenal and I wasn't getting paid to play for Arsenal. I had to go to America and better myself.

I had kept in touch with Seton Hall throughout my BTEC studies on a weekly basis via telephone. I still had to gain the right grades at college to be accepted there, so that was a big stress for me because I wasn't the best at school. But I got the grades – I just scraped through – and all that remained for me was to get on that plane.

At the age of eighteen, I felt as if I had fulfilled my life's dream overnight. In my mind, at that very moment I switched from being an amateur to a professional. It was a truly amazing feeling. This is what I had been waiting for, yet for so long I hadn't been able to see how it would ever happen for me. It wasn't going to happen to me in England, that I was sure about, and other than playing football for a living I really didn't know what else to do with my life. Only a year or so earlier I hadn't had a clue where my life was heading. It was fate that Terry Undercoffer came along and saw me play that day. I am so glad that he did.

I went to America to play football. I know that's probably not the right reason to go and sign a three-year scholarship in a lot of people's eyes because they would think that education should come first, not second. But I went there for the football. I went there to be, in my eyes, a full-time professional. End of story.

4

She's Leaving Home

I CHOSE TO GO TO SETON HALL BECAUSE I THOUGHT IT HAD A close-knit 'family' appeal. There were bigger and probably better colleges interested in me but I wanted to be in a classroom of about twenty people, not a hundred. I wanted more individual attention rather than feeling like just a number. That was important to me. This college also had a good academic advisory programme, so if I struggled with my studies I knew there would be people there to help me. That's why I chose to go there. But within twenty-four hours of getting there I was convinced I had made a big mistake.

I flew into Newark airport, where I was met by the assistant coach, Chris McDonald. The Seton Hall Pirates squad was down on New Jersey shore in pre-season training; I was due to join them the next day. In the meantime, I was driven to the campus, taken to a dorm and left there for the night.

It was quite a shock to the system. It was summer school at the time and the dorms weren't used, so the electricity was off. There was also no duvet, no pillow and no bed sheets. There was no television and no telephone either. All I had were the clothes and other items I had brought over in my bag. I had to sleep on a jumper with another jumper as a cover. I didn't know what I had got myself into or what I had just done with my life. All alone in that dorm, I cried my eyes out.

The next day wasn't any better either. After finally joining up with my team-mates down at the shore I was told that I couldn't train with them. A call had come through from the college's athletics department offices to our head coach stating that I was not eligible to train with the Pirates due to National Collegiate Athletic Association (NCAA) rules. Basically, my BTEC qualifications had to be transferred into an American points system before a decision could be made about whether I was qualified to begin studying for my degree at Seton Hall. It was a chaotic start to my life out there, and totally unexpected. They were still trying to figure out if I could play for them when I'd already gone out there!

It seemed to take ages to sort it all out. It was so frustrating for me because it could and should have all been dealt with properly before I left England. In the end, this ongoing administration process delayed everything for me. It was the best part of a month before I was cleared to play football.

Those first weeks in the US rocked me. I guess it was due in large part to loneliness. The upshot of the administrative mess surrounding my qualifications was that I had to train on my own and wait for the process to be completed. Until it was, I had to sit and watch training or go to the gym and work out alone.

It was also due to a lack of confidence on my part – and that was to become an important factor for me to recognize in my life. When every aspect was added up, all the stresses and the strains, I just wasn't mentally ready for any of it.

I hadn't really prepared myself for what I was getting into out in the USA, to be honest. I certainly hadn't expected to be left in a dorm by myself – that's quite a scary prospect for any eighteen-year-old girl on her first night in another country, regardless of how confident a person she is.

I found it really hard to deal with. I suppose that I didn't realize just how shy and timid a person I was until I was put in that situation in a foreign land. I didn't know anybody there and I found it difficult to mix. Furthermore, being cast aside from the outset didn't help me one bit. I needed to develop a rapport with the other players out on the pitch, but I couldn't do that. I couldn't play football and I struggled to make friends as a result.

It was both frustrating and damaging for me. I had gone over to New Jersey to play the game I loved, and it turned out to be the one thing I wasn't allowed to do. It isn't nice for a player to watch their team-mates play football and be forbidden to join in, particularly when that was exactly what had taken me across the Atlantic Ocean in the first place.

I was homesick. I hated my life out there in those first weeks. I couldn't play football, and because of that I couldn't fit in. I felt I had made a really big mistake in going over there. Sometimes I wanted to turn the clock back and stay in Watford.

I stayed in a beach house down on the shore. It was beautiful down there, but I couldn't appreciate any of that. I had known deep down for a good few years that I was a shy and quiet person, but there and then the fact really hit me. It hadn't been such a problem back home. Now it was a massive problem. I found that I struggled to speak to people unless they spoke to me – and even then it was difficult. At college I was asked to introduce myself, which involved me standing up and making a speech. It was awful. I hated it. I didn't want to be there. I don't think my English accent helped. I felt different from the start and I couldn't speak up for fear of my accent drawing attention to me.

I seemed to be missing everything about home, particularly my mum's shepherd's pie. Every week I would ring Mum and Dad and tell them I wanted to come home. They were great. 'Let's speak about it next week,' they would say. 'Let's just see how you get on during the next seven days out there and then we'll see.'

Before too long I found that I wasn't ringing home quite as much. I had finally begun to find my feet in America and make some friends. Life became more enjoyable as a result. But if it hadn't been for Mum and Dad I might not have reached that stage.

Both my parents knew that this was a fantastic opportunity for me, one that I had wanted all my life. They saw the bigger picture, beyond the lonely dorm and the shyness, and they didn't want me to make a rash decision that would affect my future. They really supported me during that time and got me through it. Without them I'm not sure I could have stuck it out.

Without doubt, though, if I had been able to play in the team from the start I would have been able to blend with and be accepted by the squad a lot quicker, which would have made a huge difference to me. The other players can tell if you are a good player, and of course we then have more stuff to talk about to each other. It was much easier for me after they saw that I could play football. That is how I communicate really. That is where my personality comes out – on the pitch. I found it awkward making friends with the players at Seton Hall until I could play with them. As it was, I started out with the worst-case scenario: sitting on the sidelines and becoming more and more introverted and withdrawn. Things improved quickly for me when I was able to play football and bond with my team-mates.

The college football season was relatively short in America. We played for just three months, from the beginning of August until the end of October. If you were lucky enough to make the NCAA tournament at the end of the season, you would play a little longer. But Seton Hall Pirates never used to get that far. The college didn't have a proud history when it came to women's football.

Beyond the college system there were semi-professional leagues. But the top American players didn't play in those leagues. They all trained in national camps, ultimately preparing themselves for the big one – the 1999 Women's World Cup, which was to take place on home soil. Players such as Mia Hamm, the star name in women's football at the time, didn't need to play in a league because they were in camp for months at a time, playing alongside fellow USA internationals.

Back in England, before a match we would meet up for a week or so. The USA would have all their players in camp for two or three months, training in California or somewhere. All the players had come through the college system. That was the birthplace for them all. It was college system straight into national camp, and then into national team. It was a robust system, and it worked.

The one downside at that time was that if a player wasn't good enough to play for the national team, there was nowhere for her to go. The W League changed that, and the Women's Professional Soccer league (WPS) took it a step further. Both were so good for aspiring American athletes, because young players were able to be seen playing football in a strong, competitive format.

Now that I was playing, and showing that I could play, a lot of attention was on me. That was OK, but when people wanted to talk to me in person about it all, I found that I imploded. On the field I could be myself. I could express myself in the way I wanted to and I could be what I wanted to be – a confident, smiley person enjoying life and showing off skills. But off the field I was a completely different person. I was unable to cope with any of the extra-curricular stuff that was being thrown at me. I needed to find a solution. Without realizing it, I began to find solace in alcohol.

My drinking days started in earnest at the end of my first season at Seton Hall. It had little to do with football. I just found that drinking made me a much more confident and fun person to be around – and someone I liked. I was still well under the legal drinking age of twenty-one in the USA and I would use fake ID to get served if I had to.

I roomed with a girl called Meredith Reckord, who wasn't an athlete. We had a two-bedroom dorm. Next door to us were Christine Cassano and Amy McKee, who were both in my team. There was just an adjoining bathroom between us. So, really, there were four of us together.

University life is about going away and discovering yourself. In England, lots of people get drunk in the process and do silly things. That's life, I guess. This was similar. I was living in America, I was young, and I was away from my family. I was also very introverted.

There would always be a party going on at college. It might be at a baseball player's place, a volleyball player's place, or at our place. There was an opportunity to drink every night if you wanted to take it. So it slowly got into a habit for me. I would drink most nights of the week, cheap beer that we would get from the liquor store. It was all we could afford. The refrigerator would always be stocked with cheap beer. I got into drinking it after class had finished. It was never a social thing for me, it was always about binge drinking – about drinking as fast as I could.

I would shotgun a beer. I'd burst a can with a pen and suck the alcohol out as quickly as I could. It would be finished in seconds. It was always like that for me – fast drinking from three or four o'clock in the afternoon. That would move into going out to a bar or just staying in the dorm, drinking. Various athletes would come in and go out. It was pretty relaxed, and that is how it all started for me.

I would get up for college the next morning feeling hung over. But I would go to class and get through the day and I would train hard. And then I would get home and start the whole cycle again. The drinking could go on for six or seven hours a night.

Christine and another goalkeeper, Marybeth Foran,

became my regular drinking buddies. The three of us became best friends in the team and the big drinkers in the team. If I wanted a drink, the others would be persuaded to drink; if one of the others wanted a drink, the rest of us would be persuaded to drink. It went on and on like that. It became a habit that we would rope each other in. It ended up that we rarely got a night off from it.

But I was young and fit and I found that I could do all this and still play the next day. My body recovered quickly so there was never any problem on the pitch. I couldn't do it today, but it was so easy to do it back in the late nineties.

Many times I woke up and thought to myself: 'Shit, I won't be doing that again.' But as the day went on I gradually felt better and then I would be ready to get back on it again after class.

Sometimes I wouldn't make it to class the next day. I would feel so bad physically that I would skip lessons, and then I would get into trouble for not attending class. But I would find a way out of it, saying I'd overslept or something. It was college life. That is pretty much what I did in college anyway.

I did my drinking mostly in groups and at parties. And I was always there. It was very rare that I would turn down an invitation to drink. I liked the way alcohol made me feel. The heavy head in the morning soon passed. The whole thing became a routine. It was the norm for us. I didn't know any different than to wake up at college with a hangover. It was an expected start to the day. I would simply drink a pint of water and go about my business.

Having said all that, during the short football season it

was pretty much no drinking for us because the focus was so much on football and doing well on the pitch. That was OK because those games fuelled my confidence. But in the longer off-season it was a different story. I took on the party lifestyle. I was still training and doing what I had to do to stay in shape and tick over, but in the evenings I was in full-on party mode, all of the time.

When I was drunk, I was the person I wanted to be: confident and outgoing. I felt happy. I desperately wanted to be like that all the time. It felt so good inside. I wanted to bottle up that feeling. But of course that feeling doesn't come in a bottle. It comes out of a bottle.

When I was sober I was back to being the person who couldn't cope, and I struggled, particularly when somebody came up to me and wanted to talk about football, or wanted to get to know me. When I was drunk, you couldn't shut me up. I spent my life being two different people.

There were crazy times. I would wake up with a scratch under my eye or a bruise on my face and I couldn't recall what had happened. That was funny to a degree but also scary at the same time. I would sit in class racking my brain, trying to remember if I had got myself into a fight. Deep down I would know that I hadn't got myself into a fight because my friends would have told me that I had got into a fight. But I just couldn't remember what had happened so naturally all sorts went through my head.

The hardest part with all that was going into training and my coach saying to me, 'What happened to you?' What could I say to that? I had to make up lies on the spot – 'I walked into a branch', that kind of thing. I had to create such stories because I didn't have any clear memories of the night before. Looking back, that was a big warning sign.

My first year at Seton Hall was a slow build-up to what was to come. During the latter part of my time at college I was drinking every night. Christine, Marybeth and I had to keep that to ourselves, otherwise it was a situation that would have had to be addressed by management. That would not have been good. To my knowledge, it was never brought to their attention.

Other than my drinking buddies, no one knew how much drinking I was doing. That's because as time went on I began to do it largely in secret.

5

Success in a Number 6 Shirt

IT IS HARD TO SAY WHETHER THE STANDARD OF COLLEGE football in America was higher or lower than what I had known in the FA Women's Premier League, mainly because my college team wasn't really very good at that time. I don't know if I should say that, but it's the truth. What was pleasing was the way in which the sport was accepted in the States. That was much better than what I was used to in England, and I felt much more appreciated as a result.

Under Betty Ann Kempf, Seton Hall Pirates qualified to play in the Big East conference with a best-ever 14–5 win–loss record. We were up against teams such as Boston College, Connecticut, Notre Dame, Pittsburgh and Rutgers, one of the colleges I had turned down. I went straight into the starting line-up for the Pirates once all the administration concerning my registration had been completed. I suddenly felt alive again.

Things could not have started better for me once I'd got that team shirt on my back. I scored nine goals in my first five games along with two assists. I was voted the Star-Ledger Woman Athlete of the Week – and that was the first of many accolades I was to receive at Seton Hall.

I really enjoyed my football there. I remember us beating Notre Dame, of Indiana. They were always ranked in the top five, maybe even top two, in college football. They were unbeaten in thirty-seven matches. And we beat them. It was the first time the Pirates had ever beaten them. It was glorious. I scored the first goal and set up the second in a 3–2 victory after overtime, as the Americans call extra-time. That is a big memory for me because it was such a big game for us. It was like our World Cup final. We beat a team that we weren't supposed to beat and that earned us a little bit of recognition – but not as much as I thought we deserved. We were elevated to seventeenth in the national standings. It was the first time the college had ever been placed in the top twenty.

This result gave us such a boost. It made us realize that we were not too far behind the top teams. It thrilled everybody to know that we could play with the best, compete with the best and beat the best.

As I have mentioned, the college had never been all that good when it came to women's football. When I signed for them I remember there was a lot of talk about me scoring all these goals and changing the fortunes of the team. So it was a good feeling actually to deliver in a high-profile game like that. It was in fact a fine opening season for me. I became the first athlete in any sport in the conference to be voted Player of the Year and Newcomer of the Year in the same campaign, so that was quite an achievement.

This led to my picture being used in the local newspaper. Inevitably, I started to get noticed around the place a lot more. Our crowds were on the up too. Suddenly the recognition came my way. It was a completely new experience for me. I had not had anything like it in England.

I was surprised at how much of a standout player I was in my first season at Seton Hall. But, to be honest, I was much better than the other players in my team. That will sound big-headed, but I had natural ability, and that was what allowed me to stand out. The college game was based on athleticism – run, run, run. There wasn't much of a focus on skill and technique, and of course my game was based on skill and technique. So I was always going to shine compared to a lot of my team-mates due simply to that; I was just able to offer more than them on the pitch. I got a lot of attention in the press as a result, probably because I was 'easy on the eye' – or should I say 'easy on the ball'.

I was scoring goals pretty much for fun. I wanted to take that first year in the USA by storm and I really tried to do as well as I could and score as many goals as I could. I managed to do that and it was enjoyable because I was doing it in a different environment, playing against different players in a different country.

But I had to vary my game slightly as time went on. My natural style was to run at players and take them on, but soon I was being marked so tightly that that became almost impossible. Some teams put three players on me.

I adapted well, and in the following two seasons I was the leading goalscorer in the Big East conference and all of the NCAA, scoring twenty-five and twenty-two goals respectively. I was named Big East Offensive Player of the Year in both those seasons and NCAA Rookie of the Year in my first season. I was NCAA Offensive Player of the Year in my third season there too. I scored six hat-tricks in that time. My goal-per-game ratio was 1.77. And with me scoring goals, Seton Hall's results got better and the team was regularly placed much higher up the table. So the Pirates finally started to gain some recognition at long last.

But I never felt that it was a one-woman team. I may have been the player that stood out in the side but we had talent elsewhere, goalkeeper Stacey Nagle and midfielder Courtney Wood in particular. Amy McKee and Michelle Canning were good players as well.

Under Betty Ann's guidance, we made two appearances in the Big East play-off semi-finals, which was a great achievement given where we had come from. Betty Ann was named New Jersey Coach of the Year, which was well deserved. She played an important part in my career. She decided to build her team around me, and that was a big thing to do. It was an honour for me to repay her faith in my ability in the way that I did.

One match that remains vivid in my memory from my Seton Hall days was a game against Pittsburgh, which was televised. We won 4–1 and I got all four goals. I was recognized as the best player in the team and as a result I got a lot of attention from the sports media. I didn't particularly like that, I have to say – reporters wanting to speak to me after matches and all that. Furthermore, the Seton Hall Pirates number 6 shirt was retired after I left university. It all happened in quite a short amount of time as well, and I wasn't really ready for it yet. I didn't know how to deal with the media. They had to set up media training sessions for me because there were so many requests coming in to speak to me. I was advised on how to answer questions and how to stand upright but I could have done without all that. I longed to be left alone to play football.

But, looking back, having your number retired is quite an honour. I now recognize the importance of that. I was the first female footballer to have her number retired. So that was pretty cool. It is still a really big deal in the US because only two other women in the history of Seton Hall have had their numbers retired and I am the first one not to play basketball. So to be classified in that small group is one of my proudest accomplishments. In other words, I get it now. I am part of an elite group. My number 6 banner, which says 'Kelly Smith – Soccer', hangs in the basketball arena at the university and will be there for ever.

Sometimes when I go back there and walk around the place I just think of all the good memories and lap them all up. Seeing my banner up there is massive. I think the more time passes, the more grateful I am for it. It was a good period in my life all in all, despite all the harrowing stuff I had to go through at the start – not being able to play football, and feeling homesick. Plus, of course, the drinking habit took hold then. I had no idea how serious a problem it would become in my life.

The funny thing is, the number 6 is not special to me in any other way. It wasn't a number I particularly wanted to wear at Seton Hall, it was the only low number that was available when I joined the team. It had no significance at all. It became significant, of course, but I hated the focus being on me when I didn't have a ball at my feet. I didn't feel comfortable with it at all. It didn't feel me. The person I was out on the football field was not the person I was off the football field. I was so confident on the field but I was the reverse of that off it.

The night I was named Offensive Player of the Year at the Big East awards dinner was horrible in that respect. The Defensive Player of the Year award was up just before mine, and when Kate Markgraf, who played for Notre Dame and the USA, got up and gave her acceptance speech, it dawned on me that the same thing would be expected of me. I shrivelled in my seat as I listened to Kate give her speech. I began to sweat. I felt physically sick at what would now be expected of me by this big room of people gathered here to celebrate these awards.

So I scarpered. I left the table and went and hid in the bathroom. I wasn't there to pick up my award. They had to get on and do it without me. When my name was called out, I was suddenly nowhere to be found. Betty Ann didn't know where I was – nobody did. Betty Ann had to go up and accept the award for me.

One of our players later found me. I was still hiding in the toilets, just sitting on the loo. I just couldn't physically go up there and say something in front of all those people. It was such a fear of mine to be in a room full of people like that and for them to be listening to what I said. I knew I would never be able to put a sentence together so I took the only way out and ran away.

Betty Ann came in and found me there, crying. I felt so inadequate because I knew I couldn't do what was expected of me at an occasion such as this. It is a story that the two of us laugh about now because it wouldn't happen to me today, but I was so fearful of public speaking back then and having to be the centre of attention. I was a fish out of water at moments like that, and I would do anything I could to get out of those situations – even on my big night.

6

1999 And All That

MY JOB WAS DONE AT SETON HALL. I HAD MY DEGREE AND I was qualified to teach Physical Education on either side of the Atlantic Ocean. More importantly to me, I also had the beginnings of a successful career in football. With so many Big East conference awards under my belt there was obviously a lot of interest in me in the USA. But was it right for me to stay out there or go home to England?

I had to consider my options for the future. Although there was a lot of talk, in 1999 there was still, sadly, no professional league in the USA. Still, I knew in my heart that if ever there was going to be one anywhere in the world it was going to have to be in the States.

During the latter part of my last year at college, strong rumours began to fly around that there could be a professional women's league in the USA in a year or two. That was obviously my kind of thing. It sounded exciting and it was what I was born to do. I just had to get through that one- or two-year period to get there.

I still had a verbal understanding with Vic Akers about a possible return to Arsenal and I thought a lot about that. I respected Vic a great deal. But women's football in England was still not developing as I had hoped it would or as it needed to, in my opinion. The difference between the England national side and the USA national side, for instance, was massive – from top to bottom. I think it was around this time that I was quoted as saying 'Women's football in England is a joke.' I don't actually remember saying those words but I guess I must have done. That quote has definitely stayed with me, to this day. But in my eyes it was true at that time.

It felt as though my life was at a crossroads again. I had experienced a great career in football at college level and I still yearned to play the game professionally, but there was no professional league to play in.

Luckily for me, the position of assistant football coach was advertised at Seton Hall shortly after I graduated. It was really good timing. Betty Ann Kempf knew what I wanted to do long term and she helped me a lot on my way to achieving that goal. I had no coaching experience at all, but I quickly learned. So, I drew a line under my studying and partying days and stepped into a job. The playing part continued, of course, as it had to for me. But I was now working for a living.

I genuinely felt that I had control of my drinking at this time. I could still switch off the desire to drink when I needed to. It was not out of control. I could always say no if I had to. But, as I have admitted, I didn't say no too much. Even so, at this point in my life drinking was not a big problem for me. In hindsight, I think the main question was probably this: *why* was I drinking?

Of course, working in America meant living in America and being ready for a professional league if and when it finally happened. So I found myself a new part-time team, New Jersey Lady Stallions, alongside Seton Hall. England, for now, would have to wait.

I found the coaching role at college quite hard to do because I was working with my old team-mates. Suddenly I was a different type of figure to them, something of a figure-head in fact. I had to speak up a lot more too, which I didn't find easy. I did a lot of office work, behind-the-scenes stuff, which I was much happier doing than talking to the players. But there's no getting away from it: coaching is a role that is associated with vocal people, and I found that a very challenging part of the job. I also found it really hard to be alongside friends and yet also be in the position of trying to tell them what to do with some form of authority beyond the pitch. Doing that sort of thing wasn't really me.

For instance, as half-time approached in a match I would start worrying about what I was going to say to the players in the changing room. I would stop watching play in my normal way because I was focusing too much on my half-time team talk. I knew I would get asked, 'Kelly, what do you think?' And that brought a lot of pressure my way.

I mean, what could I say to these girls? I became so fearful of messing up with them that I would sometimes panic during play. As soon as half-time was over it was a totally different feeling for me. I was back on it. And then as full-time approached it was the same thing again. I would be expected to give my input, and that meant I would have to speak up. That filled me with fear. Yes it was a living, but it was not the easiest way for me to earn a wage.

Everything changed for me after the USA won the 1999 Women's World Cup on home soil. A side led by Mia Hamm won the tournament at the Pasadena Rose Bowl in front of 90,185 spectators after a dramatic 5–4 penalty shoot-out in the final against China. It was now only a matter of time before a professional women's league was created. And I was ready and waiting for that.

Women's football grabbed America by the throat that year. Over 73,000 fans watched the USA defeat Brazil in the World Cup semi-final at Stanford Stadium in California, ahead of a Major League Soccer match between DC United and San Jose. A reported 60,000 of them left before the men's match kicked off! I was at the opening game of the World Cup, between USA and Denmark at the Giants Stadium in New Jersey. There were about 80,000 there for that one. It really is hard to put into words just what was happening to the women's game right in front of my eyes.

Later in the tournament, Sir Bobby Charlton was filmed on stage at the Plaza Hotel in Beverly Hills with another World Cup winner, Jürgen Klinsmann of Germany, discussing the best players from the tournament. President Bill Clinton was at the final. The impact went global, but on home soil it had gone crazy from the outset.

Hamm was the star name in the USA side. Within months she had become Nike's third-highest-paid athlete, reportedly positioned behind only basketball player Michael Jordan and golfer Tiger Woods. She even got her own Nike building. But Hamm is probably not the player most people remember from that successful side. That honour would go to Brandi Chastain, the player who scored the winning penalty and then promptly whipped her shirt off in the penalty box to celebrate. She appeared on David Letterman's show after that.

As a result, women's football – or soccer, as they always call it over there – became a popular sport in the States. Sure enough, it was announced that a professional women's league was about to be created. Top players from all over the world signed up to play in it. I was lucky to have a head start: I was already out there and had made a name for myself.

My future coach at Boston Breakers, Tony DiCicco, was the head coach of the USA's 1999 Women's World Cup-winning team, and he later told me that the support the team got from the press and the public was phenomenal. People went to watch training sessions in their thousands. That tournament totally blew away all the doubts and the doubters. The attendance figures were unreal. The support the USA got was astonishing. The whole game just took off from that moment.

It was sad for me only to be there to see it, not to play in it. England had failed to qualify. The media said I was the best player not at the Women's World Cup, but that was no consolation at all.

England struggled at the international level. We were in a transition stage at that time, really. We were well beaten in our World Cup qualification group, which included power-house nations Germany and Norway, losing five of our six matches. I played in both defeats against Norway and in one of the defeats against Germany. We were still some way behind both countries. I would have to continue to wait patiently before I could play in a Women's World Cup.

It may have hurt a lot to witness all this euphoria from a national pride viewpoint, but it was tremendous in terms of the bigger picture for all of us who were involved in the game, at any level. From that moment, women's football never looked back.

The USA players had become household names overnight. There were TV adverts featuring the top names in that side endorsing boots and other products. It was amazing to see our sport take off like this right in front of my eyes. A foundation was set up to help younger players come through the ranks. The money women footballers could earn rose significantly. A lot of the players who have earned a living in the States playing football in the twenty-first century are so grateful for the success of that 1999 team. They earned the game respect. They paved the way for what followed.

It was great to be there and witness it all first hand, and obviously I wanted a slice of it. It was what I had always wanted. And it was happening on my doorstep.

All twenty USA squad players were allocated a team in the new professional Women's United Soccer Association league, and they were paid a good amount of money for that. Each franchise built its team around their two or three players, which was a good idea and worked really well. A maximum of four international players could be added to those two or three USA players in each franchise, and home-grown youngsters plus the top graduating college players made up the rest. So there was a strong base of players throughout the league with successful internationals providing the core group of talent. It was also a great way to market the teams, and the league of course. It was a good, well-thought-through format, and it was to prove very successful. I couldn't wait for it to start.

7

The American Dream

IF EVER MY DECISION TO LEAVE MY FAMILY AND FRIENDS AND travel into the unknown was justified, it felt like it was now. I had been caught up in an exciting whirlwind ever since I started playing for Seton Hall Pirates in the Big East conference. The USA had won the 1999 Women's World Cup on home soil to national acclaim, and as a result of that the first ever women's professional league was starting up. Talk about being in the right place at the right time.

It felt like I was at the epicentre of the explosion. It was a great time to be involved in the game, because it was just getting so much positive attention. It was so exciting to think where it might all lead as well. At times I had to pinch myself to check that I wasn't dreaming. It was so far away from my experiences as a schoolgirl in Watford.

The player draft system, which took place in the autumn of 2000, was the first part of the new Women's United Soccer Association professional league. It was thrilling to be involved as the whole machine started to whirr into action. After all the USA Women's World Cup players had been assigned franchises, certain overseas internationals were asked if they wanted their names to go forward into the draft. I said yes without hesitation. I later received a letter asking me to list my top three teams in order of preference.

There were eight teams to choose from: Atlanta Beat, Bay Area CyberRays, Boston Breakers, Carolina Courage, New York Power, Philadelphia Charge, San Diego Spirit and Washington Freedom. I put Philadelphia Charge first because it was close to New Jersey and it was where my friends were. Incredibly, I was picked up by them. I was one of the lucky ones: there was no guarantee that a player would get picked by their number one choice.

Philadelphia is just two hours from New Jersey, so I was delighted about signing for them. It suited me well to play there. The West Coast was my nightmare scenario at the time of the draft, but luckily that didn't happen. If it had, I would probably have gone, but thankfully I didn't have to.

The league was big business: 160 of the world's best players within a $100 million set-up. Top names in the game like Mia Hamm, Sissi of Brazil, and Sun Wen of China. And I was there. In all, twelve countries were represented in the first-ever WUSA season in 2001. I was the sole representative from England.

Atlanta picked up Sun Wen, the Golden Ball winner and the joint Golden Shoe winner with seven goals at the Women's World Cup, with the first pick in the draft, and then I was picked up by Philadelphia. There were thirty or forty international players to choose from and I went second, which was really satisfying. It is just as well that Philly had second pick, I suppose. It was expected that Sissi, who had enjoyed a great World Cup – she had tied with Sun Wen as top goalscorer with seven goals – would be the next pick. But our coach, Mark Krikorian, surprised a lot of people by going for me. I can't tell you what that did for my confidence. I wanted to get out on the pitch straight away and repay all the faith that he had in me.

Mark received a lot of stick in the press afterwards. But he had seen me play and he knew the talent I had. He really believed he was picking a great player in me so he went early for me and he got me. But it was not a popular choice with everyone. Sports journalist Grant Wahl, who wrote for *Sports Illustrated*, called it 'a bone-headed move'. That has always stuck with me. It was a nasty thing to write about someone and I really wanted to go out and prove him wrong. I did that. Some while later Grant apologized, saying he shouldn't have written that. But that was years down the road, after I had established myself in the league and become a much more well-known player in the world game. At the time it hurt a lot.

I think his criticism came from the fact that although I had done well in my college career, I was still seen as something of an unknown at that time because I was apparently still 'an up-and-coming player'. I wasn't known on the international scene, so that didn't help me. But that was mainly because England hadn't done very well on the international scene. I had won plenty of full international caps, but that hadn't been noticed by the media in the USA. Even so, surely a writer can find better words to use to describe a decision they disagree with than 'bone-headed'. He didn't know me or anything about me. It was wrong of him to write it up in such a way.

When the international players were paired up, I was put with Doris Fitschen, the veteran defender from FFC Frankfurt in Germany, with over a hundred international caps to her name, so that was good. Scotland's Julie Fleeting, who later played with me for Arsenal Ladies, signed for San Diego.

The WUSA league was great for every single one of us involved in it. For me, at the age of twenty-two, it felt like I was at last living my dream. I had to pinch myself to believe it was happening. It wasn't that long ago that I was being kicked off boys' teams with nowhere to go. Now here I was, and here it was – professional football!

I knew this was a truly great opportunity for me. I would not let it pass me by without giving my all. The game was booming in America and I was playing in the same team as household names such as Lorrie Fair, Heather Mitts and Saskia Webber. These were my new team-mates. Mandy Clemens was there too. She was a young, aspiring USA player at the time. This was the core of our team, my team – Philadelphia Charge.

It was phenomenal to see how our side was put together so quickly through the draft system. After the USA players and the international players, it was the turn of the college players. I knew the USA players because I had just watched them in their moment of glory on the biggest stage there is, I knew most of the international players through playing for England, and I knew the college players through playing for Seton Hall. So I was across it all. I remember sitting there and thinking how mouth-watering the prospect of this professional league was. I couldn't wait for it to start. At long last, I was where I wanted to be.

My first game for Philadelphia Charge came on Sunday, 22 April 2001 in California against San Diego. It was a sell-out crowd of around 15,000. Before kick-off, I stood there for the national anthem and I had tears in my eyes. And this was for the 'Star Spangled Banner', not 'God Save the Queen'. It was my debut as a professional athlete and I just couldn't stop myself from showing my emotions. I couldn't stop myself from thinking: 'Wow, my dream has come true.' When the national anthem finished, all these fireworks went off. It was a grand opening. I had even more tears welling up inside me and I was trying to cover them up. But it all meant so much to me and it proved impossible to do that.

My debut as a professional football player could not have gone any better. Philadelphia won the game 2–0. I was brought down for the penalty that led to our first goal and followed that up by scoring our second goal. Live on television. I was playing on the biggest stage there had ever been, in a professional environment, and getting paid to do it, and to top it all off I had scored on my debut. It was certainly a dream come true – there is no other way of putting it. To polish things off, I picked up the Most Valuable Player award at the end of the first week of the new league, which was very nice.

Now I could afford to relax a little, although not too much.

Our home crowds stayed at around the 10,000 to 12,000 mark throughout most of the season, and elsewhere the attendances were similar. The success of the Women's World Cup had a knock-on effect that lasted for quite a while. And everybody now knew that America was the place to be for women's football.

It was an exciting time, for all of us. Whenever we pulled up in our cars for home games all the banners would be up. American fans generally turn up to sports events early, and American sports are very good at doing things with kids before games as well, so you would get this big buzz before kick-off at every game. And you would get pulled into that because all these people had come out to watch you play the game you loved.

Before this there had been so many times in my career when I had felt that the crowd wasn't there to watch me. I am talking specifically about playing in matches back in England before a men's game or after a men's game at a large stadium. On those occasions you felt like the crowd wasn't there to see you play at all. We were just token support, really. I couldn't accept those spectators as fans of women's football because I genuinely don't think they would have turned up to watch us play of their own accord.

But when I was at Philadelphia, the fans were there for us and only us. They had their Philadelphia Charge shirts on and they had their red and white tops on. They were fanatical in their support for us. And, even better for them and for us, they were there to watch elite women's football. That felt great. It was a big deal for me, especially having grown up in England with all the problems I faced. It was now a totally different experience, in every way possible.

Things may have changed in recent years, particularly since David Beckham came over to play for LA Galaxy, but when I was first in the States I would definitely say that by and large football was seen as a women's sport rather than a men's sport – and this was after the country had hosted the men's 1994 World Cup, won by Brazil. That women's semi-final in 1999 I mentioned earlier between the USA and Brazil followed by the MLS game between DC United and San Jose Clash proves that. Men's football was on the back burner at that time. The women's national team was getting much more recognition than the men's national team in the States back in the late 1990s and early 2000s, and that is a fact. I could barely name one USA men's international back then, but I could have reeled off the entire USA women's team had I been asked to do so, they were in the media that much.

In the last few years Major League Soccer has taken over a bit. Beckham's there, so that's inevitable really. Thierry Henry is also there now, of course. The MLS is booming, and as a result football is maybe seen more as a men's sport than a women's sport nowadays. Then again, the USA has still enjoyed much more success in the women's game on an international level: twice World Cup winners, once runners-up, and placed third on three other occasions. In fact, the worst the USA team has ever done in a Women's World Cup is finish third. That's some record from six tournaments.

It felt pretty weird getting all this attention and playing in front of such big crowds in the USA for Philadelphia Charge, and then flying home to play for England and finding that the sport was still where it was when I had left the country four years earlier. There was always going to be more attention given to women players in America, what with the professional league being based there, but it was still an odd one for me to get my head around.

At the end of the day, playing for my country is still the ultimate for me. You can't go any higher than that. And England is the birthplace of football. So I would come back to England and want to experience what I had in America – the attention, the exposure, the limelight. But it was flipped. What was happening in England was the reverse of what was happening in America. I would play for my country and there would hardly be anybody at the game. The support just wasn't there, not in the same numbers. My international career seemed to be spent playing at a variety of Football League grounds up and down England in front of crowds much lower than what I was used to in the WUSA league, moreover people who didn't know too much about me or the game I played. You had an England shirt on your back but you were anonymous. They wouldn't know your name, your position or your team. It felt like nobody who was there had any idea about who I was or what I had achieved. Not a clue.

That was demoralizing at times, and another world entirely from the one I was living in across the Atlantic Ocean. When I returned to America I went straight back to being something of a celebrity again. The players were well known out there. We got stopped in the streets. We got stopped in the supermarket. We were also more appreciated as athletes. What was happening in the US was not happening in England. The two countries were miles apart in that sense. That was a little worrying, but I was so young and happy and thrilled with what I had that I wasn't going to dwell on it.

It was quite normal to be seen as a young woman playing football in America. In fact, you were expected to play football. In the early days of the sport in England I got laughed at in the face on a night out for saying that I played football. That is one hell of a big cultural difference.

Thankfully, that situation has changed in England now. The women's team has achieved relative success in recent years in international tournaments and the exposure has raised the profile of the game. Fans do know who we are now. But, honestly, back then they didn't seem to care, despite the fact that steady and strong progress had been made at international level under Hope Powell.

There was still the odd sobering moment, though. I had played in an 8–0 thrashing by Norway in the summer of 2000 in our Women's European Championship qualification group, for instance. Three months after that annihilation, the Norwegians won the gold medal at the Olympic Games in Sydney, beating the USA 3–2 after extra-time in the final. But England made it through to a play-off against Ukraine and qualified for the 2001 Women's European Championship in Germany, 4–1 on aggregate. I scored a goal in the first leg away from home in Kiev – it was my first goal for England in over four years – and I picked up the Player of the Match award in the second leg, at Leyton Orient, which was won by a goal from a young rising star, Rachel Yankey.

Rachel had made headlines back home by signing professionally for Fulham Ladies. Backed by the finances of Mohamed Al-Fayed, Fulham had become the first professional women's team in England. This had been done firmly with a view to a professional league being launched in the near future. Sadly that didn't happen, and as a result Fulham faded away. They went back to being semi-professional after three years or so and then they folded. But for a while Fulham were winning everything at domestic level, and with players such as Yanks, Katie Chapman, Rachel Unitt and Kim Jerray-Silver, plus top Norwegian stars such as Margunn Haugenes and Marianne Pettersen – both Olympic gold medal winners at Sydney 2000 – playing for them, that was understandable. Later on, in the last season of their professional status, 2002/03, they did the treble, winning the FA Women's Premier League, the FA Women's Cup and the FA Women's Premier League Cup. The other English teams just couldn't compete with them. But then, suddenly, this brief period of professionalism just stopped. The plug was pulled and the women's game in England reverted to being semi-professional again.

Anyway, at long last England were through to an international tournament. The timing of the European Championship wasn't the best for me because it cut the domestic USA season in two, but I have always put my country first and after negotiations between both parties I was able to fly over to Germany and take part in it.

I thoroughly enjoyed the experience. The Women's Euro is not the Women's World Cup but it is the next best thing. Sadly, we were up against it from the time the draw was made, being paired up with Germany and Sweden in the group stage alongside Russia.

We played all our matches at the Ernst-Abbe-Sportfeld in Jena. We started off with a hard-fought 1–1 draw against the Russians but were then well beaten by Sweden and Germany, conceding seven goals without reply in the process. Not only did those two teams comfortably qualify for the knockout stage, they also ended up contesting the final. Germany won it after extra-time, 1–0.

Still, it was good for us to have qualified for our first international tournament under Hope – another important learning curve for us. Sweden and Germany were the best sides in Europe and would remain so for the next few years, so while it was frustrating to be drawn in the same group as them – and to lose heavily to them – it was another big lesson. As had been that 8–0 thrashing at the hands of Norway, not to mention the two big defeats (5–0 and 6–0) by the USA in San Jose and Portland in the last matches I had played for England against the States, in 1997. The important factor was that by reaching the Euros we had finally got ourselves into the big time – but it was going to be a long road for us. The difference between the elite teams and the rest at international level was massive back then. But under Hope, England started the climb positively and continued to steadily improve.

8

Highs and Lows in Philadelphia

THINGS WENT PRETTY WELL FOR ME ON A PERSONAL LEVEL IN my first season with Philadelphia Charge. The big headline was that I was named in the Women's United Soccer Association Global Eleven All Star Team – quite a title – after the first season of the professional league, which was a real honour for me. I may not have played in a Women's World Cup yet but I was able to hold my own against the very best in the world who had done so.

Philadelphia reached the end-of-season play-offs in the inaugural WUSA campaign, having finished in the top four. We were beaten in the semi-finals of the play-offs, 3–2, by Atlanta Beat. It was a devastating loss for us as we'd led 2–0 at one stage. I scored the opening goal, chesting down a flick-on from Mandy Clemens before striking the ball into the corner of the net. Mandy put us two up five minutes later, but then it all went wrong for us and we gave the game away. To make matters worse, late on I suffered a badly sprained ankle and had to come off, which was frustrating. My season ended there and then.

For the 2002 season I was named as the new captain at

Philadelphia Charge following the retirement of Doris Fitschen, which was another honour bestowed on me by coach Mark Krikorian. He told me one of the reasons he chose me was the strength of character I had shown in returning so strongly to fitness. And I had worked hard at it, going through a demanding training schedule with strength and conditioning coach Duane Carlisle.

I put my heart and soul into getting back into the fold as quickly as I could. I drove over to Princeton every other day to work with Duane. He worked with the Philadelphia Eagles and was the best around. He set me to work on a plan to improve my speed and strength. He was great to work with. He knew which buttons to press with me, and I responded. My goal was to be one of the best players in the world, if not the best. I told Duane that, and we got down to work.

The other change at the Charge was the signing of France striker Marinette Pichon – a truly quality player. This would have a massive impact on my positional play, allowing me to move from a forward role into an attacking midfield role. So instead of playing with my back to goal I was now able to run at the goal and create attacks. I believe my true strength is running at players one-on-one – it always has been – and I was now free to do this in the WUSA for Philadelphia. It also brought some much-needed relief for my ankles. I was the most fouled player in the WUSA, and with my back to the goal my ankles had taken a battering. Given my growing record with injuries, it was a welcome change to play in a new position.

I started the campaign well again, scoring a neat free-kick

in the opening match against Atlanta Beat. The opposition coach Tom Stone called it a 'missile'. The team played well in the new formation, and Zhao Lihong popped up in the second half to secure the win.

Although I still viewed myself as someone who did her talking on the pitch rather than off it, I found that being captain was much easier than the time I'd spent as a coach at Seton Hall. Being the leader of the team in a playmaker role came much easier to me than doing team talks. I actually found that I revelled in my new-found responsibility. I was twenty-three years old and loving life. I scored four goals and added three assists in my first seven games.

Philadelphia were riding high, and so was I. It was around this time that they made a Kelly Smith Money Box for fans. It was a promotional idea a local bank came up with to attract young family members to start accounts with them. It was a good idea to build on the strong fan base we had with younger supporters. There was a natural connection there, and the players' money boxes proved really popular. Around two thousand of them were given out before a match at our home stadium. If you get here early, you get your very own Kelly Smith Money Box! That kind of thing. I still have one at home. It was obviously modelled on me, with the number 8 on and everything. It's quite life-like, actually. It's a nice souvenir for me to have from those times at Philadelphia.

And then – crash! Everything was over again. I missed the rest of the season after tearing the anterior cruciate ligament in my right knee. This was the beginning of what would become a horror show for me.

It was my first serious injury, and it happened in a match

against Bay Area CyberRays. It was nobody's fault – it was down to the way I turned my body. When I went to put a cross in, my knee stayed where it was but my body turned. As a result my knee went 'pop'. Everybody heard it. I knew straight away that I had torn it and that I was in trouble. Brandi Chastain, who played for the CyberRays, was close to me on the field. As the ball was kicked out of play, I remember her saying to me, 'Are you all right? Are you all right?' I can clearly recall my response too: 'I've done my knee.'

I had completely torn my ACL – the middle ligament of the knee. It was totally flapping around in there. That was just bad luck due to the way I'd turned and the way the force impacted on my knee. The operation to repair it was lengthy and the recovery was a long and laborious one. The surgeon implanted a 'cadaver', which was actually an Achilles tendon from a guy who had been killed in a motorcycle accident, into my knee and sewed the ligament back together. Touch wood, it's still going strong.

The injury was a whole new experience for me. Before it, all I had known were quad pulls, muscle pulls or sprains. Nothing had ever kept me out of the game long term before. But this did. This was a major injury.

Straight after surgery I could barely do anything with my leg. I was stuck on crutches. I was told to sleep in a machine for six to eight hours per day. The machine would slowly move my leg while I slept. It was weird. I found that the only position I could sleep in and not move at all was on my back. It was still quite a difficult task. I would strap myself in and the machine would go to work, slowly moving my leg around. It didn't go particularly fast, but I struggled to sleep. Generally I would do two or three hours with it, take a break, then put it on again.

I spent the majority of my days on the couch, watching television and movies. I would do as much as I could with my leg, just to keep the movement going so that it didn't stiffen up – pretty basic stuff. The aim was to get a full range of motion back within my knee joint. Then I had to build my quad muscle, hamstring muscle and calf back up to the level I needed for professional sport. The swelling prevented me from rushing anything. I had to get all of it out of the way before I could do too much of anything, and that took several months, because sometimes I got over-keen and pushed it a little too hard and it swelled up again. It was literally a case of two steps forward and one step back throughout the whole process.

At the time of my injury I had been really happy in Philadelphia. I was with a great set of team-mates doing what I loved to do – playing football – and getting paid to do it. It was my job. It was what I woke up to do every morning. And suddenly I couldn't do that. Eventually I could get to training, but I couldn't train as I wanted to, with my team-mates. Even worse, I had to be at the training ground earlier than the rest of the team so that I could start my rehabilitation work. I would see all the players getting ready for training and I would be laid out on the treatment table, barely able to move my leg.

Just going through my routine of stretching and trying to build my muscles up again with the trainer was tough enough. It was a frustrating task. I was putting in the hours but I wasn't able to do what I was there to do. What I really wanted was to be out on the pitch getting that buzz from playing. I missed that so much.

The medical staff were absolutely great with me. There was never any suggestion from them that I wouldn't make a full recovery. But if I'm honest, there was a little bit of doubt in my mind. I was willing to do anything that was required to get back to my best, but I knew it was going to be a long road. Still, I was dedicated enough, mentally, to try and get back as quickly as possible. I never once allowed myself to dwell on the thought that I wouldn't make a successful return.

I set myself a personal goal: I aimed to be back running as soon as I could. It was a simple and straightforward goal, but it was in no way an easy one. The only way I was going to achieve it was by putting extra work in – two or three hours every day. Sometimes it was even more than that. I worked long, tedious hours with my trainer in an effort to get my leg back into some sort of shape.

It took about five and a half months, from start to finish, until I was running properly again; it was five months before I was running at all. Then I started to incorporate straight-line running into curved running. After a while I was able to run up to a cone, cut in and push off. It was a gradual process. It was also a boring process. But I desperately wanted to get back to playing football as soon as I could so that is what I had to do.

That first jog after months out felt absolutely great. Doing no exercise for such a long time is murderous for an athlete in any sport. It just felt great to be back. Once I got out on the pitch, I experienced another level of mood elevation. The team was still training without me, but at least I was there, jogging the length of the pitch at a slow pace. You get to appreciate the simple things in life at times like these. After so much time away it was a really positive feeling, psychologically, to be back out there with the girls, even though I was still essentially on my own.

After that, progress slowed again. I was told I couldn't rush it through, and I knew that I couldn't rush it through. You can't do too much, too soon. I would go to the stadium and watch the Philadelphia games on crutches. That was tough to deal with mentally. One minute I was a big part of the team, the next I was out of the game and out of the team's plans.

The team missed me, and my team-mates missed me. They told me so. And I hated missing out on it all. I hated being in the changing room before the game, sitting there by my locker, not being able to put my kit on and go out and play with them. They had their kits on and I was stuck with my crutches.

I began to miss my family again at this time. Don't get me wrong, I had good friends at Philadelphia. But it's a different deal when everybody is playing every weekend and you're not. They were getting what they needed from the game, whereas I felt lost.

The Philadelphia players were great, actually, and they made me feel as much a part of things as they possibly could. There was one game when I was sitting on the bench when Marinette scored a great goal for us. She ran over to me and lifted her shirt to show me her vest underneath with my name and my number on it: Smith 8. I had tears in my eyes. Marinette and I had built up such a great partnership and understanding on the field and things had been going so well for us before my injury. She remains one of the best players I have ever played with. We had a connection on the pitch – I just knew where she was going to be and where her runs were going to go. So I knew with that sweet gesture that she was missing me on the field. I appreciated that so much because it showed me that she respected me and that she wanted to tell me. And, my God, I was missing so much playing with her too. That's why the tears came.

But the bigger meaning of this was to remind me that I still mattered. By showing me her vest, Marinette made me realize that I was missed by the team and that I was still a big part of the team.

After a hard and intense summer programme of fitness and rehabilitation at Philadelphia, I was delighted to be named in the Charge team for the start of the 2003 season. I felt that it was going to be a big one for me. I was in really good shape, probably the fittest I had ever been in the US. I felt all was good to go for a successful third campaign with Philadelphia. Here was my opportunity to prove myself as the footballer I knew I could be in the best and biggest women's football league in the world.

Depressingly, my season lasted for just one and a half matches.

During the second match of the campaign, against New York Power, I went up for a header with Shannon Boxx and as I came down she accidentally swiped at my knee. Again I heard a sound I didn't want to hear. It was more of a 'crunch' than a 'pop' this time, but either way, I knew I had done something again. And I was right. It was the same knee too.

I immediately got a scan done, which revealed that I had meniscus damage – essentially a torn cartilage. More seriously, there was also bruising on the bone. The upshot of all this was that the damage was far more serious than had at first been expected.

A normal cartilage operation usually rules you out of action for five or six weeks maximum. I would be out of the game for another five months. This time the surgeon had to drill around the outside of my tibia a number of times, hopefully making it bleed so that calcium would re-grow and strengthen the bone.

The injuries now started to play on my mind. It seemed that I was working my butt off for no reward. What was the point? Fate was cruel. All these sorts of thoughts crowded into my head.

It was such a big blow for me. I had fought my way back from serious injury and lasted only one whole game before being ruled out for another season. I had scored in that game against New York as well. So I knew I was back and able to do what I'd done before the injury. It was frustrating and hurtful. I had done all the right things during recovery only to now have to do them all over again. It would be much harder for me second time around.

Away from injuries, some better news had come in the shape of the silver screen. *Bend It Like Beckham* was a big hit in the cinema. Featuring Keira Knightley, Parminder Nagra and Jonathan Rhys Meyers, it told the story of a young Punjabi Sikh from Hounslow in west London who has dreams of earning a football scholarship in America.

One of my goals for Philadelphia features in the film. It's the goal I scored against San Diego Spirit on my WUSA debut, and it's on screen for all of two or three seconds. There's a commentary line in there too, mentioning my name. But blink and you'll miss it!

It was really nice to be involved in something that did a lot to promote the women's game, particularly in England, where I was still something of an unknown I felt. The film was popular in America too, probably because the storyline was about the girl getting a scholarship and having to leave home to better herself in America. It could have been written about me, come to think of it! But, in all seriousness, anything to do with women's football getting coverage was good at that time, whether it was about some-one going over to America or staying in England.

But when the film came out, in 2002, my focus was completely on getting back to playing on the pitch again. As I've said, an ACL injury is a bad injury – it used to end careers – and recovery is a long and slow process. And now I had reinjured the same knee shortly after getting back to full fitness.

This was going to take a lot out of me, both mentally and physically. I soon found out that I couldn't do it on my own.

9

Numbing the Pain

MY SECOND SERIOUS INJURY WITHIN A YEAR AFFECTED ME badly. I was devastated. Why did this keep happening to me? All the strength I had shown during the months of intense rehabilitation after my anterior cruciate ligament injury now seemed to evaporate.

I didn't realize it at the time, but my drinking began to really take hold during this period. Just as in my early days at Seton Hall, because I wasn't in the team I began to struggle with my confidence again. Sometimes I would meet the girls in the bar after a game. I found that meant I would have to drink as much as I could before they arrived to enable me to feel confident by the time they all got there. I wasn't playing so I was often the first one at the bar. And I was happy to do that. When I couldn't fuel my confidence with my performances on the pitch, it had to come from my alcohol intake.

I had never stopped having a social drink with friends and team-mates during the first two seasons at Philadelphia, but not to excess. It would never get out of hand and it would never affect the way I played. But this time, recovering from a second serious injury in no time at all, I started to drink on my own. I found that drink numbed both the physical and mental pain. And this time I turned to harder drinks. The cheap beer was out and shorts were in. It wasn't yet out of control but it was the beginning of something that would get that way.

It was incredibly frustrating not only to be missing so much football with Philadelphia but some important games for my country too. England came close to qualifying for the 2003 Women's World Cup without me but fell at the final hurdle. Karen Walker scored two great goals – one of them came on eighty-eight minutes – in Reykjavik to earn us a 2–2 draw against Iceland in the first leg of the play-off semi-finals. And Amanda Barr got the goal that won us the second leg at St Andrew's in Birmingham.

That meant a two-legged final against France. We lost the home match, at Selhurst Park, thanks to a goal scored by my Philadelphia Charge team-mate Marinette Pichon. And we lost the second leg at Saint Etienne by the same scoreline, 1–0. The goal that day was scored by Corinne Diacre. The most notable difference in the two matches was in the two attendances – 5,000 or so in London and over 28,000 in France! The French went through to the World Cup. We continued to wait for our chance.

It was hugely disappointing to miss out on these crucial play-off matches, particularly as I'd been hitting good form in my last games for England before injury, scoring two goals against Portugal in a 3–0 win in Portsmouth and also finding the net against Holland in The Hague in a 4–1 victory a few weeks later. Both were World Cup qualifiers. We were unfortunate again to be drawn against one of the top sides – on this occasion Germany – in our qualification group, but this was always going to be the case with our world ranking what it was.

Due to the outbreak of the SARS virus in China, the Women's World Cup was switched to America again. The BBC came over to cover the tournament for *Football Focus* and they asked me to present some links and do some interviews for them. It was the first time I had ever been asked to do anything like that and it was good fun. It also kept me busy and positive. It was a shame England weren't there, but we were getting closer with every qualifying campaign.

I was in California with the BBC when word suddenly came through to me that the Women's United Soccer Association was in danger of folding. I was with the USA team at the time and whispers were flying around the camp that there were problems, which became bigger problems, and eventually problems that couldn't be resolved. After that it was all over very quickly. I woke up one morning and it was there, and I went to bed at night and it was all gone. I couldn't comprehend that. The day had started with me as a professional footballer, and ended with my dream job gone and me out of work.

Apparently it was all down to money. These things often are. The stories in the newspapers mentioned overspending by millions of dollars.

I burst into tears when the rumours were confirmed to be true. I felt so emotional about it because I felt that I had never got to show my true potential in the league.

Once it had all sunk in I had some serious thinking to do yet again. What did I do now with my life? I was in America only to play in a league that no longer existed. My working visa stipulated that it was for me to play in the WUSA. That job had now gone. So, in effect, had my work visa.

Germany beat Sweden 2–1 after extra-time in the Women's World Cup final and began what would be almost a decade of domination in women's football. Birgit Prinz was the Golden Ball and Golden Shoe winner with seven goals. She would soon be accepted as the best player in the world. The USA finished third, beating Canada in the third-place play-off. Third place on home soil did not have an impact on the game like the triumph of four years earlier.

Just a few weeks after the World Cup, the semi-professional W League started to recruit players from the now defunct WUSA set-up. It was a good standard of football but it wasn't a professional league, which was a shame. Still, a lot of players from the WUSA moved over to play in it. Some packed the game in and didn't play again, but most of us moved across to the W League. It was the best option available at the time.

It was certainly the best thing for me. I was at a crossroads in my life, but I didn't really want to go back to England. I wanted to stay in America. I believed in America. I wanted to keep playing football in America. That is how the W League came about really. There were a number of top-quality players who wanted to remain in the country and play in the best league there could be in the circumstances.

I joined the New Jersey Wildcats, along with Marinette Pichon. Recovered from injury again, I was able to renew the partnership we had enjoyed at Philadelphia Charge. It was good to be back. In eight games for the Wildcats, I scored eight goals and made six assists. So once more I was proving my worth on the best stage around, which the W League now was.

Marinette and I shared an apartment as well, so we were best friends off the pitch as well as on it. We had an understanding that was natural. No matter how hard you work on things, sometimes the best stuff just happens. That was the case with the two of us, both at Philadelphia and New Jersey.

But, as had been the case with my whole career in America, the dark days were just around the corner. And the days to come were to be the darkest of my life.

The catalyst was the worst tackle there has ever been. And I mean every single word of that. It still haunts me to this day, how dirty the tackle was. I genuinely believe the intention was to break my leg. That is a very big thing for me to say, but it is how I honestly feel about it. It was just so vicious and unnecessary that there can be no other explanation for it.

Whether it would have happened in a professional league is a question I have asked myself many times. I will never know the answer to that one. The fact is, due to the professional league being scrapped, I was playing semi-professionally when it happened to me.

I am pretty sure that it was the nature and the intent of this tackle that sent me over the edge. This was now my fourth injury in a row, and it was by far the worst of them – from the cause, to the injury itself, right through to the mess it made of my life.

The fact that it was my fourth injury in four seasons was a massive factor. I think I had had enough of it all. There was no point in asking why this type of thing kept on happening to me; I just had to accept it and live with it. But, of course, that is much easier said than done.

I immediately knew that my leg was broken from the way she tackled me. There was no need for it, and that made the whole thing so much more difficult to accept. As I said earlier in this book, I can't remember who was responsible for the tackle and I don't want to know. When asked about it during the research for this book, I didn't want to find out. I declined the request to do so. It is too painful for me. Even now, after all these years, I would much rather not know her name.

I know the match was against Delaware. And I know that it was a reckless challenge by a stupid player who shouldn't have even been on the field. And that is enough for me to know and for me to deal with.

I had the defender on my back and I could sense that she was close to me when the ball was played in to me. So I had to protect the ball. I received it with the outside of my left foot and I had my arm up, because I was expecting some kind of impact from my opponent and of course I had to hold her off.

As the ball came in, I took a touch, and she just came straight in on my standing leg two-footed. The crack on impact told me everything. I jumped up in the air screaming, then came back down to the ground on my left leg. I couldn't plant my right leg at all, because it was broken.

I hopped off the pitch and on to the sidelines and just sat

there on the floor in tears, cursing the stupidity of the tackle and also the horrific nature of it. And I knew that that was it for me for another season – at least.

It was incomparable to the other injuries I had suffered. This was easily the worst of the lot. There had been absolutely no effort by her to avoid causing me serious, career-threatening injury. I had my body in line with the ball and there was no way she could win it. So she had to come through me to get it. There's always a good chance a leg will get broken as a result of challenges like that. And I fully believe that she knew that. It is the only thing that makes sense to me in the circumstances.

No player should do that to another player, no matter what. In fact, she doesn't deserve to be called a player, because she isn't one in my eyes.

She wasn't sent off. I couldn't even say whether or not she was booked. I was in too much pain to notice. And literally to add insult to injury, I never even got an apology from her. Maybe it would have been a little easier for me to swallow if I had. It would have taken nothing for her to come up to me and say something. But she didn't do that. There was absolutely nothing from her. It was just like the game was over, I was done over, and she had gone home to get on with her life. For me, that says it was intentional.

I was taken to hospital. My leg was X-rayed and it was confirmed as broken. I had a cast up to my knee. All my team-mates came down to the hospital to see me. They had to wait for me to leave hospital before we could return to New Jersey.

So it was back to another slow recovery. I did my bit. I

would do some rehabilitation work for a couple of hours every day, but then it was home time. And this time, home time meant drinking on my own time.

Once again I found help in the form of alcohol. But it was different this time. This time I was getting drunk to numb the pain and block out the reality of a situation I could not deal with. I was back to where I had once been at Seton Hall. Only this time it was worse. A nightmare was beginning – one that I would endure alone.

Increasingly I withdrew myself from life. When you are out of the game for up to six months, what can you do with all your time? I had gone through that whole process twice, and for what? It seemed like for nothing. So I hit the bottle.

I used vodka to obliterate my sad life. But my life got sadder as a result. It quickly spiralled out of all control. I drank a lot – and I mean a lot: necking half a bottle of vodka on my own to put me out of my misery, downing the stuff every single night until I just couldn't function any more. I drank hard so that I could no longer feel my senses. I didn't want to feel. I didn't like feeling. I didn't like the way I was feeling. I had to numb everything, and the vodka did that.

It was really hard for me to cope this time round. It was the loss of the game that I loved again, and everything that went with it. It was all too much. I get such a terrific buzz from playing football, dribbling around players, setting up goals and scoring goals. Perhaps I would never be able to do that again.

It was such a downer for me. I was living with Marinette in this apartment. I would go along to training with her, but

I would have to sit on the sidelines again, with my leg in plaster. It would often be swelteringly hot too. It was so frustrating for me. And it felt so unfair. At the end of the day, all I could do was go home and hit the bottle.

It was neat vodka or vodka and Coke, and I would drink until oblivion. Well, until I woke up the next morning.

I hated not playing. I hated feeling like a piece of shit. And that is how I felt at that time. Vodka made me feel better. Vodka made me feel happy. Vodka felt – for a while – like it could be the answer.

Of course, I didn't realize at this stage in my life that alcohol is a depressant. So there was me thinking that the drinking was actually making me happy by getting me to forget about all my problems and worries when in reality it was making me feel worse about myself.

The situation was similar to what I had gone through at Seton Hall, only far more serious. The drinking had now got out of control. I look back now and I see it all as a big cry for help.

When I was once again able to train, I could still deal with the hangovers in the morning and I could still get through the day and do my rehabilitation work and whatever. That continued for a couple of months. Once my leg was finally out of the cast I started doing some work on the bike, and I naturally began to feel better within myself. I was working out a little bit and the endorphins were coming back. What was different this time round was that I continued to drink as I returned to some form of fitness. That was different to the previous times – a big difference.

I would try to tell myself, 'Don't have a drink today, Kelly.'

But I would fail in that quest. I found that I needed a drink. That I had to have a drink.

'Alcoholic' is a big word to use and to properly understand. But it's true to say that at that point in my life I couldn't live without having a drink. I absolutely hated myself for drinking as much as I did but I just couldn't stop myself. I would become anxious without alcohol. I would crave a drink, so I'd give in and have a drink. The next morning I would despise myself for not having the self-control to say no. So it quickly became a vicious circle – one I couldn't escape from.

One night I ran out of alcohol and I had to drive down to the local bar by myself to get a drink. I propped myself up at the bar alone, ordered the strongest drink I could think of, then downed a few of them. Eventually I managed to drive myself back to my apartment, where I passed out. I am not proud about drink-driving at this time of my life. I did it on a number of occasions. This was wrong. It was also, obviously, a very dangerous thing for me to do.

Drinking became an obsession with me. Soon I was at the stage where I couldn't stop thinking about having a drink – or, more to the point, thinking about needing a drink. While sitting at home in my apartment alone, drinking by myself, those thoughts in my head got worse and worse. I have to admit that some of them were suicidal. I wanted to end the pain. I wanted to end the loneliness I was feeling. I don't think I would ever have had the guts to do it, but the thoughts were definitely there. On a couple of occasions I went to the bathroom cabinet where I kept a tub of paracetamol tablets. I would hold the tablets in my hands and I would think about taking the lot.

Things would get worse before they got better, but luckily for me, at this point I was rescued. One day I broke down on the telephone to my dad, during one of my regular calls home, and he decided there and then to come over and bring me home. He was adamant. 'I am coming to get you,' he said. So he flew out and took me home. I had lasted seven years out there in total. It had been a long time. When I was happy, I was fine out there. When I was unhappy, I really struggled. It was a torrid time at the end and I had no choice but to return to England.

We had a lot to sort out in America. A lot of paperwork and a car to sell. All these things. But the biggest thing of all was my beloved Boxer, Bailey. It took a lot of time and money to get her to England with me. I bought Bailey out in Philadelphia so she had to go through a host of tests before she could come and live in England. There were all sorts of regulations to satisfy before she could even fly. We needed to get paperwork from the vet where I got her from. She had to fly without me. I was on a different plane with my dad. She then had to go into quarantine when she got to the UK, for four and a half months. The whole thing cost me more than £2,500.

The Americans come across as being well organized, but during that time my dad and I found that nothing could have been further from the truth. It seemed like everything we tried to do, somebody would put an obstacle in our way. As all this was going on, as we were driving around from one nightmare to another just trying to fulfil all obligations and get out of the country, we saw a car with a sticker on the back that said 'God Bless the USA'. We burst out laughing at that. I think you could call it ironic humour. What a wind-up!

We had a limited time to do things and we kept being given the wrong advice. We also had to get a form signed by the state veterinarian, who lived an hour and a half away in Trenton, New Jersey. The whole business with Bailey just added to all the stress for me. It's a wonder we all got back home safely. It was an absolute nightmare. You wouldn't believe the jokers we came across during those few days. It was chaos. My dad says he had a bigger problem bringing Bailey back than he did bringing me back.

When Dad and I arrived back at Heathrow, we had an airport trolley stacked high with about ten suitcases on it. How the hell we ever got all that on the plane I will never know. The excess baggage payment was enormous.

I guess I linked everything that had happened to me with the States. I blamed the country for it all. Would the same thing have happened in England? I will never know. All I know is that I blamed all my troubles on America. There had been too much negativity over the last three years to feel anything positive about the States. I just felt like someone, somewhere was telling me that it was a bad place for me and that I needed to get out. So I vowed, there and then, never to go back. I was done with America. I actually hated the country in the end

10

Rock Bottom

I CAME BACK HOME IN A MESS. THERE IS NO OTHER WORD TO describe it. I moved back in with my family in Garston, Watford. I was twenty-five years old and on my knees. And I still didn't really appreciate the awful position my life was in. My American nightmare might have been over, but my drinking wasn't. I was still heavily into the vodka, secretly at home on my own and at friends' houses too.

One afternoon I got my friend Lois Fidler to drink with me. Lois knew the deal with me. I had spoken to her on the telephone from New Jersey a number of times about it all. She knew I had issues with alcohol and I think she was a little concerned about me. But she gave in to my intense persuasion and agreed to have a drink with me. By the time she had had enough and stopped, I was still craving alcohol; indeed I needed more alcohol. She thought the session was over, but I had other ideas. I wanted to go on and on and on.

When Lois went to the bathroom, I quickly went to the cupboard and poured myself another drink. When she saw me, she erupted. She couldn't believe her eyes. I was oblivious to it all, really. In my world I was just pouring myself another drink.

But her reaction did strike a nerve with me. This was one of the points when I realized something was not right. I was craving more and more alcohol during the day. Lois could stop but I couldn't. Why was that? Why did I need more?

At this time in my life, playing football was a million miles away from my mindset. I didn't know if I could put myself through it all again. I didn't know if I could do it because mentally it was getting too hard for me now, after all the injuries. It never entered my head that I wouldn't be good enough any more. I was always confident in my ability and I always had the self-belief to succeed. I knew the player I was, and I knew the potential I had. But it was getting hard for me mentally now. There was this fear at the back of my mind that I was going to get crocked again. I suppose that was inevitable, really, and it never left me.

The drinking continued until my life hit a full stop – the embarrassing encounter up in Loughborough with the England coach Hope Powell. I knew after that it was either get better or get out of the game.

Lois was in Loughborough at the time of my arranged session with the England medical team. She was the one who dragged me into the privacy of the dorm room and asked me, in pretty colourful language, what I thought I was doing. But I continued drinking from my secret stash of vodka before I had my one-on-one with Hope.

The coach had a go at me, which is understandable. And she was right. I knew from the start with her that if I ever fell, she would catch me. That is a phenomenal feeling to have about somebody, particularly a national coach if you are a footballer. Within days, the Football Association had arranged an appointment for me at the Priory in Southampton.

I attended a forty-five-minute consultation with Pippa Bennett, the England team doctor. I was told by a specialist from the Priory that the best treatment for me would be a twenty-eight-day rehabilitation programme. I went home to Watford and spent the weekend with my parents. I figured out that if I wanted to get my football career and my dreams back on track it meant getting off the drink. I understood that, so that's what I tried to do.

I spent what felt to me like a very long journey down to the Priory swigging from a bottle of vodka in the car. When Lois and I arrived, I sat in the car park doing the same and constantly telling her that I didn't want to go in.

I was petrified. It felt much easier for me to drink than to deal with my shit. I didn't know how to deal with my life. I didn't know how to deal with my emotions. And I certainly didn't know how to deal with my addiction – my need to drink.

The first few days in the Priory were a very daunting and frightening experience for me. I wanted to get better, but I was so scared about facing up to the reality of the situation. I was given a detoxification programme of medication that would slowly wean me off the drink. The first few days were a blur. I felt so out of it under the influence of the drugs.

It was full on in the Priory for a couple of weeks. It is an addiction clinic, so it isn't an easy place to be. There were mentally ill patients in there and that freaked me out a little bit. But I had to accept that I had an illness too. I learned a lot about my addiction and the way alcohol affects the brain.

Most of my time was spent in group sessions with other people who were suffering with similar addictions. This involved a lot of writing and going through steps on your way to getting better. Step one was admitting that I had a problem with alcohol. Writing about it helped me come to terms with the fact that I did have a problem.

Sometimes we would have to attend Alcoholics Anonymous meetings on site, where recovering alcoholics came to talk to us about how they were now coping. They would share some stories with us too. I found all that quite difficult, not least because I was still using alcohol as my big escape, even after I had been admitted to the Priory.

While you are in residence, you are not allowed to leave. It is not an easy place to leave either; there's a long driveway for a start. But one day, early on, I slipped out of there. I didn't know which way to turn but I knew what I wanted. I managed to walk down to a local shop – it took me about ten minutes to get there – and I bought myself some vodka. I had no money on me but I did have my bank card, so I was able to use a cash machine. I got the money I needed, I got the vodka, and I returned to the Priory. Obviously I couldn't take the bottle back in with me, so I stashed it in a bush nearby.

That night I went down to that bush and I drank my vodka. The alcohol reacted in my body with all the detox medication I was on and I became very drunk very quickly. All I wanted was to be out of it. I needed a fix so that I could be somewhere different from my own world and my own

Top left: There was always a ball in the garden for me to play with growing up in Garston, or (**top right**) on the beach with my mum.

Above: Showing off my speed at the school sports day.

Right: My brother, Glen, was always good for a game, even if he did support Liverpool. I just loved my Arsenal kit.

Above: After playing for Watford Ladies, I moved with my friend Debbie Garvey to Pinner Park, and we were regular winners at the five-a-side tournament organized by the Metropolitan Police at Wembley.

Above: Pinner Park essentially became part of Wembley Ladies, but it has to be said the kits weren't the best in those days!

Left: As well as football, I was pretty good at netball and athletics, which was important for my fitness from an early age.

Below: After being spotted by a scout, it was off to America for me and a trip to New York. Here I am with my new Seton Hall team-mates at the top of the Empire State Building and (**bottom**) with my dad and my cousin Gavin.

Above: It was brilliant to play football every day and after my three years there, Seton Hall retired my number 6 shirt in recognition of my performances.

Below: My mum and dad came out for the ceremony and met my coach Betty Ann Kempf (*far left*), who was a great influence on me.

Above: The success of the 1999 Women's World Cup in America helped me to realize my dream of playing in a professional league, for the Philadelphia Charge. Injuries blighted my time in the WUSA, even if I'm trying to smile about a bruised ankle here (**above right**).

After overcoming some serious doubts, I was fit and raring to go again in 2009 when I joined the Boston Breakers in the WPS.

Top: It was also an honour to be chosen in the All-Star team, which is a big tradition in American sports. I'm standing on the far right.

Centre: The All-Stars in 2009 included my Breakers team-mates (*left to right*) Alex Scott and USA internationals Kristine Lilly, Lauren Cheney and Amy LePeilbet.

Left: Celebrating a goal with the brilliant Brazilian, Marta.

THE FA WOMEN'S CUP
IN PARTNERSHIP WITH NATIONWIDE
WINNERS 2006

Top: My years at Arsenal produced countless champagne moments. Here we celebrate beating Leeds 5–0 in my first FA Women's Cup Final, at the New Den in 2006.

Above left: None of that Arsenal success would have been possible without Vic Akers.

Above right: Scoring a free-kick against Charlton in the 2007 FA Women's Cup Final and then (**right**) getting reacquainted with the trophy. Winning the FA Cup is always special.

Above: In 2006/07, Arsenal Ladies became 'The Invincibles', winning the FA Women's Cup, the UEFA Cup (now the Champions League), the FA Women's Premier League, the FA Women's Premier League Cup and the Community Shield.

Left: At the Emirates with another 'Invincible', Thierry Henry.

Below: Tears of joy with Faye White, the Arsenal captain for so many years, after beating Umea to become champions of Europe.

head. I didn't like the thoughts I was having. I was depressed, and all I knew was that I needed to neck it to numb everything.

I felt absolutely awful the next morning. It was like ten hangovers in one. That was probably due to the drugs and the vodka mixed together. I decided that I had to tell somebody about what I had done. So I told one of the nurses. I begged her not to say anything to the counsellors in there, but obviously that's her job and her main priority. She apologized to me and said she couldn't do that, and told me straight, 'I have to go somewhere with this information. I can't just keep this to myself. I could lose my job.' I carried on begging her not to say anything. I felt let down. I'd thought this woman was somebody I could confide in. I knew I would probably get kicked out as a result. But I wasn't. It was viewed as a one-off case. I was very lucky that they did that for me. So, in hindsight, I was grateful that the nurse spoke up. Clearly I wasn't yet done with reality checks.

The lowest point of all came when I started to self-harm. On one occasion, without any alcohol to take away the pain, I just didn't know how to cope. I needed to find something to help me. With my alcohol comfort option gone, I decided to reach for a razor blade from my wash bag.

I pulled the blade out and started to cut my wrists with it. I didn't intend to kill myself, but I did want to ease my pain. Seeing the blood made me feel numb, and that made me feel better. It was a relief from my intense feelings. I cut myself a few times, on both of my wrists and on the tops of my legs too. It was a way for me to cope with the pain I was feeling inside.

It is not something I am proud of today. What more can I say? I was lonely. I was lost. I was scared. I didn't know who I was any more.

I was in a state. I had all these emotions inside me and I didn't know how to deal with them. In the past I had used alcohol to numb everything, but I couldn't do that in there. I had no choice but to come to another moment of realization, but I was too scared to do that.

When you are in a place like the Priory, you have got to deal with yourself first of all. You have to learn to accept certain things – without the use of alcohol. You have to be honest in your actions. You have to be honest with the people around you. You have to be honest with the people you have probably hurt along the way. There may be many things you've done that you now regret. It may embarrass you to talk about those things when they all come to light, but you are constantly told that the way forward is to be honest about it all. It's not an easy thing to do though. In fact I found it too hard. I couldn't do it like that. So I decided I had to leave. It had just got too much for me. I was done with the place. I think I'd lasted for about two and a half weeks.

My recovery was eventually achieved at the Sporting Chance clinic. I'd felt like I needed something different from the Priory and I found that the clinic was able to help me a lot more. I just got in touch with them and went down there for a long weekend. I felt that the people at Sporting Chance were more in tune with athletes and the way an athlete's mind thinks. I was able to get more out of the place as a result.

A lot of athletes have gone on record as saying that without Sporting Chance they wouldn't be playing sport today. I feel the same. But when you are going through treatment there, you can't allow yourself to think about the future. It is all about day to day. Well it was for me anyway. Playing for England again, playing professionally again, playing in a Women's World Cup or a Women's European Championship – none of that was even on the radar for me at that time. It was just about trying to get better and feel healthy. Furthermore, in my situation, it was about not using drink to numb everything out.

I dealt with my life on a day-by-day basis, and by not drinking I found that I was able to gain more strength to deal with things. Now, going to AA meetings gave me strength, from hearing other people talk about their recovery process to learning to live for the moment. That is what I had to do. I had to recover before I could start thinking or dreaming about football again. I also had to get my spirit back so that I could start to want to do all those things again.

I spent a lot of those meetings just sitting and listening. Somebody would get up and share their journey with the group, and if you felt comfortable enough you could get up as well and share a little bit about yourself, your life, your day. Anything that was on your mind, really. I found that that was pretty much what I needed to do to stay sober at that time.

Given my shyness and timid nature, it was not the easiest thing for me to do. I have never been one to draw attention to myself, particularly in a manner like that. But I found that it was helpful to listen to other people and to hear about their life experiences and struggles with alcohol. Relating your problems to stories about other people's drinking and hearing how they coped and got through it was pretty powerful. I drew a lot of strength from that – the sort of strength I badly needed.

I also think it helps being helped by people who have been on a similar journey in their life. I would go so far as to say that I don't think I could have got the help I needed if those people hadn't been through what I had been through. That is an important part of it all. We could help each other out along the same path.

I still speak to Peter Kay, who runs the Sporting Chance clinic, every now and again. The counsellor there, James West, became a good friend too. I used to meet him every Friday in London and talk about how my life was going – just like a counselling session, really. That helped me a lot, just so I could get my head in the right frame of mind to cope with the forthcoming week. I had that particular support for a number of years after leaving there. It was something to keep me grounded, keep me focused on the job in hand, to get me through each week as well as to help me set goals in terms of what I still wanted to achieve in my life.

The Sporting Chance clinic is situated in the middle of nowhere, at a place called Liphook, so there is not a lot for you to do other than think about your life and where it is heading. There is a Champneys health spa on site too – but, make no mistake, you know why you are in there and that is to get treatment. I think the house itself holds about five or six people so you have five or six people there in treatment at any one time. It's group therapy – getting together and talking about your problems and how you feel about your-self. Obviously it's important to be honest with the group, and therefore with yourself. There were the AA meetings too, and there were also things like yoga classes you could go to. It suited me. It was good for me.

I managed to get off the drink, which was great. I was lucky. Today, I can manage my drinking OK. I still drink sometimes, but in a controlled way. I still have to work on it, though. I have always felt the need and I still do – it hasn't gone away from me. I still have the odd fancy to neck a few and feel nice. But those thoughts are nowhere near as dark as they used to be.

That is thanks to Sporting Chance, the Priory and the Football Association. It is also thanks to my family, who brought me home and helped to get me through my recovery.

To be honest, there was a lot about my drinking that my family didn't know at the time. I kept a lot of information secret. I guess I felt that I was an embarrassment to them, really. I didn't want to tell them that I was in such a bad way. I didn't want to admit that, either to them or to myself.

Obviously my dad knew about it all because he brought me home from the US and he picked me up from the treat-ment centre in Southampton. But he didn't really appreciate how bad it was until I checked myself into the Sporting Chance clinic. Hope knew more. She was in regular contact with me throughout my recovery once she was made aware of my situation. And Lois, one of my best mates – she knew, of course. Another person who really helped me through that period of my life was Pippa, the England team doctor. She was a great support to me. My recovery wasn't just about rehabilitation, injuries, ailments and whatever, it was also about me picking up the phone and speaking to people I could trust about it all.

Few people knew about my situation because to me it was a personal problem and one I wanted to deal with privately. As far as I know my England team-mates were not aware of what I was going through and how I was trying to deal with it and recover from it. Nothing was ever discussed, that's for sure.

Five years later, in 2009, I decided to come out about it all. I did an interview with the *Daily Mail*, and overnight it became public knowledge. I guess I had got to a point in my life where I finally felt that I had the coping skills to deal with it all.

Interviews in newspapers or on television were becoming harder. Reporters would want to know how I had dealt with the succession of injuries I had suffered in my career, telling me how strong I must be to keep coming back after every setback. I just kept telling them half a story, really. And before long it felt, because of my therapy, that I was lying to them.

I wanted to be totally honest about it all. I wanted to say to the world, 'I actually got myself into a real state due to drink.' I chose the reporter I wanted to do the interview with, Ashley Gray. I felt like I could trust him. I felt that he would get my story across properly. I am glad I chose him. I felt a lot better afterwards.

11

A Gunner Again

SLOWLY BUT SURELY WOMEN'S FOOTBALL HAD RISEN IN prominence back in Great Britain during the seven years I had been away. In 2002 it had become the most participated-in female sport in the country, taking over from netball, and ten years on we are set for our first foray into the Olympic Games. It is an exciting position for us to have got to after all these years of struggle and steady improvement.

And believe me, it has been some journey for us to get here, both on and off the pitch. The Football Association has done a tremendous amount of work in terms of the development of the sport. The England coach Hope Powell has been absolutely immense. She deserves the most credit.

Media interest has increased significantly. England have reached two Women's World Cup quarter-finals in a row now – in 2007 and 2011 – plus the final of Women's Euro 2009. We successfully hosted the finals of Euro 2005 too.

To polish it all off, in 2011 the Women's Super League – an elite summer league for women's football in England – was finally launched after many years of hopes and talks. The Olympics will be a fitting climax to ten years' hard work and welcome growth. I can't wait for it, and I dearly hope that I am able to play in it.

My often-used quotation that 'women's football in England is a joke', or whatever I was supposed to have said while I was out in America in the early 2000s, has caused me a fair bit of grief over the years. As I've already said in this book, I can't actually remember saying those words but I stand by them because the statement was more or less true at that time and that is how I felt, particularly when you compared the sport in our country to what was going on across the pond.

One of the reasons why I felt so strongly about things was because I was training every day in the States and I was feeling like I was getting better and becoming more established because I was on the ball every day rather than hanging around a training ground waiting to train just twice a week. I realized that this approach had made a big difference to me. The limited amount of training was what frustrated me most at that time about women's teams in England. I needed to be working with a ball much more than that, and I'm sure the rest of the England team were feeling that too.

On those two nights a week they would have to work on their fitness as well, running without a ball and what have you. So they would get limited playing time too. That is the main reason why I felt the game was lagging behind in England. I saw all that stuff as an example of people not taking the game seriously enough. Two nights per week just wasn't good enough for me. I suppose because I was already a professional player and the game in England was still semi-professional, it all felt stale to me. I hope that people can now appreciate that.

I was the only overseas player in the England team. A few years after me, Danielle Murphy and Rachel Brown came out to the States to study and play. But at the time of my comment I was out there on my own so those particular thoughts were exclusive to me. That's why they made the press, I guess. I didn't intend to knock the system, I just spoke from my heart, voiced my feelings. It was what I felt. It was what I knew.

I returned regularly to England to play international games. I didn't go back for too many friendlies, but I was always there – when fit and able – to play in important qualification matches for Women's World Cups and European Championships.

That was a really hard thing to do when I was studying for my degree at Seton Hall. I was juggling two lives separated by the vast Atlantic Ocean, and it wasn't easy. It was tiring, and it made keeping up with my studies a difficult task. While I was away travelling I was, of course, away from college and therefore missing lectures over maybe a seven- to ten-day period, which would leave me playing catch-up when I got back for weeks afterwards. But I did it for the love of the game and, importantly, the love of my country. It was just the price I had to pay if I wanted to study and play in America and play for England as well.

Travelling like that in any job takes a toll after a while, though. Physically you grow very tired from jet lag and things like that. In fact, being a sportsperson and doing that is probably worse than other professions, for obvious reasons.

There was never any assurance that I was going to play in

those games either. I did play in most of them, but I could easily have travelled all the way to England and then sat the game out on the bench. I never knew until I arrived with the squad whether I was in the team or not.

The drinking didn't help either. Before I admitted to myself that I had a drinking problem and spent some time in recovery at Sporting Chance, I once bought a bottle of wine from a supermarket while on England duty and had a drink in my hotel room after the match. With the game out of the way, I could relax knowing that I could now drink that bottle of wine and be out of it afterwards. Nobody ever said anything to me about it. Then again, I don't think anybody in any form of authority knew anything about it at that time.

There always seemed to be a lot of talk about a possible professional women's league in England in the early 2000s. But it didn't happen. Fulham Ladies were geared up for it – they put players like Katie Chapman and Rachel Yankey on proper full-time contracts – but that venture soon fell away, sadly.

The FA Women's Cup final was covered live on BBC One in 2002 as part of the FA's new television deal. It remained on BBC One for seven years. That was a very important step for the game and an important mark of nationwide recognition for the sport.

But still all of this felt a million miles away from what was going on in my life in America at that time, where I was playing professionally with the best players in the world live on television during most weeks of the season. There were decent crowds every week too, and we were all on decent money.

It was only when I hit rock bottom in my personal life and I came back to live in England that I could acknowledge and appreciate the changes that had gradually taken place at home. The ironic thing is, by then I wasn't sure I actually wanted to play football any more.

It was seven years since I had last put on my beloved Arsenal colours, for instance. What had happened to me in those years was a real rollercoaster ride. I had some great highs, of course, but my God I'd had some rotten lows. I wouldn't want to go through it all again, that's for sure. When I search my memories of those years I struggle to separate the good from the bad.

I was in such a bad way towards the end that playing football was often the furthest thing from my mind. In fact for a while I was pretty sure I didn't want to play football. I just thought that mentally I couldn't do it. It seemed too much for me to face.

That trip up to Loughborough in the summer of 2004 was a massive wake-up call, but returning to play the game effectively and passionately was still at the end of a very long road for me. I needed to recover properly, physically and mentally, before I could even entertain such a thought, and I didn't know how I could get to that point. All I knew was that I had to start out on that road, and that if I was ever again going to become the footballer I knew I could be, I must not look back.

It was approaching Christmas 2004 when Arsenal Ladies coach Vic Akers heard that I was back in the country and he started to call me regularly, just to chat at first. His offer to return to the club I loved still stood after all those years, but it was still a fair while before it could become a reality. He knew that and he never pushed me too hard, which was very important to me.

Vic was brilliant. All he would do was gently nudge me along, saying things like, 'Why don't you come down and train with us, Kelly?' I didn't make it easy for him but he kept on: 'Come down and train with us and just see how you feel.' He was pretty persistent but kind and gentle with it.

Eventually I succumbed, and a couple of times I went training with Arsenal Ladies. I quickly found that it was great therapy for me, and after only a month or so I got back into the swing of things. I agreed to re-sign for Arsenal early in 2005. That was quite a turnaround for me, because as I said, I wasn't even certain that I wanted to play football any more.

Another thing that helped my focus and recovery was the fact that a job had come up at Arsenal at that time – assistant academy director. It was based up at Oaklands College, not too far away from my Hertfordshire home, where the club's girls' academy was created. The job was to look after about thirty girls aged between sixteen and nineteen. Once I'd begun to fall in love with the game again and enjoy being involved with the team and the girls, it seemed the perfect place for me to be. Like the position at Seton Hall after my degree was completed, I happened to be in the right place at the right time. Everything just seemed to be slotting together perfectly.

Vic was great about it all. I had a secure job offer on the table and he promised me that I could take my time returning to the pitch, which was exactly the approach I needed him to take. It was important for me that he did that.

The timing of the job offer couldn't have been better for me. I was very fortunate. I was keen to put pen to paper and secure the whole package. Before long I would be back to doing what I had done at college – playing and coaching in equal measure. This is what I had studied to do. This is what I wanted to do again. Right here, right now.

Faye White had already had a job at Arsenal for a number of years. She worked in the office at the men's training ground. A number of other players work for the club today, including Jayne Ludlow, who's a physiotherapist, and Emma Byrne, who works in an administrative role. The club really look after us and always have done. They could not have done any more for me, that's for sure. I think that after everything that had happened in my life, a return to playing football again could only have happened through Vic and Arsenal.

The first thing I did after re-signing for the Gunners was to ask Vic if the number 8 shirt was available because I desperately wanted to wear it. He told me it was, so it was happy days. I had wanted to wear that Arsenal shirt ever since I first saw Ian Wright play at Highbury when I was a young girl. It was yet another dream come true for me – and it came along just after I had been thinking that my days in football might be over for good! But now that I was back playing again, and for the club that I loved, I had to make sure that I got my priorities right. Having the number 8 on my back was just the icing on the cake.

12

Football's Coming Home

MY RETURN TO MATCH FITNESS HAD TO BE A PATIENT ONE.
Obviously my rehabilitation from alcoholism took time, as
did my recovery from the catalogue of injuries I had suffered
out in the States. By the end of the 2004/05 season I was
finally getting back into my stride. My first appearance for
Arsenal Ladies since the early summer of 1997 was as a
substitute against Milton Keynes Dons at Borehamwood in
April, when I came on for the last twenty-five minutes. Three
weeks later I scored a forty-yard goal against Charlton
Ladies that secured us the Women's Premier League title. It
was my second league title with the Gunners in just two
seasons there – and they were eight years apart!

My return to the England side after a year away took place
on 6 May, against Norway in a friendly at Barnsley. But the
big highlight came three weeks later against the Czech
Republic in another friendly, at the Bescot Stadium in
Walsall, when I scored from a similar distance to the strike I
had hit for Arsenal against Charlton.

Ten days after that, in early June, Women's Euro 2005
kicked off.

The fight to get fit for the Euros, being held in England for the first time, was a really hard one for me. I had regular meetings and telephone conversations with England coach Hope Powell in the build-up to the tournament. Everybody was working so hard to get fit and to be selected in the final twenty. There was a buzz about the place throughout the 2004/05 campaign that I sensed as soon as I got home from the US.

Some young players were staking strong claims. Karen Carney was just seventeen years old but in great form. She'd been included in the squad for England's trip to the Algarve Cup in March along with over twenty others. I was not fit enough to go. (In fact I have never played in the Algarve Cup. England only went once.) All the eight nations that were to play in the Euros – England, Denmark, Finland, France, Germany, Italy, Norway and Sweden – were there, but, due to not playing in the preceding competition and a lower world ranking than other teams, England did not play any of them. Our games were against Northern Ireland, Portugal, Mexico and China instead. We won the first three comfortably but lost to China 5–3 in a penalty shoot-out. I think the mood was good out there, and it continued through those friendly wins in Barnsley and Walsall.

My relief at returning to the team and scoring a goal, let alone a great lob from forty yards out, was immense, and the emotion was intense. I ran over to Hope on the bench and hugged her. The tears came so freely to me. Yet again I had found a way back from oblivion. And this particular journey over the past eighteen months had been the hardest I'd ever taken. I cried due to the pure elation of it all, really. It was a spectacular goal of course, in terms of the distance involved, but the tears came when I saw Hope. I just wanted to say thank you.

She had been a massive support for me. If it hadn't been for her my football career would probably have ended in 2004, because if she hadn't got me the help I needed at that time I could easily have spiralled out of control. I may not even be here today without Hope. That's how bad things had got. But she stuck by me. She knew I needed to get help and she knew I needed proper treatment. She couldn't do it herself, but she was there for me as a friend. She really cared about me as a person. Getting me right mentally mattered to her.

I remember Hope saying to me, 'I don't care if you never play football again, I just want you to get yourself back.' I had lost myself. There is no other way of putting it. Hope helped me back into a good space and into a better frame of mind. She helped me get back to the stage where I wanted to play football again. But, as with Vic Akers, there was no pressure from her. 'See how you go,' she would say to me. It was like, 'forget about the football and get yourself right'. And that was the right method to use. It was so beneficial to me that she was caring and understanding in this way. And I will never ever forget that.

I broke down in tears again during an interview with the BBC prior to Euro 2005 when I talked about this. I still get very emotional about it today. Hope was my saviour, really.

Euro 2005 was always touch and go for me. Just before the final squad was announced in late May I had to go for a scan on my left foot because I was still in a lot of pain, mainly because I'd started to play again. I had been suffering from a navicular stress fracture and I experienced a lot of discomfort during those Arsenal games and England friendlies. I was passed fit, took my place in the final twenty, and was given squad number 12. But I wasn't yet match fit so whether or not I would get to play any part in the tournament I didn't know. Still, I was in the squad, and that felt really good.

The 2005 Women's European Championship was amazing for women's football in England. It was very successful in terms of crowds and television viewing figures and it played a massive part in the growth of the sport in our country. The players felt it from the off. In the lead-up to the tournament we were doing interviews for national newspapers, magazines, television and radio, sometimes making pull-outs and back pages. It seemed the whole nation was getting behind us. It was what I had dreamed about for so long – what, if I am honest, I'd wondered for a long time if I would ever see in my own country. America, yes; England, I wasn't too sure. But Euro 2005 changed all that. It proved that fans wanted to go along and support their national women's team and enjoy the game. Supporters were turning up at grounds in England shirts, their faces painted with the St George cross. Some of them proudly came to matches with our names on their backs. The red and white flags were every-where. The atmosphere heading to the grounds on the coaches was terrific, and the atmosphere inside the stadiums was something I thought I would never experience.

The tournament was held in the north-west, at the City of Manchester Stadium, home of Manchester City; Ewood

Park, home of Blackburn Rovers; Deepdale, home of Preston North End; Bloomfield Road, home of Blackpool; and at the Halliwell Jones Stadium, home of Warrington Wolves rugby league team. We were drawn in Group A with Denmark, Finland and Sweden. Germany, the Women's World Cup holders, the European champions and the tournament favourites, were drawn in Group B with France, Italy and Norway. The top two from each group qualified for the semi-finals. On paper, Germany and Norway were expected to qualify from Group B and Sweden were fancied to go through from our group – all three teams were ranked in the top five in the world – but the other semi-final spot was thought to be wide open.

We kicked off our campaign against Finland on a balmy Sunday evening at the awesome City of Manchester Stadium. It was a match we really had to win if we had any realistic hope of progressing, for the Finns were considered to be the minnows of the competition with the lowest world ranking of all the teams involved. I was told ahead of the game that I was going to start.

Walking into the changing rooms at Manchester City was like moving into another world for us. There was just so much room. It was the biggest changing room I had ever been in in my life. There was so much space to put all your stuff and everything. It felt like the team-mate next to you was far away.

To be playing the opening game in such a stadium was amazing for all of us. For so many people to turn up was even better. A crowd of 29,092 was out there waiting to watch us. We were overwhelmed. It was a record attendance for an England women's international and for the Women's European Championship. A further 2.5 million people were watching live on BBC Two. I'd never imagined that so many people would turn out to watch a game of women's football in our country. When we walked out, it was just buzzing out there. I could clearly see the face paints on the kids in the stands; I could see loads of England flags and England shirts too. The fact that people were wearing such things and wanting to wear such things for us was a real 'wow' factor. It was like, 'Our time has come!'

They were all fantastic that night. You knew that they were there for you, and that was a tremendous boost. There weren't too many Finnish fans around. It was red and white all over.

I played for forty-five minutes – I just wasn't fully match fit due to the stress fracture in my foot. I got frustrated with myself from time to time, because I wasn't able to do things I knew I could have done had I been 100 per cent, but I felt that I did all right. We took a 2–0 lead in that first half through a Sanna Valkonen own goal and Amanda Barr. I had a long-distance strike that hit the bar and bounced out and Amanda was on hand with a quick reaction to score from the rebound.

But Finland came back strongly in the second half and Anna-Kaisa Rantanen got them a goal back. They drew level with just a few minutes remaining. Laura Kalmari was their danger player and she got the equalizer. They also hit the bar and the post and, to be fair, they were on top for most of the half.

Amazingly, in the finale of all finales, Kaz Carney made

her name with a brilliant winning goal for us in injury-time. It was such a dramatic and fantastic finish and it kicked off the tournament in style. Everybody seemed to be talking about it the next day. We were all over the papers, and Kaz, who was still at school at the time, was doing interviews left, right and centre with media from home and abroad. I was so pleased for her, and I was so happy to see that all this was happening in England.

As a squad, we had a real feeling of togetherness during that tournament. England had been the first to qualify, after being named hosts back in 2002, so it had been in our sights for three years. The team was developing nicely with players such as Faye White, our captain, Katie Chapman, Fara Williams, Rachel Yankey and myself. And then we had a number of younger players coming through, Kaz being one of them.

The one thing we didn't really have as a team was international tournament experience. Added to that, we hadn't had to go through a qualification process to play in this competition. We were there as hosts. We hadn't actually played competitive football at international level for over two and a half years when we walked out on to the pitch against Finland. I hadn't played a competitive match for England for over three years, since the March 2002 Women's World Cup qualifier against Holland in The Hague.

With one win and three points under our belts, we went to Ewood Park knowing that another victory, over Denmark, would put us into the semi-finals. Before another big crowd, Fara gave us a first-half lead from the penalty spot after Yanks had been brought down by Mariann Knudsen. We were just ten minutes away from the last four when, cruelly, Denmark grabbed the first of two goals to beat us. Merete Pedersen's free-kick was a great strike, and two minutes from time, Cathrine Paaske Sørensen headed home past Jo Fletcher from Johanna Rasmussen's cross. The pressure had been mounting the longer the match went on. I'd come off at half-time again and watched it all unfold from the bench. It was heartbreaking not to be able to do anything to help.

We were down but not out. We got a little bit of luck later that evening when Finland drew with Sweden, which meant we were still placed in the top two in the group. But we had to now go out and get a result against Sweden. We knew that a win would definitely put us through while a draw might do. We also knew that a defeat would put us out – and Sweden, one of the strongest outfits in Europe, had to win the match to go through.

In the end, a draw would have been enough for us because Finland went on to beat Denmark in Blackpool. But we lost to an early goal from Anna Sjöström, so that didn't matter a jot. Rachel Brown, another player returning from injury problems, came into the team in goal and was beaten in the first few minutes by a flick-on from a corner. We felt that she had been fouled. As far as we were concerned she was pushed into the goal by the goalscorer.

Sweden's experience counted for a lot, and that one goal was enough to send them through at our expense. We never recovered from that third-minute setback. This time I played for the whole ninety minutes. But we couldn't get into our rhythm. The best chance I can remember was when I touched on a Yanks cross for Kaz, but the Swedish goalkeeper,

Hedvig Lindahl, pushed the shot wide. It was a frustrating match to play in, particularly as I still wasn't fully match fit. But I couldn't beat myself up about that. I'd done my best in the circumstances.

I think we were too naive in this match. We were too naive regarding their goal, that's for sure. Because of our inexperience, we just allowed the play to happen and didn't even think to complain about it. We didn't appeal to the referee or anything like that. The Swedes obviously had experience of doing that sort of stuff and getting away with it – getting their own way in the penalty box, I mean. We didn't play the game like that. We didn't come close.

Sweden were ranked third in the world at the time and were World Cup runners-up two years before. Some of their star players, like Hanna Ljungberg, were brilliant. A goalless or 1–1 draw would have put us into the semi-finals. As it was, we finished bottom of the group. That's how tight it was.

There was an incident in that Sweden game that I still remember well today. A lot of us still laugh about it in fact. At one of our corners there was an opponent marking me at the top of the box. Just before the corner was taken, as we were jostling around, she firmly stepped on my foot – the one where I had my stress fracture. I felt that she'd done that on purpose because it was well documented at the time. And she got me right where the pain was. I turned round and pulled at one of her hair bunches. She squealed. One of our players – I can't remember who it was – said, 'You can't do that, Kelly,' and this girl was screaming her head off, trying to draw the referee's attention. Nothing was done about it and I stood there in shock for a little while because

I couldn't believe I had actually responded like that. I mean, I had literally yanked some girl's hair! It just shows you what can happen in the heat of the moment. It was quite a physical game, that one.

We were gutted. It was an opportunity spurned. We certainly felt that way, and a lot of press people said that too. We had these big crowds behind us and a semi-final spot – and who knows what afterwards – had been there for the taking. The country had taken to us and to the game as a whole, so it was very disappointing not to repay that with a good run.

Looking back, as I have said, I think we were pretty naive during that group stage. That is the best word I can find to describe it. This was the first international championship pretty much any of us had played in, and maybe that showed. The stakes were high too, of course, because there was so much interest in us. Yes, I think there was a lot of naivety and inexperience on everyone's part. I just don't think we were ready for it. Because we were hosts, the build-up was too long as well. And then all of a sudden it was 'Bang, off you go!' Almost before we knew it we were right into it and off and running.

It's obvious, but it's true: you need to play in international football tournaments to experience international tournament football, to get the knowledge you need to succeed. Once we had that learning experience under our belts, it was a different story. England have progressed a lot since 2005 and fared much better in tournaments as a result. We learned an awful lot that summer, and we moved forward.

But it's still a shame that it happened like that for us on

home soil, and we did feel that we'd let our fans down a bit. It had genuinely felt like something good was just getting going, and then it was cut off and finished.

Germany won the championship again, beating Norway 3–1 in another well-attended match, held at Ewood Park. I was a guest for the BBC at the final, alongside Sue Smith and Gavin Peacock, but I wished I could have been out there playing in it. It was the same ground where we'd got knocked out by Sweden too.

Our participation in the finals only lasted for six days. That wasn't what we'd wanted and it wasn't what the people deserved, really. They had been superb again – 25,694 watched the match against Sweden. Our three matches were watched by an aggregate of 69,481 fans. On average, that is over 23,000 for each match. Our group games were also watched by a television audience of 8.2 million viewers in total, with a peak of 3.6 million watching the final stages of the Sweden match – an audience share of over 20 per cent on a Saturday evening. Overall attendances at Euro 2005 were healthy: 118,403 spectators at fifteen matches.

We had made a name for ourselves. But we were still a young team and, as I said, inexperienced in international football. I was twenty-six, Faye was twenty-seven and Yanks was twenty-five. Along with Mary Phillip, who was twenty-eight, we were the senior players. Katie was still only twenty-two, Fara was just twenty-one, Alex Scott was twenty, Eniola Aluko was eighteen and Kaz was seventeen. We certainly had a youthful look about us. Players such as Gill Coultard, Marieanne Spacey and Karen Walker – huge players for England with huge amounts of experience – had all gone.

But, here's the important factor to mention in this respect: the England team that played in that Women's Euro 2005 was largely the same team that played in the 2011 Women's World Cup. We had a consistent line-up for a good part of a decade, from one to eleven. Euro 2005 was our first real public outing in a sense, definitely to a much wider audience.

We are now so familiar with each other's play and have much more of an understanding. Back then it was a case of us wanting so much to do so well and working hard to get the results but coming up short. As a group, we had very few caps at that time. That is no longer the case. Half of us are now above or near to the one hundred mark.

But we needed to do well in this tournament to help keep the profile of the game on the up. If we made a real impact, it could one day lead to international success and a professional women's league. That's what all of us felt at the time: we knew that we had to do well. And we didn't do so well. Well, we did OK, I suppose. The Finland match was a great occasion, but we didn't build on that and therefore we didn't make the most of the opportunity that was presented to us.

I'd felt a big responsibility on my shoulders to try and move the game forward and get it into the public domain more. It wasn't sink or swim, but it was a golden opportunity. So it was frustrating for me to have to be fighting to get fit when the tournament was happening all around me. And it was heartbreaking to go out so early, for all the usual reasons.

Hope was great about it all. I remember her telling us that 2009 would be our year. That was her vision. I think she knew then that the core of youngsters in front of her would be the heart of the England team for years going forward. She knew that with more tournament experience and more caps under our belts we would grow, both as individuals and as a unit.

Having said all that, Euro 2005 was deemed to be a great success for England and the Football Association. The figures at the time indicated that over two million girls were now taking part in some form of football activity in our country. UEFA president Lennart Johansson said that taking the tournament to England had been the right decision, which was good to hear. And the whole England squad was invited down to a reception at the House of Commons, which was a special occasion for us all.

I think the tournament started something in our country that exists to this day. There's now a general public awareness that in every year ending in an odd number there is an international women's football tournament, just like in every year ending in an even number there is an international men's football tournament. English people love to get behind their national teams, especially in football; happily, that now extends to us. That all began in 2005, in my opinion.

13

The Invincibles

In 2003/04, Arsenal's men's team was known in English football as 'The Invincibles'. Under Arsène Wenger, the Gunners won the Premier League and went unbeaten through the whole season. Nobody could touch them.

In 2006/07, Arsenal's women's team became known in English football as 'The Invincibles'. Under Vic Akers, the Gunners won the quadruple: the FA Women's Premier League, the FA Women's Cup, the FA Women's Premier League Cup and the UEFA Cup (the Champions League of women's football). We too were unbeaten in all our fixtures that season, winning twenty out of twenty matches in the league. We also won the Community Shield for good measure. Nobody could touch us either.

At that time, Arsenal Ladies provided the backbone of the England team as well, which probably went a long way to us achieving more success at international level. We also had the likes of Emma Byrne, of Ireland, Julie Fleeting, of Scotland, and Jayne Ludlow, of Wales, in key positions. We were a very good team – the best I have played in.

We in fact won the Premier League and FA Cup double

three seasons running, from 2005/06 to 2007/08, and were only denied once, by Everton Ladies, in the League Cup during that time. We won four Community Shields in a row too. But the big highlight was that UEFA Cup win – even though I wasn't allowed to play in the final.

For an English women's team to win the top honour in women's European club football is really something. For years those competitions have been ruled by German and Scandinavian sides. But we were too good for all of them in 2006/07 with the side we had, even though both Faye White, our team captain, and I missed the final: Faye through injury, and me through a stupid suspension.

We'd played Brondby, of Denmark, in the semi-final. The first leg was away from home and I picked up a yellow card during the second half for kicking the ball away, which was ridiculous. We were winning 1–0 and, with the tie being away from home, I was penalized. A little while later I made a strong challenge in our own half. I felt that I'd won the ball but, probably because I went to ground in doing so and caught the player as well, the referee gave me another yellow card. So I was sent off for two yellows, which I thought was unfair in the circumstances.

As I was on my way back to the bench, the home fans started jeering at me. So, without thinking too much about it, I stuck my middle finger up at them. I also kicked a chair quite vigorously when I got back to the Arsenal dugout.

I was frustrated, with myself and the treatment I'd received. I genuinely didn't think I deserved to be sent off. And then I was being wound up by the fans. So I told them where to go and subsequently had to face the consequences, which included missing out on the most important match of the season, and what would have been the biggest club match I had ever played in.

The fourth official ushered me away on the night. He had seen everything. And he put it all down in his match report, of course. The sending-off got me a two-match ban, which kept me out of the home leg against Brondby and the first leg of the final, should we make it. The added offence of the middle finger got me a further ban of one match, which in effect ruled me out of both legs of the final. Without the gesture I would still have been available to play in the second leg.

Vic appealed on my behalf. Arsenal vice-chairman David Dein also tried to help me. We sent a letter of apology, tried to wangle a deal somehow, but all efforts were to no avail and I ended up missing what would have been my biggest game for the Gunners as a result. I was gutted.

I am still gutted all these years later. For this remains the only occasion when an English women's team has won what in effect is the European Cup in women's football. The competition has been renamed the Champions League now, in fact. I was devastated at the time, and that level of hurt doesn't leave you very quickly. I felt I had done my bit on the field in the group games, the quarter-finals and the first leg of the semi-final to help the team get through to the final. And then I had to swallow the fact that I would play no part in it.

I felt rotten in the changing room that night, but I was still made to feel part of the team. I was there in the changing rooms before both legs, first in Sweden then back at

Borehamwood. But I was not allowed to sit on the bench during the games, because I was banned. I had to sit up in the stands, away from it all.

Marta, the Brazilian super talent, was the star player for our opponents in the final, Umea. The team was also stacked with Swedish stars. Both matches against them were hard-fought encounters, but we prevailed. Alex Scott scored a cracker for us from thirty-five yards in injury-time which won the game out there. Alex also kept Marta very quiet. She had her in her pocket, actually. But we were under the cosh a lot.

Borehamwood was packed for the second leg – probably the most packed it has ever been for one of our matches. It was three or four people deep at some parts of the ground. It was a great atmosphere, quite intimidating for our opponents but terrific for us.

Umea played very well in the second leg. They hit the bar, they hit the post, and Emma Byrne made a few good saves as well. On the day they probably deserved to score, but it was just one of those times when you get the feeling that the ball will never go in. I think it was one of those moments when it is written in the stars that a certain team is going to come out on top. And that year it was Arsenal Ladies.

I still regret in a big way missing out on it all for doing what I did. But I can't change that now. It's in the past, and life has to go on. I might not have played in the final, but I still felt that I was part of the winning team. Vic made sure of that. He is brilliant like that – another great boss and a good friend.

We were the first, and so far only, English women's team

to win such an honour. I think that is fitting because I believe that team was the best women's football side ever to have come out of England. Winning that trophy said it all. We did the quadruple, including the big one in Europe. I don't really see an English club doing that again for a while. Not with the strength of women's football in Germany, France, Sweden and even Russia today. I think it will be a hard task. That Arsenal Ladies side was very special. The number of quality players we could field plus the experience they had was something else, it really was. We knew how to win matches, at home and abroad. And you can't bottle that.

We dominated women's football in England for three years. The FA Women's Cup finals, shown live on BBC One, were real thrashings: 5–0 versus Leeds United Ladies, 4–1 versus Charlton Ladies, 4–1 versus Leeds again. It was like cruise control for us. They were good, fun days, but I was sure we would win those matches before we had even kicked off. Sorry if that sounds arrogant. It's just that we were so much better than the rest.

My first FA Women's Cup final for Arsenal was at the New Den, home of Millwall, in 2006. It was a really hot day, and as we walked out to inspect the pitch and stretch, Leeds, our opponents, were vigorously warming up at the other end. They had been doing this workout for about twenty-five minutes before we even got out there. Vic took us out to see it for ourselves. I thought it was a bit dumb for them to be doing that, personally. I think we all did.

Vic explained to us that all we were required to do, in order to conserve our energy levels, was a limited warm-up and stretch – in the shade. He had been watching Leeds warm up in the sun and he knew that they wouldn't last in the heat. To me, this was an example of Vic's experience in big games like this. By contrast, it was Leeds' first final, and their inexperience showed.

We stretched out in the shade at the other end of the pitch, and we only did that for fifteen minutes or so. From that moment on I knew we would win the cup. We all did. That is the mentality we had in the team. And we were right to be confident. It was good to win the FA Cup at a London venue too. We wore the redcurrant Arsenal anniversary kit as well, and I scored a penalty. It was a fantastic day.

That was my first ever FA Cup winners' medal. And it is true what people say: there is no other game like it, for both men and women. League matches are different; the FA Cup final is a one-off game and it is played in front of the biggest audience. It is, by far, the most-watched game of women's club football on television. The women's final is normally played on a Bank Holiday Monday so you always get a good crowd, whether it's in the north or the south. The FA Cup final was always the one game I wanted to be involved in when I was growing up. Winning the FA Cup is special, and it meant a lot to me.

For me, our best performance was the last one we all played in together, in 2008, when we beat Leeds at the City Ground. I got two goals that day, Jayne Ludlow and Lianne Sanderson got the others. We beat Southampton's record of eight wins in the competition too, which pleased Vic a lot. To win a match like that in such style in front of a large live television audience was really pleasing. In total, I scored five goals in those three successive FA Women's Cup final wins for Arsenal.

As I said, we were almost unbeatable in those days. We became so used to winning matches that we hardly ever lost. In fact, the only domestic defeat we suffered during that very special three-year period was against Everton in the 2008 FA Women's Premier League Cup final.

I suppose we knew that if we weren't mentally right then a surprise could be on the cards. Charlton had taken the lead against us early on in the 2007 FA Women's Cup final, for instance, up in Nottingham, but we powered back to win comfortably. Importantly, we were always secure in the knowledge that tactically and technically we were sound. We also knew that player for player, nobody could touch us. As time went on, it must have been mentally tough to play against us too.

Some of the scorelines we were recording were massive. It can be a challenge to keep that going when you are not being tested as such. But we prided ourselves on our professionalism. We never got bored. We never slacked. We always set new targets.

For us, it was always a target to try and score a goal as early as possible in games because we knew that some of the teams were already beaten before they had even got off the bus. They were coming to Borehamwood to play Arsenal, and that was enough to intimidate them into a defeatist attitude. So we knew that if we got an early goal we had pretty much won the game there and then. Vic set us the task to score as early as possible for that reason, and a lot of our games were won within the first five or ten minutes.

The biggest test for us came when we failed to score in the early part of a match. When that first goal didn't come, it was a case of us waiting to find an opening. We knew we would get chances with the attacking personnel we had, and we knew that that talent would take those chances. We just had to stick with it and be patient sometimes.

Everyone bonded and everyone clicked in that team. We all had the same goals and we all worked hard to achieve them. It is an old adage, but hard work does pay off. We knew we were a good side and it was a lot of fun to play for Arsenal Ladies in those years. We were buzzing in training, buzzing in the league, and buzzing in the cups. I scored 100 goals in 112 games for the Gunners in those years. It was great.

We were very attack-minded and so good at going forward that the opposition didn't really stand a chance – not English opposition anyway. There's always the possibility of a surprise for any team, no matter how good it is, but as I said, we were surprised once in three seasons. We had Karen Carney on one side and Rachel Yankey on the other. We were just so strong on both flanks. Karen and Rachel played in those positions for England too. Julie Fleeting was our target up front. And what a target she was. She always found the right position to be in. She got a lot of goals for us. She was like some sort of hunter in the box. If you could find her, she could put her head on it and it would be in the net. Julie is one of the best goalscorers in and around the box there has ever been in the women's game.

Our game was on fire at that time. Every one of us was an international. Katie Chapman was so strong in the midfield. She is solid and breaks everything up, making everybody's job so much easier, and gets things moving as well. Alex

Scott and Faye White were at the top of their games too. Every position in that Arsenal side oozed quality. The list of potential goalscorers seemed endless. We had so many options, so many different players capable of scoring goals from anywhere on the pitch. We were the complete side.

It was so nice to play in a team like that where every one of us was on the same page. Back in my college days, it was down to me to score the goals and create the chances. That brought a lot of pressure. But the rest of the team at Seton Hall were lacking in certain areas. At Arsenal, nobody was lacking in talent. And if they had an off day, the rest of the team would cover for them. There never came a day when we were all off our games. One of Julie, Kaz, Jayne, Lianne, Yanks and me would always pop up and score a goal for the team.

Vic deserves all the credit for the Arsenal Ladies success story. He is Mr Arsenal. He is also the kit man with the men's team, and for twenty-two years he was the brains behind the success of the women's team. He created it, he cherished it, and he made it what it became. Any advice you ever needed, any concerns or problems you had, you just went off and found Vic and had a chat. He was always available, to every one of us. He was based at the training ground and that was ideal. He was a father figure to us.

He started off the Arsenal Ladies team more than two decades ago. He had a hunger for the game and he wanted to see it grow. He is a major reason why the game has grown like it has. He still complains and moans about certain aspects of women's football because he just wants to see the game developing properly, and for it to get the respect it deserves. Vic has always tried to push the game forward and he has always strived for better things for us, both on and off the pitch. Put simply, he is just a great guy. He's a funny guy too. And a cuddly guy! He reminds me of a teddy bear. I have told him that.

But, seriously, he is someone to be trusted. He is a friend for all days. He is a nice fellow who always wants to have a laugh and a giggle. He is devoted to Arsenal Ladies and always has been. If it hadn't been for him, there wouldn't have been the same success story. The team would not be in the position they are in today. No way.

14

Kiss This

IN MY OPINION, THE ARSENAL EFFECT WAS ONE OF THE MAIN reasons why England began to perform better and started to climb the world rankings like we did in the second half of the 2000s. As I have said, the majority of the Arsenal team at that time were England players. That helped both teams immeasurably. We played together week in, week out and we trained together week in, week out as well. About six or seven of us were never away from each other. That bred even more confidence in us all: we knew all the runs, all the passes and all the moves in each other's games. After a while you just get a natural understanding with each other. And when there are more than half a dozen of you – Alex, Faye, Katie, Kaz, Yanks, Anita Asante, Mary Phillip and me – plus a few more on the bench, that is going to have a really big positive effect at international level.

Having said that, the national team was maturing nicely and some key non-Arsenal players, such as Rachel Brown and Fara Williams, were also vital to that progress. Our coach, Hope Powell, had her sights set on us reaching our true potential in 2009 or 2011. Several years before then we were well on target.

I felt that we were already at a new level as an international side within a few months of Euro 2005. The experience we gained from that tournament meant we grew up a lot. The qualification campaign for the 2007 Women's World Cup, to be held in China, saw us cement our position and build on that growth.

We started off in September 2005 with a 4–1 win in Austria. Thankfully, I was now back to full match fitness and I scored a goal in that victory. That felt great: it was my first competitive goal for England in three and a half years! My sickening run of serious injuries had cost me two and a half years of international football – eighteen months between spring 2002 and autumn 2003 and a further twelve months from summer 2004.

Our second match in the group, against Hungary, was surreal. We played away at a small sports ground in Tapolca, close to the beautiful Lake Balaton, the largest lake in central Europe. No more than a hundred people were there to see it, but we set a new Women's World Cup record by winning 13–0. We were two up after five minutes, four up after a quarter of an hour, seven up at half-time, and so on. I got a hat-trick – the first one I had scored for England – and Eniola Aluko, Alex Scott and Fara Williams got two each. It was a scoreline you sometimes got at school but not in international football. The result earned us just three points, of course, but it did a lot for our confidence. We never stopped in that game, we never let up for one moment. We were searching for a fourteenth goal in injury-time. Other teams would have noticed that result. They couldn't have missed it.

After Hungary, we won away in Holland. So, three wins out of three games, and all of them away from home. But our next match was the big test – France at home.

We hadn't beaten France since 1974. They were one of our bogey teams. They had knocked us out at the last stage of qualification for the 2003 Women's World Cup. They were top seeds in our group and the favourites to qualify as winners.

In an edgy game at Blackburn in March 2006, we held them to a 0–0 draw. As they had been surprisingly beaten at home by Holland earlier in the campaign, we held the upper hand.

Our target was now clear: beat Austria, Holland and Hungary at home and then go to France in our last match to seal the deal. Given that qualification this time round would be decided on head-to-head results not goal difference in the event of two teams being level on the same number of points, we would still have to get a result out there if neither of us slipped up from now on.

And neither of us did. For our part, we beat Austria 4–0, Hungary 2–0 and Holland 4–0. I got a second hat-trick of the campaign against the Dutch. So it was all down to a one-off match at the Stade de la Route de Lorient in Rennes, in north-west France. We were three points ahead in the group and had a goal difference that was sixteen better than the French, but a 1–0 defeat would mean we would have to go into the play-offs again. We needed a draw to be sure of qualification.

We decided to go for the win. No mean feat, given that we hadn't beaten them for over thirty years.

I remember being in the changing room before that game and never feeling so confident before a match. I was sure we were going to get the result we needed, not necessarily a win but the right result for us. I just couldn't see them beating us, not after the disappointment in our backyard at Euro 2005 and what we had gone through as a squad. We had had a great qualifying campaign and we had grown so much as a unit. I think that mood was felt by everybody who was in the changing room that night. We had done so much work on the training ground beforehand and our mental preparation with our sports psychologist was spot on. We all felt ready for the game, up for it.

I think it also had that extra bit of bite to it because they were the team that knocked us out in 2002, which meant they went to the World Cup in the USA in 2003, and we missed out. We had to bide our time and wait for our chance. Well, this was our chance.

Revenge did play a part in it, I think. They hurt us back then; now we wanted to do that to them. We wanted to go to the Women's World Cup instead of them. It's funny how fixtures sometimes work out like this in football. This was our opportunity for some payback.

There was a buzz and positivity about us when we walked out into the tunnel. We were stood on the right and they were stood on the left. I wasn't really paying attention to any of them but you could just feel the energy within our line-up, this confidence that we had. There was such strong belief that we were going to get whatever we needed to get out of that game. We were shouting out 'C'mon!' as we headed down on to the pitch. It was as though we all knew it was going to be fine. Of course we knew we'd have to put a shift in and that it was going to be extremely hard, but we felt that this was our time. England had last played in the Women's World Cup finals back in 1995 – I had not even been capped yet back then. From our squad, only Mary Phillip had been involved, and she was an unused substitute during the tournament.

The match was shown live on BBC Three. Faye White, our captain, was up in the commentary box in the stand alongside Guy Mowbray. She was recovering after knee surgery. She was up there with a microphone and crutches, shouting for us of course, along with a few hundred England fans who had travelled across the Channel. But the majority of the 19,674 crowd were French.

We silenced that crowd when we took the lead just after the hour, Hoda Lattaf deflecting Fara's header into the net. It was the first goal we had scored against them in seven meetings. Far too long. France pushed and pushed but didn't score until the eighty-eighth minute when substitute Ludivine Diguelman equalized. It was too little too late. We would have loved to beat them in their own country, but a draw was enough for us.

I had never before felt such a feeling of jubilation as when the final whistle blew that night. To go to France and get the result we needed was a brilliant achievement for us. I could see in all of my team-mates' faces just how much it meant.

The small group of England fans, plus some families and friends of the players, that had travelled over to Rennes made a massive difference that night, cheering so loudly throughout the game. At the end, we all went over to that part of the stadium to say thank you.

There were photographers and television cameramen covering it all. Faye even came down from the commentary box to join in with the celebrations. The atmosphere in the changing room and on the bus back to the hotel was awe-some – we were singing songs rowdily and all sorts. We just couldn't get enough of that moment.

England had qualified to play in the Women's World Cup for the first time in twelve years. And I was through to play in a World Cup finals at long last. I would be twenty-eight going on twenty-nine when China came round, but it was another dream come true for me. And one that I wouldn't have thought was possible during my darkest days just a couple of years earlier. I scored seven of our twenty-nine goals in qualification, which was a return I was happy with. Equally pleasing was the fact that ten other players had found the net too.

Hope took us out to China in January 2007 so that we could experience the country and the culture before playing in the World Cup in September. We competed in the China Cup against a few other teams that had also qualified: the hosts China, Germany and the USA. The matches were played in Guangdong, on the South China Sea coast. We lost to China, 2–0, but drew against the other two countries. We saw those last two results against good opposition as real progress.

Being out in Guangdong was very, very different to what any of us had ever experienced before anywhere in the world. So we were very lucky to have had the opportunity to get over there and get used to it all before playing in a World Cup there. In fact it was so different to what we were used to that it was unreal. For a start, the stadiums we played in and visited were absolutely massive. It was pretty mind-boggling for us. We were left to imagine what they would be like at a World Cup. I was one of the England players who had travelled the most and I found some things quite shocking. There were just loads of people rushing around everywhere, and busy, busy roads with lots of traffic on them. The air was different too. It was heavy and smoggy.

Food was another issue. The only local produce I ever ate out there was rice. The other food on offer just wasn't the sort I knew from Chinese restaurants back home. I might find myself faced with a duck's head in a stew for breakfast, that sort of thing. We ended up living on cereal, bread and rice for ten days. The USA team stayed at the same hotel as us, and on a couple of nights I saw that they'd ordered in from Pizza Hut instead of having food from the hotel. The situation was so bad that team meals were cancelled.

That experience alone was essential to us. When we came back for the World Cup, we brought our own chef with us. It just made everything so much easier for us, and it was one less thing – and a very big thing too – for us to worry about. He went out to China two weeks before the squad and prepared everything for us, in line with our normal diet: chicken, rice, pasta, salad – all the right stuff that we needed to perform. My dad, bless him, and some other family members weren't as lucky as me. They struggled a lot. On one occasion my dad had to order a shark's tongue for dinner. He couldn't eat it. In the end, the Football

Association allowed all the family members to come to the team hotel after matches and eat with us. That is how bad the situation was for them. They were sometimes starving when they met up with us!

We were again drawn in Group A for this tournament. Our draw wasn't too bad, even though we had Germany, the perennial tournament favourites, in there with us. Japan, ranked two places higher than us at ten in the world, and Argentina made up the numbers.

The Women's World Cup holders kicked off the tournament, and essentially kicked Argentina out of it with a spectacular 11–0 win in Shanghai. It was a record scoreline in a Women's World Cup finals match. Germany's captain Birgit Prinz scored a hat-trick. They looked very good.

This result meant that whoever won the match between England and Japan would likely go through to the quarter-finals with Germany. No pressure, then, in our country's first match on this global platform for twelve years. 'Shanghai or Bust' I believe the newspapers put it back home.

We were confident that we could get a result against the Japanese. And I was very confident in my ability to help England achieve that. I had worked so hard to get myself to peak fitness and I felt strong after having overcome all my problems on and off the pitch. For me, going into a World Cup with England without an injury was an immense boost. Psychologically, that gave me real strength. I was absolutely buzzing.

This was the ultimate for me – representing my country on the biggest stage. It was a massive achievement for me after everything that had happened. Walking out at the

Hongkou Stadium that day was a very proud moment.

The stadium was huge, and it was almost full. I had goose-bumps as I left the tunnel. I kept thinking to myself: 'Well, this is it – this is what it's about.' I tried to lap up everything that was in front of me.

I spent a short while trying to find Dad in the crowd. I just wanted to make sure he was there. Then I wanted to spot all the other family members. As a team, we always wanted to know where our family members were. It was very important to us. It was particularly important to me.

The national anthem hit me, as it always does, in the throat. All the hard work I had put in, all the training, all the time I'd spent in recovery . . .

On paper, we weren't expected to win the game. As I mentioned, Japan were ranked higher than us and they were ever-presents in the Women's World Cup finals. They had also beaten China in the qualifying tournament. This was our first Women's World Cup as a nation in a long while. It was a big step up for us as individuals and as a unit.

We went into the match as underdogs but that was perhaps the right thing for us because the pressure was on them as a result. However, once they took the lead through Aya Miyama, we knew we had it all to do to get a result and keep our World Cup alive. We had to get something out of the game. But, as hard as we tried, we just couldn't make the breakthrough.

All of a sudden the clock was counting down fast. I was moved to centre-forward for the last quarter of an hour.

With just nine minutes remaining, we were still trailing. I felt confident that if I could get a chance, I would put it away. But the chance wasn't coming.

Then Kaz got on the ball, and as soon as she did I knew there was some space in front of me and that I had to get myself into the Japanese box. Kaz played a neat through-ball along the ground to me. I had a couple of players close to me but I took one of them where she didn't want to go so that I could then do a version of the 'Cruyff turn' on to my left foot. I almost pirouetted 360 degrees to give myself some space and a shooting opportunity.

I had about a second to score. No more. Suddenly, my mind was on fire. 'This is it! Just do it!' And I did it. I placed the ball coolly into the bottom left-hand corner of the net.

My mind went blank. It was a pretty euphoric moment for me. 'Oh my God!' I had just scored my first ever goal in a World Cup finals and I really didn't know what to do or how to feel. I was not prepared for it to be like this. I simply had no idea how to celebrate the goal. Filled with elation and pride, and without thinking, I took my left boot off and kissed it. I then held it aloft and ran to the corner of the pitch. It wasn't planned. I don't suppose the best things are. But it's an image that has stayed with me. I guess it sums up my life for me, both my struggles and my achievements. Scoring that goal on the biggest stage I could ever play on was a beautiful moment in my life. After everything that had happened to me, it was a poignant moment too.

Actually, I had visualized myself on the pitch, moving with the ball and playing out certain scenarios the night before, as I lay on my bed in my hotel room. I had asked myself, 'What celebration will I do if I score in this game?' I wasn't going to take my top off because Brandi Chastain had already done that – and it wasn't really me either. I did fleetingly think to myself: 'I might take my boot off instead.' But that was it. I never thought about it again from that moment on.

When I scored the goal, it was just an instinctive reaction. I didn't think about it. I didn't recall my thoughts the night before until much later. It just felt right for me to take my boot off at that moment. I then kissed it, of course. I genuinely don't know where that came from! I suppose it's fair to say that I marked the occasion.

Two minutes later my boots were off. I had scored a second goal. This time I slipped them off and Kaz picked one up. And that reaction was unrehearsed on her part. Looking back, you think to yourself: 'Where did that come from?'

The ball had come down the left from Fara and I followed it into the Japanese penalty box. I knew that if I could get hold of the ball I could score again. But first I had to get myself into the right position to receive the ball and get it under control. I got hold of it. I started to dribble with it. I needed to accelerate and get into some space, so as one defender came across, I beat her. Then another one came at me. I cut the ball inside and took a shot. But I didn't really angle it the way I wanted to and it came back to me off the goalkeeper. The second time I managed to strike it hard with my right foot, and it hit the back of the net.

Pure pandemonium. Both my boots came off. We were all ecstatic. I have some great pictures of those celebrations in my private collection and they help to keep alive memories that are very special to me – memories of the two goals I scored against Japan in my first ever World Cup finals match.

Sadly, those goals did not win us the game. Five minutes into injury-time, Miyama hit a free-kick from way out that rattled into our net. It was no fluke. She was something of a free-kick specialist. Years later I saw her score a similar goal for Atlanta against St Louis in the Women's Professional Soccer league. She could score goals like that with ease, it seemed.

But to concede a goal like that in the dying seconds of a game after coming from a goal down ourselves to take the lead was heart-wrenching. We had worked so hard to get ourselves into a winning position at 2–1 so it felt like we had lost the match at the end.

I remember looking up at the scoreboard before Miyama took the free-kick and thinking to myself: 'This is a really good result for us.' And then, bang, she fires the ball into the back of our net. However, when everything had sunk in, I think we accepted that a point was a good result against Japan. We were still in the competition and our destiny was still in our own hands.

Once we had recovered from the match and got it all out of our system, Hope sat me down and told me not to do the boot celebration again. She told me she didn't like it. So, even though I enjoyed it, I couldn't do it any more. I understood her reasons. She told me that I already got enough attention from the opposition without them wanting to kick me for my goal celebrations. I accepted her point of view and retired that one. To be honest, I don't think I would have done it again anyway because it was such a one-off moment. Then again, I wouldn't change the fact that I did do it for anything in the world.

The Women's World Cup was being shown live on television back in the United Kingdom for the first time. All our matches were going out on BBC Two in the daytime schedule. So a lot of people saw it, of course. It certainly caused something of a stir for a day or two.

I did a lot of press about the goal celebration afterwards, answering lots of questions about what it meant and who it was for. There was talk that I had celebrated with the boot on purpose for sponsorship reasons. That was all nonsense, as I hope I've already explained. I admit that I did speak to Umbro out there after the match and they were very pleased that I'd done it because it got their boot a little bit of publicity, but there is no way I would do that sort of thing in a planned way. It's not in my nature. It's all about emotion out there for me, nothing else.

Germany were our next opponents. What can I say about them? They were the reigning European and world champions. They had the former women's World Player of the Year in Birgit Prinz, plus other world-class players such as Kerstin Garefrekes, Renate Lingor and Sandra Smisek. Added to this, they had started the tournament with an 11–0 win. Oh, and we had never beaten them before.

They also knew all about us. They had certainly seen our match against Japan and taken some notes. Their coach, Silvia Neid, said in the press that if she had been the referee in that match she would have shown me the red card for celebrating like that with my boot.

We played our hearts out against them and were rewarded with a fantastic 0–0 draw. It was our best ever result against them. Defensively, we were sound and solid. Faye was a rock for us at the back. She was brilliant, in terms of her leadership and play. She pretty much marked Prinz out of the game. She hardly let her have a kick.

Beyond Faye, who was the Player of the Match, the whole team battled hard to earn that result. It was an awesome effort. And it was another indication of how far we had come as a team in such a short space of time.

Japan beat Argentina 1–0 to keep us on our toes. But as long as we could beat Argentina, who were now out of the tournament, Japan would have to get a result against Germany to send us home. So it was down to us to go to Chengdu and do a job, which is what we did.

There was a fair amount of pressure on us going into that game because we still needed a win, and sometimes when you are favourites – especially when you are not used to being favourites – that can go against you. We had done the hard bit against Germany, so we didn't want to waste all that and throw away our opportunity to progress. Mentally, the Argentina game required a different approach from us after two very tough games.

In the end, in front of 30,730 spectators – the biggest crowd we played in front of in the whole competition – we won comfortably, 6–1. It took us a while to carve out the first chance, but once we did it was straightforward for us.

I got two goals to move up to four goals for the tournament. I was really enjoying my football and the whole squad was gelling together nicely. Jill Scott – another real find for us, and a good addition to the 2005 squad in midfield – got a goal in this game too. The only disappointment was the loss of Fara for the quarter-finals due to her receiving her second yellow card of the tournament. That was really frustrating for us because she was one of the players we needed in our team. Katie Chapman was back, after serving a one-match ban against Argentina, but we really needed both Fara and Katie in midfield to take on the best in the world.

Still, we were into the last eight of the Women's World Cup and we were feeling confident as we moved north to Tianjin to take on the USA. We were hearing that back home interest was mounting, and the live showing of the match had been switched from BBC Two to BBC One as a result. This was another gilt-edged opportunity for us to make a difference.

It was the first time I had come face to face with some of the footballers I had played with and against in the Women's United Soccer Association league in America, players such as Shannon Boxx and Kristine Lilly.

The USA were the favourites to win our quarter-final. But we held our own in the first half and went in goalless at the break. The game changed when Faye was elbowed in the face by Abby Wambach and suffered a broken cheekbone. Then Wambach, Boxx and Lilly scored to put us out of the competition. It was an intense match, and a disappointing one to lose, but on the day they were better than us. They were much more clinical when they had their chances. We weren't as naive as we had been two years before, but at times like this I saw that we still had lessons to learn.

The USA just have this never-say-die attitude. They never let their heads drop. They just keep going and going. They keep trying to pummel you into the ground until you succumb. We learned from that afterwards. Our progress as a squad seemed to be punctuated by these big learning curves once in a while.

Admittedly we let our heads drop a little bit in that match against the USA. We just didn't have the same mental strength – plus the belief at times – as the Americans. I don't think they were better than us technically, but in terms of mental strength they were much better. Our mental strength was stronger in China than it had been at home in England in 2005, but it was still developing and it was some way short of where it needed to be when we came up against a big nation like the USA. But you don't know that until you go through it. We went through it that day against some hard, fierce opposition.

This quarter-final appearance matched the achievement of our predecessors back in 1995. But with more experience and some improvements we were sure that in four years we could surpass that.

Germany won the World Cup again with a 2–0 win over Brazil in the final. Marta, who played for the losing finalists, was the star of the tournament. She won the Golden Ball and the Golden Shoe for being the top goalscorer in China with seven goals. She is a talent to behold.

Another big disappointment hit us a few weeks after the World Cup when it was confirmed that although we had qualified (as one of the three best-placed European teams) for the 2008 Olympic Games women's football tournament, we would not be able to take part. FIFA refused to allow an England team to represent Great Britain in the Olympics on political grounds, so we couldn't take our place in Beijing. With London already confirmed as the host city for the 2012 Games we could only hope and pray that there would be a change of heart among those who mattered before then.

Away from football, the one regret I have about China is that the players weren't given the opportunity to see the sights. I would have loved to visit the Great Wall, but we weren't allowed to do that in camp. So I had gone all that way twice and never seen China's most famous attraction. We had an afternoon or two off to walk around and see the immediate area where we were staying, but no further than that. But I suppose we were there for football, not for sightseeing.

We were the only team in the entire tournament to take any points off Germany, and we were the only team to keep a clean sheet against them. We took great pride in those achievements when we got home, when the tournament was done and dusted and we could consider what those statistics meant. Above all, they told us that we should approach the qualifiers for Women's Euro 2009 – the next big international tournament on the agenda – with confidence.

15

Jonathan Ross, Take That
and the Queen

THINGS FELT A LITTLE BIT DIFFERENT WHEN WE ARRIVED BACK IN England after the 2007 Women's World Cup. There seemed to be more interest in us. This was underlined when I was invited to appear on the *Friday Night with Jonathan Ross* show on BBC One.

I think the request came through the Football Association. Everybody was quite excited about it. But I had never really watched the show, if I am honest. I had only been back in the country for a few years anyway so the programme had passed me by a little bit. Obviously I made sure I watched it once the request was made – and then readily accepted. It was a massive compliment to the team's achievement in China and, of course, a great opportunity for me to promote the game further.

Was I nervous? Yes. This is the person who ran away to the toilets rather than pick up an award and speak when I was at college, so you can imagine how meeting a television presenter like Jonathan Ross and being interviewed in front of millions of people was going to feel.

I took my mum and dad with me. I wanted them to be there. It was a big thing for them too that I was on the show, of course. My aunt came along as well. When I arrived at BBC Television Centre, I went straight to the green room on the basement floor. As I waited there, I was given some flowers. That felt nice, like I was in a professional environment and I was going to be looked after properly, which was important to me.

I was given some preparation as to how the format of the show would work. Then I went into make-up. While I was in there, Jonathan popped in and made himself known to me. He told me that he had watched all our games in the World Cup, which was great to hear. He also said to me that he thought I was a really great player, which was nice of him too, and that he wanted to get an insight into women's football and to help take awareness of it to a larger audience. It was actually his idea to get me on there; he told me he had asked personally for me to come on the show. So you can imagine how all that made me feel. It was a really nice gesture by him. He didn't have to come in and say all those things. It meant a great deal to me that he did, and it relaxed me a lot. Well, a little anyway!

I remember saying to him, 'Don't make too much fun out of our sport!' I had heard enough about Jonathan and now seen enough of his show to realize that this was a possibility. I feared he might ridicule women's football to this big audience of his, like some guys tend to do. But he assured me he had no intention of doing that and that was not why I was on there. Jonathan's reasons for getting me on there were genuine: he wanted to talk to me about the sport, learn something and help to make it a little bit more popular.

Take That were also on the show – they had re-formed the previous year – and they were really friendly to me. When I was growing up, I liked them. Mark Owen was always my favourite so I was made up when he spoke to me first of all. I actually walked out on stage to a version of 'Could It Be Magic', performed by the show's in-house group 4 Poofs and a Piano.

I talked to them all about football. I tried to mention this during my interview but I made a big hash of it all, saying that I couldn't remember if I had spoken to Howard Donald or Jason Orange backstage about my playing technique. I panicked for a second but Jonathan was great and, as quick as a flash, he saved me from my embarrassment. 'Don't worry, even Gary Barlow can't tell them apart,' he joked. This brought a roar of laughter from the audience and I could relax again. Later he said that Mark had played for Tottenham Hotspur's ladies team, and that got a laugh too.

Obviously he has his own style of doing things. He is a funny man. There was one little comment in there, about women taking their shirts off in the changing room, that led to him throwing in a joke about masturbation. But it was OK. Overall I was really happy with the interview.

But I tried not to think about how it was going when I was talking to him. Actually, when you walk out into a television studio, it seems like the audience isn't there because they're in the darkness. For me, sitting on that couch felt like it was just me and him having a chat. Obviously there was some applause every now and then, and a bit of laughter too, but I was concentrating so hard on what I was being asked and what I was saying that I didn't think about the outside world. It did feel as though there was nobody else in the room. The heat of the studio lights reminded me that wasn't quite the case, but the 'millions at home watching on TV' thing didn't enter my head at all during our interview.

I had recently been taught a technique for sitting that gives you enough strength and power and enough space to make you more comfortable. So I sat in that position and had my hands in a comfortable position too. That was all very important to relax me, because it was a pretty big thing to do when I think about it. But it was good. Once the first minute was out of the way, it just felt like a normal chat between two people.

Having said that, there was a certain amount of pressure on me because this was such a big platform for a discussion on women's football, particularly after our quarter-final appearance in the World Cup. It was, I guess, the biggest platform the sport had ever had in our country. And I was the one being handed the microphone and being asked to sell it.

The show reached such a big audience at that time that it was important I did that in the right way. I really wanted to come across as feminine and to promote the game in a good way. And I think I did that. I hope I did that. It was light-hearted and it was fun. I really enjoyed the experience.

But the show is definitely the scariest television programme I have been on. I suppose that's mainly because I was out of my comfort zone a little bit. *A Question of Sport* was cool, but that's a sports quiz with banter going back and forth between two teams. My only worry when I appeared on *A Question of Sport* was that I wouldn't get any of my questions right. But I held my own so that was all OK in the end. It was another interesting experience to see how a show like that is filmed. You get so much time to answer the questions, you would not believe it. It is cut down a lot for television. That surprised me a fair bit. It didn't seem quite as daunting when I was there.

I was on Matt Dawson's team with James Toseland, the world Superbike champion. Dame Kelly Holmes was on that show too and it was a thrill to meet her – a double Olympic champion.

I have appeared on *Gladiators* as well. That was great. I had always wanted to go on that show. I used to watch it every Saturday night and I desperately wanted to get on there as a contestant and to be up against one of the Gladiators. So when I was approached about doing it, I didn't hesitate for a second. I was definitely doing it.

I did feel a little nervous about telling Vic Akers and Arsenal Ladies about it, because I didn't know how they would take it. But they were fine about it, probably because I took part for charity: I did it for former Arsenal goalkeeper Bob Wilson's charity, the Willow Foundation. Vic had his concerns because the show is by definition a high-contact physical game. But I stressed to him that I wouldn't be stupid; I would take part in the less combative games. He said that he was OK with that – but he did also tell me not to come back injured.

It was filmed at Shepperton Studios. I was like a big kid in a playground that day: climbing on the monkey bars, swinging down the zip line and running up the 'travelator'. I loved every moment of it. The only game I did on the show that was quite physical was Powerball, where you have to dodge and run to the other side, putting foam balls in pods. Funnily enough, that's where I scored all my points. I think my quick feet helped me in that one. I did the Wall as well; Hang Tough, with the monkey bars over the water; and Duel and Eliminator.

I was competing against Karen Pickering, the swimmer. Rugby player Kyran Bracken and Olympic boxing champion James DeGale also took part. So it was all good fun with good banter – a great thing to do. I came away uninjured and of course I got to meet my hero, because Ian Wright was the host of the show alongside Caroline Flack. He knew who I was too. I was over the moon with that. I had my picture taken with him, cuddling him. I was in my element.

All this exposure on television was great for putting me and women's football in the spotlight. But in terms of prestige, nothing could beat being recognized by my Queen and country. Being awarded the Member of the Order of the British Empire in 2008 remains my biggest honour of all.

I was informed that I had been recognized by the Queen for my services to women's football by a letter in the post. It wasn't too long after the Women's World Cup in China, so I think my performances out there may have had something to do with it. I was invited to attend Windsor Castle to receive the award. I was delighted. It isn't every day that you get a letter with the Queen's hallmark stamped on it. I'd had absolutely no idea at all that this was going to happen so it was quite a shock to receive that. I literally just picked it out of the mail one morning.

I had to list certain dates on which I could attend Windsor

Castle. It was so exciting. I later received another letter, telling me that I was to go along on such a date, advising me what to wear, and so on. I was also told that I could take three guests with me, so I asked my mum, my dad and my brother. My dad and brother got all suited and booted for the occasion in top hat and tails. They loved it. I went out and bought a special outfit – a new blue dress – and my mum bought herself some new clothes too. We were intending it to be a big day out for all the family.

We all drove together to Windsor Castle on the morning of the special day. I had a VIP car park pass so we were allowed to drive through the gates at Windsor. We had to go through all the security checks and then we were there. I remember it as a freezing cold day because I had this little dress on. I really wanted my big Puffa coat, which obviously I couldn't have on me.

Once we'd walked into the castle, my parents and my brother were ushered away to their seats. I had to go into another room where I was told to wait. At this point I had no idea what I was doing. Everybody seemed a lot older than me, which did make me wonder if I was in the right place for a minute or two.

I got myself a glass of orange juice and just stood about talking to other people who were in this room with me. It was really interesting to meet all these different types of people who were being recognized for different things. There were about fifty of us in all. The only other athlete among us was the Northern Ireland footballer David Healy. We had a good chat.

A guard then arrived to talk us all through the procedure

of the day. I had something pinned to the top of my dress at that stage. I was told that when the Queen presented me with my medal, she would clip it on to this. The ladies in the room were then shown how to curtsey.

When I was called, I had to walk out in front of the Queen, curtsey, stand upright and then wait for her to address me. You are strictly told not to speak until you have been spoken to.

We all joined a long line of people waiting by the entrance to the room where all the presentations would be made. Some of us were trying to peep in to see if we could see what was going on in the room. I saw the Queen immediately. She was stood directly in front of us all with her Beefeaters behind her.

As I got nearer and nearer to this room I grew more and more nervous, thinking to myself: 'What is the Queen going to say to me? How am I going to react to what she is going to say to me?'

I entered the room, then waited for my name to be called. When it was, I was ushered along and followed a path straight to her. We said hello. She asked me how long I had been playing football. I said, pretty much my whole life. She then asked me, 'Isn't it a physical sport?' And I remember saying, 'Yeah, very much so.' She said she wanted to congratulate me on my achievement. I said thank you. She then pinned my MBE on to my dress, shook my hand and, in a very polite way, gently pushed me. That was my instruction to take three steps back and curtsey again. I never turned my back. You are told beforehand that you can't do that and you mustn't do that.

The Queen was a lot like I'd expected her to be. Actually she looked a lot younger face to face than I thought she would. I was just stood there thinking: 'I am two feet away from the Queen.' So I started studying everything about her: her glasses, her hair, everything. The whole experience was absolutely perfect. I couldn't believe I was so up close and personal with her. I mean, I am just Kelly from Watford.

As I left the hall, I started balling my eyes out. It had been such a touching moment. Again, everything came back to me – all the highs and lows of my past. To have come through all the bad times and to have just been standing face to face with the Queen was amazing. Actually, it had all hit me when she said the word 'congratulations' to me. That was when all the emotion surged out.

To be at the point in my life where I was standing before the Queen blew me away, maybe because things could so easily have been so different for me. When my drinking was spiralling out of control, my life was spiralling out of control. I was lucky. I got the help and the support to get through it. I had to learn and grow before I could move forward. I had to become stronger in myself so I did not have to rely on drink for my happiness. I had to learn coping mechanisms in order for me not to need drink in the way that I did. So, to come through all that and to be stood there with the Queen blew me away, it really did. It might easily never have been possible.

On leaving the room I had to give my MBE back for a little while; it was later returned to me in a box. I then re-entered the room through the back entrance, to where all my family members were. I sat down and watched the rest of the presentations with them. They were as emotional as me. Afterwards, the Queen walked out down the middle of the room, passing us as she did so with her guards and Beefeaters in tow behind her. So that was another little treat for us all. I was in awe again, studying everything about her and them.

As soon as the Queen left the room, she disappeared. It was like she had never been there with us. I don't know where she went. The castle's so vast, there might have been a secret, special room she went through or something. Whatever she did, she just seemed to vanish.

We went outside for our official photographs and then we went for lunch at a nearby pub. It was a lovely day and a very proud day.

16

Pelé, Ronaldo and Torres

ACCOLADES WERE SUDDENLY COMING MY WAY THICK AND FAST, both inside and outside the world of football.

One morning I was sat at home watching Sky Sports News when the nominees for the men's and women's FIFA World Player of the Year came up on the bottom of the screen. My name flashed in front of me and then it was gone. So I waited for it to scroll around again and, sure enough, there it was. It was quite exciting to find out in this way. I was listed in the top five women's footballers in the world. Things were just getting better and better for me.

I was a little shocked at the thought of it all, to be honest. It is quite an achievement at the end of the day. But I was totally ecstatic to have been recognized in this way. It was another proud moment for me.

I am also proud to see how women's football has grown so much over the past few years and is now so widely accepted in the sport as a whole. The last ten years have seen a massive change. The fact that the women's World Player of the Year stands beside the men's World Player of the Year is a massive watermark in terms of recognition for us. The result of this is that we all get to go along to the awards gala in Zurich. And it's not just the nominees who attend. Iconic names from the past are there too, such as Pelé.

My dad and I actually shared a car with Pelé. It's a funny story. We boarded the same plane as him from London Heathrow to Zurich. It was an early flight. My dad saw him first, as he got on the plane. When we were getting seated, Dad said to me, 'Kelly, you're not going to believe who's on this plane.'

I was like, 'Who? Tell me?'

'Pelé,' he said.

'Pelé?' I then said it even louder: 'Pelé?' I couldn't believe it.

But he was there on the plane, sitting about five seats behind us. It then dawned on us that he was probably going to the World Player of the Year awards as well.

It was such a thrill for me to be sharing a plane with Pelé. So imagine my excitement when I got to share a limousine with him. As we approached Zurich airport we were told that there would be a special car service to take us to the check-in terminal. We were to be taken to the front of the line of passengers at passport control. We would then collect our luggage before taking another organized car to the hotel that was hosting the gala. So, after landing, we were ushered down some stairs and straight into the limousine that was waiting for us. Dad and I were just sitting in it when suddenly Pelé and this other guy got in and joined us.

This was now totally unbelievable. I am sitting there, my dad is sitting alongside me, and Pelé is sitting directly in front of me. It was crazy. We had a little conversation with him and his friend. Not too much, but enough.

Dad was desperate to get his autograph. He really wanted

to ask him, but he couldn't bring himself to in those circumstances. He feared that it would be a bit cheesy. It all happened so quickly, and the moment was then gone. Dad never did get his autograph, which is a shame because Pelé is one of his footballing idols. Still, it was an amazing experience for us both.

Once I was at the hotel, I was told how the day would run by my personal guide. We were given a tour of FIFA headquarters – we saw the World Cup and all sorts. Every FIFA tournament trophy was on show. We were also given a tour of the city, which is pretty.

The hotel room we stayed in was amazing. It had remote control blinds – I hadn't seen those before. There was a massive bathtub in there too. Dad shared my room and he hadn't experienced anything like it either. It was a top five-star hotel. The Liverpool (as he was then) and Spain striker Fernando Torres was in the next room to ours. I didn't recognize him at first. My dad had to tell me that we had just walked past him in the corridor. I should walk around with my eyes open a little bit more.

When I got to my seat, I found that Torres was sat next to me. We were both on the front row – with all the other World Player of the Year nominees. So it was obviously not that much of a coincidence that our rooms were next to each other's, right? I had a conversation with him and I remember saying to him that he should win the award in the future if he carried on playing like he was. He was absolutely brilliant that season. Funnily enough, a year or so later a friend pointed out to me that those comments I'd made were in his book. He had remembered what I said to him and included it in his book.

I also met Cristiano Ronaldo. He was there with his entourage in tow. Kaká, Lionel Messi and Steven Gerrard were there too. Big, big names from the world of football. It was such a great occasion because all around us there were so many high-profile players and stars. I met up with Germany captain Birgit Prinz when I got downstairs before the actual awards ceremony and we both did some interviews and had some pictures taken. Marta was there too. She deservedly won the women's award. I came third. Messi won the men's award.

At one point I had to get up and go on stage and speak, answering questions put to me by a FIFA official. It didn't last long. They showed some clips of me, asked some questions and that was it, I sat down again.

The following year I was shortlisted again. And Marta won again. Xavi was there this time, and John Terry too. I spoke to him briefly after the event and he told me that he was heading back to London on his private jet! The late England manager Bobby Robson was given a posthumous award that year and his wife came to Zurich to accept it. She gave a really nice speech. She was lovely.

It was all so hard to take in for someone like me. You do take it in your stride to a degree, but sometimes I have to pinch myself, especially when I look back to how things were when I was at school, and of course everything I had to go through to get to awards ceremonies like these. These players were the elite men and women in our sport. You couldn't go any higher if you tried.

Take someone like Marta. In the USA, I wouldn't be too far behind Marta in the recognition stakes, but there would be a gap. She is renowned as the best player in the world these days.

I would say she is now a global star; she's the biggest name in women's football by far. She can't go anywhere in Brazil. She won the World Player of the Year award five years in a row, from 2006 to 2010, so that's understandable. And rightly so. She is a supreme talent. The technical abilities she possesses are very rarely seen in a woman. I can't recall ever seeing the like in another woman. Not in the same way. She is exceptional. Being Brazilian obviously helps to achieve that level. She is very much on her own in the women's game.

I played alongside Marta in Atlanta once. It was in an All Star match between Marta's XI and Abby Wambach's XI. Players, coaches and fans voted for which players were selected.

Marta picked her team with FC Gold Pride coach Albertin Montoya and Abby picked her team with Philadelphia Independence coach Paul Riley. Abby went mainly for USA players while Marta went international in her picks. It was like choosing players from the playground. We had the likes of Sonia Bompastor of France, Aya Miyama of Japan and Christine Sinclair of Canada in our side.

It was good to be involved in something fun and different and we all wanted to win! Who plays a game and doesn't want to win? Not me. I set up Marta for the first goal in the seventh minute and then she did one of her mazy runs two minutes later to make it 2–0. The match ended 5–2 to us. I really enjoyed myself. It was great to play alongside such talent in a one-off game.

From the mid to late 2000s, it always seemed to be Marta, Prinz and me vying for these top awards. Another Brazilian ace, Cristiane, was always in the mix too. In a sense I have been unfortunate to be up against such excellent players. But coming third behind the likes of Marta and Prinz is no disgrace. It has actually been a great honour for me to play at the same time as them. We all vied for that top spot for four or five years in a row. We are all different types of players too, with different talents. So that's good for the game.

Prinz was just so big, strong and powerful. Her statistics speak for themselves at international level – 128 goals in 214 appearances. When you have that strength element in your game and you also have good players around you – as she did with both FFC Frankfurt and Germany – you can put your technique and finishing qualities to the fore. She had those in bundles, and that set her apart from everybody else. She also worked so hard for her team. She was a strong leader too, and a very good captain. Germany ruled the game when she was at her peak.

Players relished the chance of playing against her because she was the best centre-forward in the women's game for a number of years, the biggest test of all. My Arsenal and England team-mate Faye White would always have the bit between her teeth when she played against her. She would be out there trying to stop her and trying to prove a point by stopping her. She did that so well in that famous 0–0 draw we got against Germany in the 2007 Women's World Cup.

But Prinz had this aura about her. She knew she was the best at what she did and she was very much a confident player because of that.

Marta is the flair player in women's football. In terms of the stuff she can do with a ball, she has no peer. Not many female footballers can do anything like what she can do. As a player you can try and emulate it, of course, but I think it is such a natural gift to her; she is so tuned into it. She has obviously worked at her game – we all have to do that – but it seems to me that what she does comes very easily to her. I'm a bit like her in that sense. What I do comes easily to me.

You are born with that sort of talent. I genuinely believe that. It is, as I said, a natural gift. Sure we all have to work a little bit in certain situations, but when you possess the sort of composure and vision the top players have you are really playing the game at another level. There's a higher comfort factor on the ball. You are always aware of other players coming in and the space that is around you, and you always fancy yourself in those situations. I don't think you can actually teach that. It has to be an instinct that you have within yourself. The more you play the game, the more you can fine-tune that talent. But I don't think you can teach it to players who don't have it, not to the same level those who are born with it enjoy – the few lucky ones. You can't buy being born a Brazilian, either!

Together with my England caps and my MBE, the World Player of the Year nominations are the proudest achievements in my career. These personal accolades are now getting to a level I could never have imagined when I was a young girl. Playing for my country was a dream. But meeting the Queen and mixing with the best male footballers in the world – past and present, on an equal footing – were never in my wildest thoughts.

In terms of women's football, being talked about in the same breath as players such as Marta and Prinz is the bar I always aimed to reach. And that is a great achievement in itself. But meeting the Queen, the monarch of our country, our leader, is something else. It doesn't get much more special than standing there face to face with her as she pins to your chest an award in recognition of your services to a game you have loved all your life.

My past will always help to put everything into perspective for me, because I had to work so hard to achieve these things, off the field as well as on the field. All my rehabilitation work, getting myself into a better frame of mind and into better shape, staying fit and healthy so as to allow myself to reach for those goals again, the goals I always believed deep in my heart one day I could achieve. The goals that looked for a long time to be lost. I always had this vision of being one of the best players in the world – and now here I was, posing for pictures at a FIFA gala.

I strived to be number one in the world and to be one day recognized as the best women's player in the world. That didn't happen. But I came as close as I could to it. I mean, I was pipped to the post by two of the greatest women's players that will ever live. No other player from England has come as close as I did.

To be frank for a moment, it is just so bloody pleasing for me to be able to say all this after all the shit I have been through. Despite all the obstacles I managed to prove to myself, and to others, that I could reach the levels I always believed I could reach.

After all my trials and tribulations – with boys' teams when I was a schoolgirl, loneliness when I was in America, and a horrible rollercoaster of injuries, depression and alcoholism – I had managed to get to where I wanted to be. It had been a hell of a journey, but I was now definitely living the life of a footballer.

17

Boston Calling

WITH THE SUCCESS OF THE ENGLAND WOMEN'S TEAM AND THE increased profile of the game as a result, rumours began to re-emerge about the creation of a new semi-professional women's football league, backed by the Football Association.

At the same time, across the Atlantic Ocean, there was talk of a professional women's football league being formed in the USA.

There was absolutely no way I could ever envisage myself going back to America. So as far as I was concerned, stories about another league starting up out there remained out there, so to speak. My memories of my time in New Jersey were just too painful for me to consider a return. Joining any new set-up over there was just not an option for me.

One day my former Philadelphia Charge team-mate and good friend the USA international Heather Mitts contacted me on Facebook. She came straight to the point: 'Would you be interested in coming back here to play in a pro league if it came back?' I sent her a reply straight back: 'No, my time is done. I am not interested.' She understood the reasons why.

But, as time went on, the rumours about the American women's professional league grew stronger while talk of an English equivalent seemed to stall. Heather had stayed in regular contact with me, so she asked me again. This time I replied, 'I'll see.' It wasn't exactly putting my hat in the ring, but I was no longer ruling it out either. And I suppose that was a big step for me to take, given everything that had happened to me over there.

The difference this time round was that other English players' names were being linked to it. Possibly frustrated with what appeared to be another delay to all our dreams of playing professionally in England, players such as Anita Asante, Karen Carney and Alex Scott seemed quite keen to find out more about the options that could be open to them in America.

A lot of feelers were being put out and about to see if any of us were interested, and as I said, a few of my England team-mates were interested. When it got to the stage where they were asking for telephone numbers, I found myself thinking: 'OK, let's see what's on offer.' I wanted to know what kind of money they were offering and how the new league was going to look. But I was still at the stage of thinking it was very unlikely that I would go over there again.

I received two telephone calls, from Boston and Chicago, asking if I would be interested. If I said yes, my name went into a draft again. Boston Breakers seemed very keen. I had an agent at the time, Steve Kutner, and when he started to negotiate possible figures with them, they started to talk about a lot of money. My viewpoint began to change a little bit when I weighed all that up.

It was a bit of a dilemma for me again. The money was massive in relation to what I was earning at Arsenal, playing for the Ladies and working for the club. I sat down with my mum and dad and we discussed at length the possibilities out there and the obvious pitfalls too.

I was happy at Arsenal. The only issue – if there was one – was that the matches were easy. We were so dominant then that it was no contest most of the time. It wasn't challenging me, I had to admit. There were perhaps four or five guaranteed competitive games per season: Everton Ladies and Chelsea Ladies, home and away. And then there was the FA Women's Cup final, which was always good to play in whether it was a contest or not. But other than that it was thrashing teams most of the time.

So when the American opportunity became more and more real I began to consider it. But this time, given all that happened the first time round, it had to be a family decision. I owed that to Mum and Dad.

My mum was dead set against it. 'Don't go back,' she said. But I was now swaying in favour of doing it. It was a better standard of football, it was much better money, and there were going to be quite a few England players out there with me. I started to fancy it. I wanted to do it.

But then I began to panic about the thought of being there again. Then, just as suddenly, the enthusiasm would take over again. My mind was going backwards and forwards over it time and time again. I couldn't make a decision: it was 'I should go and give it another go, I want to be a professional footballer again' versus 'I don't want to go back, I'm not comfortable there, I've got a good job at Arsenal, I love playing for Arsenal'. It was to and fro all the time. It was a nightmare of a decision to make. I even wrote down a long list of pros and cons.

I said no to my agent at first. 'Kelly,' he said, 'you would be foolish to turn this down.' So I thought it all through again. Steve saw the opportunity whereas I was perhaps blinded by what had happened in the past. I told him to say no to Boston – but instead he told them to give me a couple of weeks to make a decision.

When they called back, I said no. But they came back again, and something – I don't know what – gave. I think I felt I might be missing out on something if I said no. The Brazilian maestro Marta had said yes. Her international team-mate Cristiane had said yes. Canada's Christine Sinclair had said yes as well. A lot of the top English players were agreeing deals and signing up as well. It was a mouth-watering prospect if the top players from around the world were going to be in this one league, I had to admit that.

So I found myself agreeing to give it a go again. It was a very difficult decision for me to make, though. That's why it took me a month to make it. Mum and Dad couldn't believe I was going. I think they were just very concerned, as parents, you know? Still, they said that they would support me whatever my decision was. As they always have done.

England did get their league, the Women's Super League, but in 2011 – two years later than its American counterpart, which was great. Had it been ready to go in 2009 I think the chances are I would have stuck around. I think I speak for a lot of the girls who went over to play in the USA when I say that.

I was moving into the latter stages of my career, and I wanted to feel fulfilled. At that time, early 2009, England still could not provide that for me. I'd been looking forward to a change in the league set-up because, as I said, it had got so predictable. The players I was with at Arsenal were fine. We were a top team. But the majority of the opposition up and down the country was largely uninspiring for me. Cutting the number of teams in the new Women's Super League down to eight was a good move, in my opinion. It would make the league more elite.

Back in 2009, it had sounded like the plans for this new, improved league were in motion, but nothing was happening. The American option was on the back burner, really, but as time went on it soon took over. I recall that those of us who did go over to America were like, 'Is this league in England going to happen or not?' And then it became, 'If it is going to happen, it needs to happen soon!' Of course, it didn't happen – not then anyway – so the decision to go to the States was made for us all there and then.

The delays in setting up this new league, which sounded such an exciting prospect, were so frustrating for us. It was frustrating for women's football as a whole in our country, because it needed a change, it needed spicing up.

In all, Arsenal lost three players to America – Karen Carney, Alex Scott and me. And so, ironically, the Women's Premier League finally became a little more competitive as a result. Alex and I went to Boston and Karen signed for Chicago Red Stars. But there were England players every-where: Eniola Aluko, Anita Asante, Karen Bardsley, Lianne

Sanderson and, later, Katie Chapman all joined up with the WPS.

It wasn't an ideal situation for Arsenal to lose three key players all at once. I think if Vic Akers could have done anything to keep us there, he would have done it. But he couldn't do anything for us, so he couldn't do anything to stop us leaving. As footballers, we all had this huge desire to play the game professionally. If you can't achieve that in your home country, you will naturally go elsewhere, to some place where you can.

As for the England team, the effect wasn't as clear. At the time it was felt that it wasn't a good thing for half the national team to be leaving the country. But I think that in the long run the experience and the improvements that came with us playing over there, with and against the best players in the world, definitely helped us. Domestically it can perhaps be argued that it would have been better if the likes of Alex, Kaz and I were playing week in, week out in England, but playing in America helped us as individual footballers on the international level. We would soon see evidence of that at Women's Euro 2009.

Playing against top-level opposition every week forces you to learn a different mentality. Playing in a top league among world-class players is the best education around, I have always believed that. All of the players who made the trip over there developed their games and fitness levels.

Anita is a good example of that. She joined Sky Blue, in New Jersey, and played centre-back for them. She didn't usually play that position for England so she has now got a much better understanding of the game. She has played in different positions against top-level opposition and she has benefited greatly from that experience. Anita was probably one of the hardest defenders I played against in the American league.

This time round, my dog Bailey wasn't with me in America. I couldn't risk going through all that quarantine and paper-work business with her again. She stayed behind in England with Mum and Dad during the season. I missed her like crazy.

But Alex was there with me, and that was very important to me. In fact I don't think I would have made the trip to Boston had Alex not been there. She knew everything that had gone on in my past so she was a big factor in my decision to say yes.

Alex wanted to go to America to progress her career. Boston really wanted Alex. And Boston wanted me. So it turned out to be an ideal situation. Being on the same team was a big thing. She has always been a great support to me. Finding a team we could play for together involved us getting both our deals right, which wasn't easy. Thankfully, we managed it.

America had been such a daunting, scary experience for me first time round. I left home to go there when I was so young. I didn't know anybody, which was probably a mis-take looking back. That was the hardest bit. This time, with the improvements I had made within myself, and with Alex there to bounce things off – somebody who knew me inside out – it was a totally different prospect.

Of course, Alex was young herself. At twenty-four she was

a few years older than I had been, but she had me as a support. I'd been through the whole thing out there. So, if it was needed, I could help her along the way too. It was the right move for the two of us.

There was an even bigger picture too: a host of other ex-Arsenal players were out there, playing in the league with us, like Anita and Karen. So in several ways my second stint in the USA was a completely different experience for me. I now felt I was in a different place to the one I had once found myself in. There would still be times when I would have a drink, but I wouldn't be drinking every day. It was under control.

You don't live through something like I did and not recall going through it. But since those bad old days in America I had grown up a little bit. I'd enjoyed being back at home with my family and friends, and it had made me stronger. I was also a lot older – thirty as opposed to a teenager. Life experience is an important factor.

I believed I was now much better equipped to handle certain situations. I felt I had strong coping mechanisms in place. Once I got out to America again I made sure that I continued to get the help and support I needed. I just picked up with somebody out there on a weekly basis. I needed to ensure I would stay on track. And I managed to do that. I also knew I had other outlets near me, friends to talk to if things were going bad, whereas previously I would shut down and not speak to anybody about anything. I was still in contact with the Sporting Chance clinic too. I hadn't had that previously either. So I was in much better shape to deal with whatever life in America threw at me. I had a good base and I had grown a lot in important areas. I knew myself much better. I didn't feel as vulnerable as I had done.

Another aspect that helped me was the strong sense of Englishness in Boston's character. When Alex and I flew out there together for a recce before signing, we noticed that. It was a big factor in us deciding to play there.

I'd had an opportunity to play for New Jersey again. But having spent three years there while at college I didn't really want to go back. I fancied a fresh start, but I wanted to stay on the East Coast, mainly because it's only a five-hour journey to England from there. I didn't want to end up based deeper in the country, in, say, Atlanta or Chicago. Boston ticked a lot of boxes.

I love Boston. It's one of my favourite cities in the world. I absolutely adore the place. There is just so much going on in the city. There's always something to do or to go and see, whether it's a band playing in the park or going for a trip along the beautiful Charles River. You can ride your bike down there during summer too, which is really cool. You can also take part in a lot of sporting activities down on the river – yachting, kayaking, whatever you want really. There are volleyball nets down there as well. So, a lot of outdoors activities to get involved in and enjoy, which is ideal for an athlete or someone who loves sports. And if you like your food, there are lots of nice restaurants downtown. Boston is just a vibrant city where there's always something happening. So I was very happy with my decision to join the Breakers.

Playing-wise, the Women's Professional Soccer league was a lot more physical and faster than the first professional league, the Women's United Soccer Association, back in

2001. We had the best Chinese, German, Norwegian and Swedish players in the league back then, but I think the overall standard was better second time round. And that's saying something. Players have developed so much in terms of fitness and technique over the last decade or so. Marta, and players like her, didn't really exist in women's football ten years ago.

It was great to be a professional footballer again. Your whole week is totally different to when you are playing as a semi-professional. Playing for Arsenal and working for the Arsenal academy allowed me to train with the team on just two evenings per week, whereas playing for Boston involved me training every morning, Monday to Friday, from ten o'clock. We also had time to do video sessions, receive treatments and take part in long team talks as part of our training schedule. Things like video sessions – where we would watch opposing teams play, and study them – would only happen at Arsenal ahead of important European matches. Once or twice a season perhaps. In Boston, we were completely focused on football. It was our job. It was our life.

I should say that when I was at Arsenal, even though I was only training twice a week with the team, I was still on an England fitness programme, which was also undertaken on my own. It would come to me direct from our fitness trainer, our exercise scientist. Each England player was given an individual programme and that was what we focused on between international games. We would also have video sessions at England get-togethers. But, of course, the England set-up was a professional set-up. The national league still wasn't.

I find that being a professional athlete is such a great life because I get to do what I love to do every day. And I am able to do that with other people who share a common goal. We are all hungry to play, and we are all hungry to win.

In Boston, it was like a big, happy family. Everybody got on so well. The coach, Tony DiCicco, moulded us into a close-knit group. Obviously we saw each other every day, but we also did a lot of stuff together away from football, such as visiting children's hospitals in the area or taking part in coaching sessions with young girls' teams. We were all friends together. We would grab lunch in the city on our days off, or go out and watch movies as a group – things like that. Harvard Square was a favourite destination for us. There are plenty of coffee shops and clothes shops down there and a few too many ice-cream joints. Many of the players liked to get their nails done down there too. There are several universities nearby, so that makes for a young and vibrant area. It was just a cool place to be. Sometimes the players would get recognized. But a lot of the time we would be left alone.

The Breakers also had an arrangement with certain families to put up some of the players in houses in the area, which was really nice. We made the most of that, going over and having dinner at those places some nights. A lot of the time, after enjoying a night out I would come home and go to bed early. I was in control of my life now. And I always wanted to be fit and healthy for the next day.

We did all right in our first season of the WPS. I did all right too, tying for fifth at the end of the campaign in the league's goalscoring chart with six goals. I played in fifteen matches. I would have played in more but suffered another knee injury late in the season. The worst fears flashed through my mind for a moment – but, thankfully, it was nothing serious.

The attendance figures were not as high as the ones WUSA had got shortly after the USA's success in the 1999 Women's World Cup, but they were OK. We played in front of 6,000 or so during our first season at the Harvard Stadium, right in the heart of the university's athletics facilities. We would have liked the crowds to be bigger, but, again, these numbers dwarfed what we used to get at league games at Borehamwood.

In my second season at Boston, in 2010, I feel that I did much better, scoring eleven goals in the league, which put me fourth overall in the scoring charts. More importantly, for me, I was an ever-present, playing in all twenty-one matches. The pick of the bunch was a 2–0 win over Chicago Red Stars, where I scored both the goals. We reached the end-of-season play-offs but lost 2–1 at home to Philadelphia Independence. Some consolation came with me being named in the WPS All Star Team.

I was really enjoying my life. The spotlight was on women footballers in America. Fox Soccer showed a live match from the WPS every Sunday at 4 p.m. nationwide. Television coverage is so important to our sport, whether it is in America or in England, and Fox's coverage was great. They made it quite personable to the viewer, getting a player to introduce their team before the match and things like that. I did it once. I had to face the camera and say, 'Hi, I'm Kelly Smith from the Boston Breakers and this is your starting line-up.' It was a good way of taking the game to a new audience and relating the players to the viewers.

One difference I did notice coming back to the States was the growth in the men's game. Let's call it the David Beckham effect. Men and women now love soccer in equal measure in America: they support their women's team and they support their men's team too. Major League Soccer has grown enormously and helped the profile of the game a lot. Americans seem to really love it now. Admittedly the big star names who have gone over there to play are coming to the latter part of their careers, but they can still do it on the field. They are still great to watch, and people enjoy watching them.

The local MLS side in the Boston area is New England Revolution. A lot of the Breakers would go along and support them when we didn't have a game. It's now approaching twenty years since the USA hosted the World Cup, in 1994. It has taken this long for the game to take root. The next stage will be to see young talent coming through the ranks, through the college system perhaps, like it has in women's football for many years now. If that starts to happen in a big way, it might not be too long before the USA are contenders for the top prizes in the men's game too.

18

The Year of Truth

ENGLAND COACH HOPE POWELL HAD ALWAYS INSTILLED IN US that 2009 would be our year to blossom. She had nurtured the team for several years by now and the Women's Euro, to be held in Finland in August and September of that year, was our best bet yet to do something special on the international stage.

Bizarrely, our qualification programme had actually begun a few months before the 2007 Women's World Cup in China. We played Northern Ireland at Gillingham and beat them 4–0. I scored one of the goals in that one, although the score-line was not as comfortable as it suggests. The match was goalless at half-time.

We didn't play again until later in the year, at the end of October. But the qualifying group was well under way by then, with the other teams – Belarus, the Czech Republic and Spain plus Northern Ireland – all having played two or three matches.

Belarus were seen as the weakest team in the group, but they then went and walloped Northern Ireland 5–0 at home, beating our scoreline against them. However, they were well beaten by both the Czech Republic and Spain before they travelled over to meet us in Walsall. It was another resounding 4–0 win for us. Again, I got one of the goals.

By the end of the year it was clear that the Czech Republic and Spain were going to be our rivals for an automatic qualification place. They both had 100 per cent records until they met in Pilsen, where the outcome was a 2–2 draw. But we were ranked well above both of them. We were playing well and we were confident.

However, we struggled against both of them. Spain held us for over an hour at Shrewsbury, in front of a decent crowd of 8,753, before Karen Carney grabbed us a winner. And then, on a freezing cold night at the Keepmoat Stadium in Doncaster, we were held 0–0 by the Czechs.

In March 2008 we recorded a 2–0 victory in Lurgan against Northern Ireland, and we followed that with an impressive 6–1 thrashing of Belarus in Minsk. But both the Czech Republic and Spain did the double over these two countries as well. So, with two games left, we knew that it was going to be the head-to-head matches that would decide the group. This was not what we had expected when the draw had been made.

Things got interesting when Spain thumped the Czechs 4–1 at home in Madrid, leaving us level on points with the Spanish but with a game in hand over them. We next travelled to Prague to take on the Czechs in the hope of making up for that dire draw in Doncaster.

We fell behind to a Katerina Doskova goal. And trailed at half-time. It was the sternest half-time team talk we had received in a long time. It worked as well. We came out in the second half and scored five goals without reply. I got two, Emily Westwood, Kaz Carney and Jill Scott got the others.

This meant that a draw in Zamora, close to the Portuguese border, against Spain would be enough to put us through to the Women's Euro finals in Finland. A defeat would mean it would go to head-to-head. We had won 1–0 at home so Spain would have to better that result against us.

At half-time we were 2–0 down. Kaz pulled us one back at the start of the second half, and I notched the equalizer fifteen minutes from time. But it had been far too close for comfort. When Spain were thrashed in the play-offs, 4–0, by Holland, it did make me wonder whether we had gone backwards a little. But the main thing about qualification groups is to qualify, and we had managed to do that.

The Euro finals had now been extended to twelve teams, with three groups of four. The top two in each group would go through to the quarter-finals along with the two best third-placed teams.

If our qualification campaign had been a little hairy at times, it was nothing compared to our experiences in Group C in the competition proper. We were drawn against Italy, Russia and Sweden. The scheduling of the matches gave us our hardest game, against Sweden, last. So we had to hope that by then we would have done enough to reach the last eight.

Before the competition got under way, a Swedish football magazine published an interview with one of their players that insinuated that I was a dirty player. The pigtail-pulling incident from our match in Blackburn four years earlier was dragged up again. I was a cheat and all sorts, apparently. It made me laugh that someone had thought to talk about this, never mind write it up. I had to remember what Hope told me about these things: I must ignore them. It was probably published to get a reaction from me. Well, they weren't going to get one. Not a negative one anyway.

When I saw it, I thought it was a stupid article. Somebody posted it to me on Facebook. It featured a cartoon that showed a caricature of me pulling at this girl's hair. I had clearly hit a nerve in the Swedish camp by doing that.

Hope caused a surprise by not naming Rachel Yankey in our squad for Finland. Yanks was probably one of our highest-profile players so this generated a bit of publicity in the press. People were asking us if this meant that nobody's place in the team was safe. We just had to ignore all that and focus on the task in hand.

I was personally a little bit surprised by Rachel's omission from the squad, just because her name within the game was so big and there is always the matter of what she can do for you on the pitch. At times she had been a match winner for England, so it was a bit of a shock to find out she wasn't going to be there with us. Then again, Sue Smith was play-ing really well. We had two top-class players challenging for that position on the left flank.

Hope obviously had her reasons for leaving her out. I don't know the full story. But, as the papers said, nobody's place was safe in the team any more. We all knew that we had to keep producing the goods or we might be out of the squad as well. We talked about it privately, of course, among ourselves. It was a big surprise to a lot of the players in the group, and it gave a few a kick up the bum as well. But the fact was, if we were going to reach our potential in 2009 – a prospect that had been bandied around for a little while now – then we were going to have to do it without one of our most influential players of the last decade.

We started off the tournament against Italy in Lahti. I remember that we had a toy mascot, a cuddly moose called 'Bruce'. He was to attend all our games in Finland. We had had 'Yolanda the Panda' in China. This tradition was started by Rachel Pavlou, who is the national women's football development manager at the FA. Bruce was sat on the top of the perspex roof on our dugout for that match. I was sat underneath him, struggling with a slight knee injury. By the time I got on, at the start of the second half, we were a player down, Casey Stoney having been sent off early in the game for a so-called 'push' on Melania Gabbiadini. We felt that it was harsh.

Despite playing with ten, we'd still taken the lead when Fara Williams scored from the penalty spot after Kaz had been brought down by two players. But in the second half, we kind of imploded. Patrizia Panico equalized for them, and then, with eight minutes remaining, Alessia Tuttino scored a wonder strike from way out.

We were speechless after that result. Obviously you don't want to start any tournament off with a defeat. It made us realize that we had to really buck our ideas up if we were going to progress. Italy were not the best team in our group by any stretch of the imagination. So it was a big shock to the system; we weren't prepared for anything like that. It was a very bad result for us, whichever way we looked at it. And it meant that it was going to be a hard job for us from now on. We couldn't afford any more slip-ups.

Things got worse before they got better. In Helsinki, against Russia, the lowest-ranked team in our group and a side that had been beaten 3–0 by Sweden in their opening match, we somehow found ourselves two goals down after just twenty-two minutes. Ksenia Tsybutovich and Olesya Kurochkina were the Russian goalscorers – names we won't forget.

I started this match – Jill Scott dropped to the bench; Lindsay Johnson came in for Anita Asante and Rachel Unitt replaced Casey, who was suspended. So we looked quite different at the back from the opening match. We got ourselves into a real big hole in that game. But it turned out to be the making of us.

As the scoreline suggests, we were atrocious in the early part of that game. We just weren't at the races. There was no other way to look at it: we were going out of the tournament. At that point in the match it did enter my mind that if we didn't do something spectacular, we were going home. It was as simple as that. Actually, if we continued playing like that, we deserved to go home. Nobody in our side was doing the basics right. We were playing – every one of us – as if we had never played the game before. It was awful.

I don't know if that was nerves on our part or the effect of too much expectation placed on us to put on a show after the Italy result, against what was felt to be inferior opposition. I couldn't say to this day. We all knew that we had to win the game, so it is inexplicable, really, and indefensible.

For some reason, we just didn't play our normal game in

the early part of that match. We were very anxious on the ball. And with those two goals going in so early on – we had conceded the first one after just two minutes – I think we were shell-shocked for a little while.

But when I looked around the pitch, into some of our players' eyes, I just knew that we were so much better than what we were showing out there. At that moment, something happened to us. Something clicked inside us and we bucked our ideas up. We started playing with little touches. We started moving the ball around quicker. We started to believe in ourselves and each other more. Once we started to do that, our confidence grew. And you could literally feel it coming back. I don't think I ever quite allowed myself to believe that we were going to lose that game, even at 2–0 down, but, obviously, we had it all to do.

To come from two goals down in any match, let alone in the finals of an international tournament, is a very big ask. A massive ask, in fact. Never mind the opposition. We went in at half-time 3–2 up.

Kaz had pulled one back a few minutes after Russia's second goal, and she then played in Eniola Aluko for the equalizer for us just after the half-hour mark. With a few minutes remaining before the half-time whistle, I'd rocketed one in from near to the centre circle to put us in the lead. The goalkeeper had kicked the ball straight at me. I had one touch and then lobbed it back, over her head and into the net. It was a sweet goal to score – a bit of quick thinking, a bit of skill, and a neat execution. The timing of it could not have been any better either.

We came in at half-time and Hope told us that we were

very lucky to be where we were because at 2–0 down we were going out of the tournament. She reiterated that to us. But she was positive. She told us that we had now pulled it around and that we had to go out there in the second half and keep it that way – that we had to keep that belief in ourselves.

Incredibly, after such a mad first half, there were no more goals in the second half. So we had pulled it out of the fire. Two games gone, and we were won one, lost one. We were still very much in the tournament, with the Swedes up next.

Our confidence was back. We had done a lot of work on the mental aspect of our game, and I think that tie with Russia was really the first big test for us in that respect, definitely in tournament football. Having so much more experience and so much more knowledge had enabled us to cope with something like that much better. We were able to stop, think and analyse the game, and then go again. That period was such an important stage in our growth as a team. If we hadn't had that, I don't think we would have been able to pull out a result like that. We showed such great character, determination and fight to turn that match around and save our tournament. I believe that the England team from the previous Women's European Championship, four years earlier, would have struggled to do that.

We always seemed to like to do things the hard way rather than the easy way, for some reason. Why couldn't *we* have gone 2–0 up in twenty-two minutes? We didn't do things that way. We didn't do comfortable and cruising. No, it was much more like us to go a couple of goals down and then have to produce a miracle to win the game.

Luckily, we now had the players who could do that, with the experience to do that. There is no greater pressure in an international tournament than knowing that you have to do something otherwise you are going home. That match made us realize that we could do that when we had to. When the chips were down, as a team we now knew that we could produce something special. You couldn't buy the extra belief and confidence that gave us.

Due to the complexities involved with eight teams going through to the quarter-finals from a group stage involving twelve teams, mathematically it was actually easier to go through than go out. After the Russia game we were in third place with a win, but the group had been so unpredictable that there was nothing to suggest the Russians could not go out and beat Italy in their final game. So we knew we needed to get a result in Turku against Sweden, who were already through with comfortable wins over both Russia and Italy.

We wanted to do that for many reasons anyway. We hadn't played them since the last Women's Euro, and all of us who'd played in that game in Blackburn remembered that day only too well. I am pretty sure that the Swedish girl with the pigtails could remember it as well!

Casey came back into the team after her one-match suspension, and Unitt moved to the bench. Otherwise it was the same team that had started against Russia. Sweden had some players in their team who had played in Blackburn, but not as many as we did. I am pretty sure that that match meant much more to us than it did to them.

We felt confident going into the match. We had now started to believe, as a team, that we could match the top nations in the world. There wasn't the same fear factor when coming up against the likes of Sweden that there had been in the past for us. I recall us going into this particular game and genuinely believing that we could beat them.

Faye White put in another awesome performance for us in this one. She was Player of the Match again, as she often was in the big games that mattered. She also gave us the lead, in the twenty-eighth minute, when she towered over Charlotte Rohlin to score with a great header past Hedvig Lindahl.

We held the lead for twelve minutes, until Katie Chapman was adjudged to have fouled Lotta Schelin in the box and Victoria Sandell Svensson scored from the penalty spot. We thought the penalty decision was harsh. Sir Trevor Brooking, the head of development at the Football Association, was sat in the stands, and he agreed.

Our defence was rock solid in this match and overall I think we were the better team, but we ended up with a 1–1 draw. A good result, really. We also felt that we had played our best game of the tournament, by far, against the best team we had faced, so far. And without the penalty, we would probably have beaten them.

Italy defeated Russia 2–0 in the other match in Group C, so we finished in third place on four points, with a win, a draw and a defeat, behind Sweden and Italy. We had improved with every game and we were feeling confident going into the knockout stages after an admittedly very shaky start.

In fact it began to feel to me as though we were on the verge of being able to make a breakthrough at the top level of women's international football. I had never felt quite like that before. Over quite a few years now we had built up such a strong base and togetherness in the England camp. Previously when we had played the likes of Sweden, Germany and the USA, it was a case of damage limitation against them. Now we were feeling down as a team because we hadn't won a game against one of them, which we'd really deserved to do. The goalless draw against Germany in the 2007 Women's World Cup had been a watershed for us; the longer Euro 2009 went on, the more I felt that we were reaching another level. And that felt absolutely fantastic. I had moved from playing in an England team that seemed to lose all the time to the best teams in the world to playing in an England team that was able to compete and was unlucky not to beat one of the best teams in the world.

We had some very good players in that squad, with the right level of age and experience. The fact that we had been together for quite a while was a big plus point. Mentally, physically and technically we were so much better than before. There was also the fact that many of us were now playing professionally in America. I believe that made us a much stronger team going into that tournament, fitter and more skilful in key areas. The core of our team was now playing at an elite level. That meant training on the ball every day. That was so important for us going into that tournament.

Having said that, those of us who were playing in the States were just coming off the back of a hard six-month summer season, so there was a bit of tiredness in there too. Kaz seemed to be living on jelly sweets in Finland due to this. I remember that she had to be given these Lucozade gum boosters all the time to help her fight fatigue. I think she was just wiped out after a full-on league campaign; she needed a sugar high and some extra energy when she went out and played for us.

I began to feel that way too. I felt absolutely drained at times. I felt that I was trying to give everything but I also felt like I didn't have anything more to give. There was no more fuel in the tank. This is a horrible feeling at the best of times, but when you are playing in a major tournament for your country it's even worse. Given that I genuinely felt this was our time and our chance, it was hard to comprehend and to deal with that at times.

Luckily, there were a number of key players in our team who had been well rested over the summer. They were probably in a much better physical condition than those of us who had been playing in the Women's Professional Soccer league over the pond for the last few months. So it was swings and roundabouts, really. The WPS had definitely improved those of us who had gone out there in a lot of ways, but it had also wiped us out a bit, and a few of us struggled.

Despite all that, this was the best England team I had ever played in. That was due to a combination of factors, but the main one, for me, was the coach. I will talk more about Hope a little later. I want to devote a whole chapter to her because she is 99 per cent of the reason why I am here today, why I have been able to do what I have done in my career. The improvements that have been made in the England team over the years all come down to the hard work Hope and her staff have put in since she has been in charge, getting us to understand the system that we play, making us defensively sound, and making us fitter. Without doubt she is the reason we are where we are now. And we started to show real evidence of that during those three weeks in Finland in August and September 2009.

By the time of the quarter-finals, Finland was going football crazy. They are a small nation but they came out firing in the tournament and the crowds turned out to support them. In the group stages, the Finns were consistently watched by crowds of more than 16,000. Compare that figure with the lowly 1,462 that saw us play Russia.

Finland had played all their group matches in the Olympic Stadium in Helsinki, which hosted the 1952 Olympic Games, where Czechoslovakian Emil Zatopek was the star of the show, winning gold in the 5,000 metres, 10,000 metres and the marathon, and the famous Hungary team featuring Ferenc Puskas, Sandor Kocsis and Nandor Hidegkuti first came to international prominence when they won the gold medal in the men's football tournament. More recently, it had hosted the 1983 and 2005 Athletics World Championships. In such a setting and with such support, Finland had won their opening two matches, beating Denmark 1–0 and Holland 2–1. But our quarter-final with them would be held in Turku, not Helsinki, and we hoped that this would help us. We stayed put for a few days as we didn't need to travel.

It surprised me that Finland didn't stay in Helsinki. But the draw didn't work like that. They had won Group A, so it seemed odd that they had to sacrifice that advantage and head over to Turku and the smallest stadium of the lot – the Veritas Stadion, with a 9,000 capacity – to play against us.

We knew all about the Finns, of course, from that magnificent match at the City of Manchester Stadium during Euro 2005. Striker Laura Kalmari was still the star of the team. She was their main goalscorer. But they had a number of capable players in their side. They had reached the semifinals four years ago, of course, and they were a better team now than they had been back then.

Due to an injury to Alex Scott, Lindsay moved over to right-back for us in this match and Anita came back into the team to partner Faye at the centre of defence. Otherwise we were unchanged.

The midfield pairing of Fara and Katie was now so strong when they played together, allowing me to do what I enjoyed doing best – roaming around the pitch with the ball at my feet and making penetrating runs.

Eniola was flanked superbly up front by Karen and Sue, who had certainly proved that the decision to play her was the right one. We had gelled so well as a team that when one of us had to drop out, somebody could come in and take their place and do the job for them. We were a strong unit now.

What we needed was an early goal to silence the crowd. And what we got was an early goal to silence the crowd. We put together a really slick move; I helped on Katie's pass, and Eni was on hand to finish it off. There were fourteen minutes on the clock.

Fara popped up to stab home a second, and the crowd now fell very quiet. But then a horrible injury to Faye, after a clash of heads, rocked us. For the second international tournament in a row we had lost our captain and leader with a fractured cheekbone. Jill Scott came on for Faye, and Katie dropped back to join Anita in central defence. We got to half-time with the two-goal lead intact but we were in a fair bit of disarray.

The Finns became even more physical in the second half – and that's saying something. They were a strong team and, as sometimes happens in football, accidental and unfortunate incidents such as what had happened to us can change the mindsets of both sides. Sensing this, the crowd became more raucous and more vocal, despite the electronic scoreboard still showing 2–0 to us.

We survived a hell of a lot of pressure in the first part of the second half. I seemed to be spending much more time putting tackles in and dropping back to help the team out than surging forward and trying to create attacks for us.

I could not remember us being put under such consistent and intense pressure from corners in a match before. The height of the Finnish strikers was causing us huge problems in terms of keeping out headers and shots from knockdowns.

Finland brought on another big striker in Annica Sjölund, for Essi Sainio. The pressure mounted. Within a few minutes, Sjölund's height had got them back into it. The goal, unsurprisingly, came from a corner. The noise that greeted it was extremely loud.

What happened after that was one of those moments in football that you want to play over and over again on your DVD player or video recorder, or on YouTube. Straight from our kick-off, Eni picked up the ball and ran at the Finns at pace. She was dribbling, jinking, twisting and turning, and left three or four defenders in her wake. As she entered the penalty box, she looked up and drilled the ball past Tinja-Riikka Korpela in the Finnish goal to restore our two-goal lead – after about ten seconds!

We all went mad. What a goal! What a time to score it! We all ran over to her to celebrate, jumping up and down. Everybody was off the bench doing the same. The match had been turned round, back in our favour.

But the Finnish onslaught just dusted itself down and started all over again. They were forcing corner after corner after corner, realizing that this was their best option. And it was. Linda Sällström scored for them from another corner on seventy-eight minutes to make it 3–2.

The remaining twelve minutes saw such a display of fighting spirit and strong defensive play on our part that it seemed to last for an hour or more. Those of us who were aching with tiredness probably felt it the most, but the adrenalin kicked in and got us all over the line. Rachel Brown made a great save in the closing minutes from Kalmari to seal our win.

We'd held out. It was a magnificent performance. Finland were a tough team to beat, particularly on their own patch. We were elated at the end.

The crowd was so partisan. We had a little section of family and friends, but that was it. The rest of the crowd was Finnish through and through. Any time they went forward, you would hear this noise. I wouldn't say it was hostile, but it was definitely very loud. Every time they won a corner – and they won a lot of corners – they put four or five of their biggest players around our goalkeeper. They tried to hit the near post with every one and then tried to bundle the ball in.

The noise of the crowd got louder with every corner. They really got behind them. It began to affect us a little. Every time they got a corner, the nerves rose in your body. We just knew what it meant, where the ball was going to go and everything. And, of course, if it dropped for them in the right way, there was a good chance they were going to score.

It was another massive game for us in terms of our development. For us, being able to win in a cauldron like that against opposition playing like that was another big step on the learning ladder. Again, we couldn't have done that a few years earlier, I am certain of that. Grinding out a result like that with a performance like that in an environment like that to reach the semi-finals of a major international tournament for the very first time was phenomenal.

19

So Near Yet So Far

TO MAKE THINGS EVEN SWEETER FOR ENGLAND, THE DRAW FOR the knockout stages at Women's Euro 2009 had really opened up for us. Strangely, finishing third in our qualification group had put us in the easier half. Both Sweden and Italy, who had finished above us in our group, went into the top half with Germany and Norway. We'd gone into the bottom half with Finland, France and Holland.

Our semi-final opponents for a place in the final of the Women's European Championship, then, were going to be either France or Holland. We sat down together – sadly without poor Faye, our injured captain, who was travelling back to England to undergo surgery – and watched the second quarter-final, from Tampere, live on television. After a goalless draw, Holland won on penalties.

The next day, in the other two quarter-finals, Germany beat Italy 2–1 and Norway beat Sweden 3–1. We were now the sole survivors from Group C. It's quite funny how these things work out sometimes.

We had avoided Germany – the one team everybody probably wanted to avoid – and that was the main thing, I suppose. Even though if we were to go on and win the tournament then of course we had to beat them all. And we now started to believe that we could go all the way. Holland were definitely there for the taking, we knew that, and a victory against them would put us into the final – where more than likely we would face the Germans.

The mood in the camp was electric. But, sadly, there was still no terrestrial television coverage of the tournament back home in England. British Eurosport were showing all the matches live on satellite television but the BBC, ITV, Channel 4 and Channel 5 were showing nothing. Television coverage is vital to women's football. Our game was given a tremendous boost when the BBC covered Euro 2005 and the 2007 World Cup so extensively, not to mention several FA Women's Cup finals as well.

But the BBC was no longer the broadcast partner of the Football Association. I don't know whether that had anything to do with it. There were a lot of rumours flying around, obviously, at the time. All we knew, as players, was that every game of ours in those international competitions in 2005 and 2007 had been shown live on free-to-air television in the United Kingdom, but now, in 2009, there was nothing. We were on the verge of reaching the Women's European Championship final yet nobody back home could watch us unless they had satellite television, which a lot of people don't have.

We really felt that we were doing something for our nation and we really wanted the people of our nation to be able to see us achieve this. This was our greatest opportunity yet to put women's football firmly on the UK map. Obviously we wanted to win this tournament for ourselves, but we also wanted to win this tournament for our country.

We couldn't really understand it, because the television coverage of those two previous international competitions had been really well received and got decent viewing figures too. We had been invited to the House of Commons after Euro 2005, and I had appeared on Jonathan Ross's show after the World Cup in China, so it was a bit of a mystery to us all, to be honest.

It hurt us, actually. On the one hand we felt as though we were making great progress, and then suddenly it all seemed to grind to a halt. So, why was that? Had we done something wrong? We had actually got better, so it didn't make sense to us. We certainly didn't feel that it was justified. But we didn't know the details of why things were the way they were. And we couldn't do anything about it. All we could do was play our game. It might have been a disappointing and frustrating situation for us, but we couldn't allow it to affect us. We just had to keep playing, beat Holland, and hope for a change of heart from somewhere.

When we lined up against Holland at the Ratina Stadion in Tampere it was obvious to me that it was a massive game for both teams. Holland had been of a similar capability to us for many years in women's football, probably just further down the scale. The Women's European Championship final usually featured Germany, Norway or Sweden. This year it was going to feature one of the two of us.

So we expected a hard game. We knew that Holland played very defensively. They liked to keep players behind the ball. And in this semi they often had ten or eleven players behind the ball, soaking up pressure. They played on the counter-attack. But we knew all this, and we were ready for it.

Dutch coach Vera Pauw had once publicly stated that I was the best women's footballer in the world – after I scored a hat-trick against Holland in that 2007 Women's World Cup qualifier at Charlton – so she knew all about me and the England team. She is actually one of the best coaches in the world in our game and very highly respected. She made sure that her team was set out in the best way for them to get a result against us. It wasn't a particularly pretty style of play, but it was effective. She was criticized a little during the tournament for it, but it worked for them and it got them to the semi-finals, so you can't really knock it. We knew that we were going to have to be patient against them and slowly break them down.

Alex returned from injury to play at right-back. Anita and Lindsay played in central defence, which was a big ask for them in the absence of Faye. Jess Clarke, of Leeds, came in on the right flank in place of Kaz. There were no other changes. Fara was given the captain's armband. We were an international squad – playing for each other, working for each other, and helping the team out in whichever way possible. Tournament football is not about one to eleven, it's about the whole squad. We had strength in depth – and four games down, we needed to have that.

It was goalless at half-time. The game had gone as expected. We remained patient. Hope made one change at half-time, bringing Kaz on for Sue down the left flank. We began the second half in the same way as we had played the first half, and we were rewarded with a goal on fifty-one minutes.

It was my second goal of the tournament. Kaz made a good run, Eni cut the ball back to me, and I struck it home to finally break the deadlock. I skidded on the turf with my arms aloft in celebration. I couldn't see Holland getting back into it. I genuinely thought my goal would be enough for us.

I was wrong. Within three minutes it was 1–1, Marlous Pieëte equalizing after a quick run and break by Manon Melis. It was a lack of concentration on our part.

After that goal, it was back to us pressing and them sitting back and holding on. It was like that until the end of normal time.

My mind and body were tired now, as tired as they had been at any stage during the tournament, but the adrenalin levels were higher than ever. I also remember that my knee felt quite sore at the end of the ninety minutes, and the pain never left me.

Jill came on for Jess at the start of extra-time; Lianne Sanderson had replaced Eni after seventy or so minutes of normal time. We knew that we needed just one chance, one opportunity. We didn't want penalties. We didn't think it would get that far anyway. We were confident that we would get the goal we needed.

It came in the second half of extra-time when Jill powered home a header from Kaz's corner kick. This time we kept our concentration and defended as though our lives depended on it. The job was done. We held out for the last few minutes and sealed our place in the final.

I was so thrilled with our achievement. I struggled to put my feelings into words at the final whistle. I was rewarded at the end with the Player of the Match award. That was nice, but it came nowhere near the jubilation of reaching the Women's European Championship final. We now had to recover – and for me that meant ice, treatment and a bit of rest – and focus on winning it.

Germany beat Norway the following night, as I knew they would, by three goals to one. As expected, we would be facing Birgit Prinz and Co. – the biggest test of them all – in the final. So there was no celebration and no resting on our laurels. We drove back to Helsinki and prepared for the most important match any of us had ever played in.

It was a massive match for us. From day one we had said that we felt we could reach the final in Finland, and here we were. We had come so far in such a short time. So much hard work had been put in by so many people – and it had paid off. We had grown into the tournament as we progressed. We had learned so much about ourselves in just a few weeks and we had got better and better. Our performances had peaked at the right time, and that is ideally what you want. We had learned from the disappointment of the defeat against Italy, showed our mettle in coming from two goals down against Russia, stood up to Sweden and more, played out of our skins with such great spirit against Finland, and now we had gone through the whole extra-time experience in the semi with Holland.

We knew it was going to be tough against Germany, but just to have got there, just to be playing them in the final, was out of this world. It was our biggest achievement and the biggest test we had ever faced rolled together in one.

As we prepared for the final, we heard that the BBC had

bought the rights to show the match live to the nation. It was such a thrill for us to hear that. We were delighted. Obviously we wished that decision had been made sooner so that people could have watched those games against Finland and Holland, but we no longer felt that we were out on a limb and that nobody really cared. So that gave us a boost.

Another boost came in the shape of the return from England of our team captain, Faye. Incredibly, she had been passed fit to play in the final, provided she wore a specially fitted protective face mask. This was less than a week since she had fractured her cheekbone.

England had actually played in the first ever Women's European Championship final, back in 1984. There was no finals competition as such, so the final was played on a home and away basis. We lost to Sweden on penalties. But it didn't rank as an official UEFA competition.

In 1991, UEFA took over the running of the Women's European Championship, and Germany won it that year. It was a once-every-two-years competition then, and Norway triumphed in 1993, but after that it was Germany all the way, in 1995, 1997, 2001 and 2005. The tournament was held once every four years from 1997 so our opponents had, in fact, won the last four Women's Euros. Make no mistake, we knew that we had our work cut out.

Germany might have been the top nation in women's football, and might have been at the top for many years, but we could only focus on us. We had felt really confident when we played against Sweden and we now had to build on that approach, because Germany were another step up from that level. We remembered the 0–0 draw in China in September 2007 and we used that to build a positive mental mindset going into the final.

Personally, I definitely felt they were beatable. There was no fear factor in me going into that match. I did an interview the night before the game and stated, 'It's about time somebody else won something!' I hoped that could be us. They had no divine right to be European champions or world champions. We had to realize that they were human beings. Forget the records, forget the history, it was eleven versus eleven on the day: England versus Germany.

There was suddenly a lot of media interest in us out in Finland: newspapers, radio and, of course, television. We made a lot of the back pages in the UK, which was great. The final was being sold as this big England–Germany rivalry thing again in some places. Some of the English reporters out in Finland appeared to be more nervous than us. 'Are we going to get thumped?' they asked. Seriously, what can you say to a question like that? That certainly wasn't in my mind going into the final, and I hope it wasn't in the rest of my team-mates' minds either. I genuinely don't think it was. We were there on merit. And we were now a good team as well. We were going to take the game to Germany and see what we could do. No fear.

One thing that Hope did make us aware of before the match was that the Germans had already planned their celebration party after the game. They had booked a restaurant in Helsinki, and apparently they also had T-shirts with 'Euro Championship Winners' or something like that printed on them. We seethed when we heard about that. That's how much belief that team had in itself. I suppose that comes from winning time and time again.

I can't comment on what made the Germans do something like that. I don't understand the arrogance involved because it's just not the sort of thing we would do. But certainly that business with the celebration party added extra fire in all our bellies. It certainly pepped me up. The cheek of it, and the total disrespect to us as a team! I guess that Hope knew it would get that sort of reaction from us. That's probably why she told us about it.

But that arrogance, that supreme confidence if you like, comes from years of being the top team in the world. Every time we played in a tournament, Germany was always fancied to win it. So, wholeheartedly, they believed that too.

Hope changed things around a little bit for the final. Faye was obviously back, so Lindsay made way; Anita played at the back with Faye. Jill, after her winning goal in the semi-final, came into the starting line-up, and Kaz started too. Jess and Sue were the ones who were left out as a result. The midfield was now packed with Fara, Katie and Jill. I was moved into the centre-forward position, and Eni was switched to the left flank with Kaz coming in down the right.

Germany, obviously, had all the big names out: Nadine Angerer, Kerstin Garefrekes, Simone Laudehr, Melanie Behringer, Kim Kulig, Birgit Prinz, Inka Grings, and on it went. The list never seemed to stop. As you would expect, there was quality everywhere you looked on the team sheet.

Our plans were quite simple. We knew that we had to keep Germany's forward line quiet if we were to stand any chance at all of winning the match. Obviously that would be quite a feat in itself. But that had to be our starting point whenever we played them. Prinz, in particular, was at the top of her game at that time. We had managed to keep them out when we played against them in China and we had to do something similar in Helsinki.

So we knew we were going to have to close them down quickly at every possible opportunity, and we knew that we couldn't allow them to have time on the ball. We also had to do our best to limit the number of crosses coming into our penalty box. Garefrekes was a big threat to us, she always was. We accepted that we were going to have to work very hard for ninety minutes, without letting up for a moment. So, whenever we got the ball, we needed to keep it and then move it – quickly. We had to look to get numbers forward whenever we had the opportunity to do so. And we had to take every chance that came to us.

If we were going to be European champions, it was not going to come easy.

As kick-off approached, I left the changing room and walked out on to the pitch in line with the team, as usual. I could now experience the historic Helsinki Olympic Stadium for myself. The famous observation tower, near to one corner of the pitch, is its most memorable feature. The feeling inside me at that moment was an intense mixture of excitement and pride.

I had never before felt as passionate as I did on hearing our national anthem before that final. This was not only my moment, it was our moment – it was England's moment. If ever there was a stage to play my best, this was it. I knew that.

We started really well, and the game was pretty even for

the first twenty minutes. But then we conceded two quick goals within two minutes. The first one was scored by Prinz and the second one by Behringer.

This had now become a true test of our new-found strength and character. And we responded magnificently. I won the ball, went down the left and cut it back inside from the byline. Kaz was there to prod it home. It was 2–1 with twenty-four minutes on the clock. Game on.

After three goals in a matter of minutes, the game went back to the pattern of the first twenty minutes. We largely cancelled each other out. It was very even in all areas across the pitch. After the flurry of goals, Jill actually came closest to scoring again before half-time when she had a header cleared off the line by Behringer. It remained 2–1 to Germany at the interval.

We were definitely in this match – and it was the match of our lives.

Fara and Katie had worked so hard throughout that first half. They did really well for us because they faced a tough time defensively due to Germany's movement being so good. They are such strong, physical opponents that if you win the ball from them you really have to try and keep hold of it because if you lose it, they will hurt you. The concentration level in our side had to be at the maximum. And those two were in the thick of the battle.

Hope seemed happy at the break. There was advice and reminders as always, but the overriding message was to keep doing what we were doing. We were holding our own and we were playing well. And, every now and again, I would think about those T-shirts . . .

The Germans came out firing on all cylinders after the

Above: I made my England debut in November 1995, shortly after my seventeenth birthday, and scored my first goal against Croatia two weeks later.

Above: This was taken when England played in the USA in the summer of 1997. We used to get heavily beaten by them in those days.

Hosting Women's Euro 2005 was great for the game but results didn't go our way, unfortunately.

Above left: After Euro 2005, we had reached a new level, and qualification for the World Cup was sealed with a draw against France the following year. Here (**above right**) I celebrate after the game in Rennes with Rachel Yankey.

Left: My dad was pretty happy too!

Below: Modelling my favourite England kit.

Above: With Hope Powell in China before the 2007 Women's World Cup. We were in great shape going into that tournament.

Above: Walking out to face Germany in Shanghai. The 0–0 draw proved that we could compete with the best.

The famous goal celebration. It's an image that has stayed with me, and it was a beautiful moment in my life.

Above left: I had Hope to thank for guiding me back after all my injury problems.

Above right: Another of my forty-five goals for England (so far!) took us past Switzerland in a playoff to qualify for the 2011 Women's World Cup.

Left: At Women's Euro 2009, we came so close, and I had three goals to celebrate, including one from the halfway line against Russia.

Pure elation as Jill Scott's header in extra-time against Holland put us into the final.

Left: Sweden are always tough opponents but we beat them in a warm-up game for the 2011 Women's World Cup.

Below: Beating the USA at Leyton Orient was another massive result and we were full of confidence going to Germany.

Bottom: I slammed home the first penalty in the shoot-out against France in the World Cup quarter-final in Leverkusen, but it was heartbreak for us again.

Above: A great England team. Back row (*left to right*): me, Faye White, Karen Bardsley, Jill Scott, Casey Stoney, Fara Williams, Kaz Carney; front row: Rachel Yankey, Alex Scott, Rachel Unitt, Ellen White.

Left: Receiving my hundredth cap with Hope and Yanks.

Below: Hope's impact on the game in this country has been massive.

Right: My parents' house on Kilby Close in Garston is decked out for the day I received my MBE in 2008.

Below: So proud. With my mum, dad and my brother, Glen, at Windsor Castle.

Bottom: The whole experience of meeting the Queen was absolutely perfect.

Top left: Being named one of the top players in the world by FIFA was another massive honour, and gave me the chance to hang out with the likes of Lionel Messi (**top right**).

Centre: I was also invited to participate in the draw for the Olympics, with some more famous faces.

Right: Promoting London 2012 – another fantastic opportunity for women's football in this country.

break. The pace of the game became quite hectic. Five minutes into the second half, Kulig snatched at a half-chance in our box after our defence had failed to clear a shot from Laudehr, and the ball was in our net. We were 3–1 down with forty minutes to play.

But our heads didn't drop, and once more within a few minutes we had scored again. I picked up a great little ball from Kaz in the box, turned neatly and smacked the ball past Angerer. It was the first time I had ever scored against Germany, and what a time for me to do it!

We weren't going to let the Germans out of our sights. The dream was back on. Fifty-five minutes on the clock in Helsinki and it was now 3–2.

Now, if there is a moment in my playing career where I want to pause the tape and start again, it is right here.

Make no mistake, with an hour gone, and the scoreline at 3–2, this final was anybody's. We were in it and, looking back, we had such a great chance to win it. But, annoyingly, we then went through a really bad period of play. We kept giving the ball away and allowing Germany far too much space and time on the ball. Against a side like that you just can't afford to do that. You get punished – and we were punished severely.

Grings got on to the end of a cross from Garefrekes to make it 4–2 on sixty-two minutes, and she added another ten minutes after that. Prinz then finished it all off just a few minutes later. Germany won the final 6–2.

No way were they four goals better than us, but that is what the result says. Maybe the hard work and effort that had gone into the previous five matches just took its toll on us all at the end – in the last thirty minutes of our tournament.

I think that when Grings scored her first goal – Germany's fourth – something stopped within us, as a team. Maybe we lost a little bit of belief. I don't know. We definitely allowed our heads to drop a little bit. And we never got the game back after that. We just couldn't claw our way back into the match again, as we had managed to do twice before. So 4–2 became 5–2, and 5–2 became 6–2.

In my opinion, we had a really good game for an hour and then we let ourselves down. We crumbled for some reason. We definitely stopped playing as we knew we could, and that was yet another tough learning curve for us to get our heads around. We had to learn that you can't play for just sixty minutes in a European Championship final. If we want to lift trophies, we have to do what we were doing for ninety minutes and more. Never stop. Never give in. I remember it as a close game. We certainly weren't steamrollered, regardless of the result.

After the dust had settled, we could appreciate what we had done during that tournament. We were losing finalists in the Women's European Championship. That stood as quite an achievement, particularly when you consider that, as a nation, we weren't qualifying for such tournaments not that long before.

We took a lot of pride out of that achievement, and also out of the hard work we had put into it all as a squad. We were delighted and disappointed in equal measure, I think. We had reached our first final; hopefully it won't be our last. We got a silver medal. We wanted a gold medal, but we will have to wait for that.

20

Journey to Germany

WITH EVERY INTERNATIONAL TOURNAMENT THAT CAME ALONG, our performances were getting better and better: last eight at Euro 2005; quarter-finalists at the 2007 World Cup; runners-up at Euro 2009. So when we faced up to the first of our qualifiers for the 2011 World Cup, our ambition had justifiably grown to a new level. The 2011 Women's World Cup was a tournament we felt we could win. There were no more barriers left for us to cross.

Before the qualification campaign got under way, shortly after the completion of Euro 2009, I realized that this might well be my last bite at the World Cup cherry. I was into my thirties and would be approaching my thirty-third birthday when the finals were held in Germany. Add four years on to that and I was looking at thirty-six going on thirty-seven for the 2015 tournament.

The qualification system for the 2011 Women's World Cup was involved and rather tedious. With so many European countries now playing women's football, winning your qualification group was not enough to reach the finals; now you had to win your group just to reach a two-legged play-off. If you won through your play-off, *then* you qualified for the finals.

We were pitched against Austria, Malta, Spain and Turkey in Group 5. We won all our matches against Austria, Malta and Turkey comfortably and conceded no goals in the process. But, once again, the Spanish provided much more difficult opposition. Spain also beat those three countries home and away and did so with a better goal difference than us. So it all came down to two head-to-head matches with them again.

We won at home, 1–0, a Katie Chapman goal separating the sides at the New Den. And in June 2010 we managed to secure a nervy 2–2 draw in Aranda de Duero, near Valladolid, to top the group. Two defenders, Rachel Unitt and Faye White, popped up with the goals that night.

But we hadn't made it easy for ourselves. A two-goal win for Spain would have essentially put us out of the World Cup and put them through to the play-offs in our place. And with twelve minutes left Spain were leading 2–0 after two first-half goals from Sonia Bermudez and Adriana. Faye had vented her feelings at us at half-time in the changing room, telling us that none of us was doing what we were capable of on the pitch. She was dead right. But we left it very late to rectify things. Unitt's goal came on seventy-eight minutes, and Faye netted the equalizer just two minutes from time. Thankfully, we now had a clear path into the play-offs.

I didn't play in all of the qualification matches and I didn't score a goal until our fifth match, a 6–0 win away in Malta at the Ta' Qali National Stadium. I also scored twice in a 4–0 win in Krems, seventy miles north-west of Vienna in Austria.

I scored in both play-off matches against Switzerland. In the first match, played at Shrewsbury, we achieved a comfortable 2–0 victory with goals from Fara Williams and me. But the second leg, away in Wohlen, was a naughty affair. Ramona Bachmann got our goalkeeper, Rachel Brown, sent off when she fell to the floor holding her face moments after scoring a goal for the Swiss and following through into the net to collect the ball. It was a very strange piece of play-acting and cheating. But it worked, and Rachel was shown the red card.

Down to ten players and with a pretty hostile crowd on our backs, we showed great strength and character to win the match 3–2. Eniola Aluko and Fara Williams got the other goals. So we won 5–2 on aggregate and qualified for the Women's World Cup again as a result – our fourth international tournament in a row.

The strength in depth in the England squad was underlined by our statistics for that qualification campaign: twenty-eight players were used in the ten group and play-off matches and six players scored three goals or more.

In October 2010, shortly after we'd dispatched Switzerland, Hope Powell took us off to South Korea to play in the Peace Cup against New Zealand and the host nation. We drew both matches 0–0. The following month we were drawn alongside the Kiwis in our Women's World Cup group, along with Japan and Mexico, so it proved a very useful trip from that point of view.

Japan was the seeded team in Group B. They were ranked fourth in the world. It was felt that we had got lucky because we had avoided the three other seeded teams – Germany,

Brazil and the USA. We had also avoided Norway and Sweden. So it was a good draw for us.

In March 2011 we flew to Cyprus to play in the Cyprus Cup, where we met South Korea again, Canada, Italy and Scotland. Only Canada had qualified for the Women's World Cup, and we lost to them. We were also beaten by Scotland, so it was not the best preparation trip for us in terms of results, although we did beat Italy and South Korea. On the occasion of my hundredth international cap – as part of the celebrations I was made captain for the day – I scored against the Italians, as did Ellen White, a young centre-forward at Arsenal Ladies and a very exciting prospect.

The results may not have been great, but in terms of a bonding exercise the Cyprus Cup was really good for us, particularly because so many members of the England team were now playing out in the States. Only once had we entered another European spring tournament, called the Algarve Cup. I didn't go on that trip but I know that it was a frustrating time for the girls because we weren't allowed to compete against the best teams. As a result, we have played in the Cyprus Cup ever since.

When we played our next friendly match in preparation for the Women's World Cup, the result could not have gone any better for us. At the beginning of April we beat the USA – the number one ranked team in the world – 2–1 at Leyton Orient. Jess Clarke and Rachel Yankey got the goals. The match was shown live on ESPN in America too. That was a sweet victory and another performance to suggest that we could compete with the best.

Katie Chapman caused a surprise by announcing her

retirement from international football at around this time. She would not be an easy player for us to replace and the timing of the announcement, a few months before the beginning of the World Cup, rocked us a bit. Despite this, the England squad that was selected for the World Cup was packed full of experience. We had 1,053 international caps between us. Fifteen of us had gone to Euro 2009 and thirteen of us had gone to the previous World Cup. So that underlines the consistency we had in the squad.

Of course we were all getting a little older, but we were still a young squad. I think the average age was twenty-six. I was one of the older ones, along with our team captain, Faye White, and Rachel Yankey, who was back in the England set-up after surprisingly missing out on Euro 2009. Ellen White, who had impressed me so much in Cyprus, was one of the five new call-ups to a major international tournament.

We got together in the middle of May and secured another impressive pre-tournament friendly win over top-class opposition when we beat Sweden 2–0 in Oxford. Jill Scott and Karen Carney got the goals. We now had so many players who could consistently find the net for us from all over the pitch. It was another strong performance, and another good reason why we could go into this tournament with the world's best with confidence.

Our main concerns before flying out to Germany were the injuries to two of our best players. Both Faye and Fara were recovering from knee injuries at the time, but they were both in the squad and we hoped that they would be fit for our opening matches.

To me, our squad looked even better than the one we had

taken to Euro 2009. There had been a few changes in the team since we had reached that final in Finland.

Karen Bardsley, who was playing in the Women's Professional Soccer league with Sky Blue, was our new goalkeeper. She had taken over from Rachel Brown since the turn of the year. She stood five feet eleven inches tall and was a big presence in the penalty box at set plays.

Rachel Unitt was now back as our regular left-back with Casey Stoney partnering Faye in central defence, when our captain was fit. Sophie Bradley, of Lincoln Ladies, would deputize for Faye. Alex Scott was at right-back as usual.

In midfield we would be missing Katie, of course, and that was a big loss. But alongside Fara, Jill Scott was now a regular at international level. And Anita Asante was another good option for us.

I remained at number 10 with Eniola Aluko usually playing up front and two from Kaz, Jess and Yanks playing down the flanks.

On the bench, waiting in the wings, was the exciting Ellen. At just twenty-two, she went into the tournament with four goals from seven matches from our World Cup qualification campaign and four goals from six games for Arsenal in the first half of the recently launched Women's Super League. She was tall and powerful and was already being spoken about as a player with a big future ahead of her.

So, our squad was a mixture of players from the Women's Professional Soccer league in the USA and the new, semi-professional WSL in England. Five of us were out in the States, and there were four Arsenal players, four Everton players, three Birmingham players, three Lincoln players and two from elsewhere. So I think it was a good mixture.

A lot had been made in the press about fitness concerns regarding the English-based players, because the WSL had only kicked off a few weeks before. But the girls were in full training, so I thought that was nonsense. And I have already explained the other side of the coin, which a few of us learned about to our cost in Finland after a long, hard season in the States. If anything, maybe an argument could have been made against the lack of competitive football they had played, but you can make arguments for either side. I don't think it affected us too much.

I definitely felt that there was a new maturity about us going into the tournament in Germany. The experience we had gained in our last World Cup, in China, had been bolstered by our experience in Finland, as a group, and the fact that every one of us was now playing in the WPS or the newly formed WSL was a big bonus.

We felt good. Secretly, because we didn't want to go public with it all, we felt that we could progress in the tournament and do well. You have to believe in yourselves if you are going to win a World Cup and I think we had that belief going over to Germany. I was convinced we could go and do something special out there.

We enjoyed a four-day training camp in England a few weeks before the tournament. We did a lot of team bonding exercises during that time, played fun games, and training was relaxed and enjoyable. It was nice to have the squad together before heading off.

We had the following weekend off so that we could go home and spend some time with our families before meeting up again and travelling to Germany for a week of intense preparation prior to the competition getting under way. During that time we played Australia and South Korea behind closed doors in unofficial friendly matches.

All our focus was on the first game against Mexico on 27 June. For the whole week before then we worked on our defensive and attacking strategies. We knew everything about them. We had been given so much information on the Mexicans that it felt a bit like overload at times. But you couldn't say we weren't prepared. We were all raring to go.

The organization behind the 2011 Women's World Cup took the competition to a new level. I suppose it was fitting in a way that the Germans were behind it. The opening match was held at the Olympic Stadium in Berlin – the same stadium that had hosted the men's 2006 World Cup final between Italy and France. It had also hosted the 1936 Olympic Games.

The attendance for the opening fixture, in Group A between Germany and Canada, smashed all previous women's football records in Europe to smithereens – 73,680. It seemed the same thing was going to happen in Germany that had happened in the USA in 1999. The country was going football crazy. Everybody seemed to be dressed in red, black and gold and a lot of supporters were painted in red, black and gold as well. National flags were everywhere too, of course. It was a party atmosphere, and for the next three weeks it would make national headlines. The sport's growing status was underlined when the Panini group brought out the first-ever women's football sticker album ahead of the World Cup.

Germany beat Canada 2–1 in Berlin. But they didn't look as powerful and awe-inspiring as they had so many times before in recent years. Birgit Prinz was very quiet, in fact. So that was interesting to observe from our initial base in Wolfsburg, home of the famous Volkswagen motor car factory.

Japan and New Zealand kicked off proceedings in Group B the next day. The Japanese won narrowly, by two goals to one. Aya Miyama, the player who had produced a superb free-kick to deny us victory in Shanghai four years before, did the same thing late on against the Kiwis to win the match for the group seeds. A few hours later it was time for us to kick off our campaign against Mexico.

Mexico had surprisingly beaten the USA 2–1 to qualify for the Women's World Cup at their expense; the Americans subsequently had to go through some play-offs to reach the finals. So they were not a team to be underestimated. And there seemed to be a lot of support for Mexico in Wolfsburg. I'm not sure it was all Mexican either. We had our loyal supporters there too, of course, but it did feel to me like most of the stadium was against us – maybe because we were an England team playing in Germany? That's what it felt like to me.

Fara gave us the lead on twenty-one minutes and we were in control of the game until a wonder strike from Monica Ocampo flew past Karen and into the net. Karen was crest-fallen. After that we struggled to find our rhythm again, and in the end I think a draw was probably a fair result. Although obviously not the result we were looking for from our opening match in the tournament. We were expected to beat Mexico quite comfortably, and because we only drew with them that was considered a disappointing result for us. We felt that too. But we hadn't been beaten by them. Hope told the BBC after the game that she was 'glad' we hadn't lost the match. I knew what she meant by that. But that again received some scrutiny in the media.

Elsewhere, all sorts of criticism and in some instances abuse were flying around after the match regarding our performance. A lot of it was directed at some of the England players. Eniola, in particular, received a fair amount of it on the social media network site Twitter. She decided to hit back and answer her critics, and that then became a big news story in its own right. She was quite upset by some of the remarks, and she said so. If I remember rightly, she used the word 'poisonous' to describe the messages she had received.

I think Eni would admit that she didn't have her best game for England against Mexico, but that's no reason to send an abusive message. And that is what happened. Tweets like that aren't going to help anybody play any better. They're not going to help Eni or England. She did think about shutting her account down as a result of it all. It got that bad.

Should she have replied to the abuse? I think that is a question that can only really be answered by the individual who is on the receiving end. But, obviously, it can become a never-ending cycle if you are not careful.

But what happened to Eni was cruel, hurtful and un-necessary. Yes, fans can follow you on Twitter – I am all for that – but they shouldn't really be using that platform for that kind of stuff, in my opinion. Either way, I suppose we all had to accept that, even in just four years, the climate had completely changed since our last appearance in a World Cup.

Luckily, I don't think it affected Eni as much as it could have affected somebody else. That is because she's a strong person and she can shrug things like that off. But that doesn't mean she thought it was right, and she wasn't going to stand for it. She had the full support of all of us, her teammates, which was important. It wasn't a nice thing to have happened. We felt it as a squad because we were in camp together. And it wasn't just Eni who received messages like that. But, thankfully, it didn't happen to a lot of us.

Many of the England players use Twitter. I do. It can put you in touch with the general public and that is usually a good thing. But people follow you, and you allow yourself to be followed, and therefore you are allowing people to contact you directly. Facebook is a little bit different because you can accept who you want to accept as your friend. On Twitter, anybody in the world can follow you and see what you are up to, and what you're writing about. It's a modern-day problem, and I'm not sure there's an easy solution at the moment.

It was hard to know what to make of New Zealand before we played them. We had drawn with them out in South Korea, but that didn't really tell us too much – other than that it had been a tough match. They had also gone close to getting a draw against Japan in their first game, and Japan had now gone and thrashed Mexico, who'd got a draw against us 4–0 in Leverkusen.

There has always been a rivalry of sorts between England

and New Zealand. I think it's a bit like a cup final for them whenever they play us. They really rise to the occasion. So we knew that it wasn't going to be a straightforward game for us down in Dresden.

All we had to do was focus on going out there and beating them, particularly as Japan now had two wins and six points and had comfortably qualified for the quarter-finals while Mexico, who New Zealand still had to play, were bottom of the table and looked to be possibly the weakest team in the group.

Hope made changes to the line-up but she did not drop Eni, as the newspapers had speculated. She dropped Kaz instead, and gave Ellen her first start up front.

The New Zealand coach, John Herdman, came out and said some stuff that wasn't too nice about us. That revved everything up pre-match. My recollection is that he was quoted as saying that New Zealand much preferred to play England rather than Japan, because we were rigid and predictable and the Japanese played like Barcelona! Apparently he fancied his side to get a result against us. It wasn't too complimentary, so Hope wrote all of it down, word for word, and put it up on the wall in our dining hall.

Hope is big on quotes. And this one had the same impact on me as the premature German party plans in Helsinki. Things like that always seem to get me going.

Whatever I had expected from New Zealand, I hadn't expected them to be quite so physical in every part of the pitch. They were certainly not the most technically gifted side around, but they were very well organized and they were more than happy to put the boot in. I'd thought they would be tough, but they were also pretty dirty. They fouled us a lot: I was kicked a lot, Yanks was kicked a lot, and when Kaz came on, she was kicked a lot too. There were a few free-kicks for us but, remarkably, no cautions.

The fact that the referee, Thérèse Neguel of Cameroon, did nothing about it still makes my blood boil. There is not a lot of protection in women's international football, particularly for the flair players such as myself, and I am sick of it. If you are a skilful player and you are playing at a level where you come up against players who are not so gifted – for want of a better word – this type of foul play is absolutely rife and nothing ever gets done about it. In my opinion, the skilful players are the ones who need some form of protection in the game, both in men's and women's football. Flair players are the ones people pay to watch, so if they are not able to play, the game is doing a disservice to the paying public. I have felt that for a long time, but in this particular game, at World Cup standard, it was ridiculous. On one occasion I got absolutely raked down the side of my leg and nothing was given.

I think referees really need to start stamping this sort of thing out as early as possible in a game, because the longer it's allowed to go on, the worse it gets. It gets out of hand – as it did in this particular match.

The big problem for me is that you can't react. I will admit that I am one to react sometimes and I have had to learn to deal with that. It is often the case that the flair player gets sent off for reacting to something that has gone unpunished.

Look at a player like Wayne Rooney. I think he is a really great player. But he also has that fire in his belly, and that sometimes gets him into trouble. David Beckham was the same in the World Cup in France in 1998. I actually believe that most, if not all, of the top, elite players in both men's and women's football have that. We can flip at any time. I certainly have that, and it has been shown often enough in my career. I have been sent off for some stupid things, and that's because I haven't been able to keep my cool in certain situations.

But, honestly, if you are not protected and you are not allowed to protect yourself, then what are you supposed to do? The fear of getting injured is massive to me. I have been injured too much in my career. And when you have experienced that and you are not protected, on occasions you are going to snap.

Sadly, I am now used to being marked heavily and kicked a lot. It is an unfortunate part of the game that seems to accompany the type of player I am and the type of game I play. Opponents set out to stop you – that is their main purpose – and some of them will use whatever way they can get away with to accomplish that. It is no coincidence in my mind that the England players who were fouled in that match against New Zealand were Kaz, Yanks and me. It doesn't take Albert Einstein to work out what the game plan was there.

Early in the match I rolled my left ankle when I went up to challenge Jenny Bindon, the New Zealand goalkeeper, at a corner. To be fair, it wasn't her fault. But it was really painful. It was touch and go for a while whether I would continue, but with the adrenalin pumping inside me and the fact that this was a World Cup match, I wanted to play on, and the pain did ease a little bit. But the injury would come back to haunt me later on in the tournament.

To add insult to injury, literally, we then fell behind in the match to a goal from Sarah Gregorius, against the run of play, after something of a defensive mix-up between Casey and Unitt.

At half-time we were still behind 1–0. But we were calm in the changing room. Jill joked with Alex that if she received a decent cross in the penalty box she would get us a goal. And on sixty-three minutes, that is exactly what happened.

Jess came on for Yanks just after the goal and she was our super sub, smashing the winning goal high into the net from a crowded penalty box nine minutes from time, prompting wild celebrations on both the pitch and the bench.

After the match I had to deal with the pain in my ankle. I had it iced and strapped in a bid to keep the swelling down as much as possible so that I could play in the final group match against Japan.

I wasn't 100 per cent going into the game. Obviously, that is not ideal. But the one thing I didn't want to do was miss out on the biggest tournament in the world. It was a difficult one for me, because by this stage every match could be our last in the competition. There was nothing I could do to change that. Had we already qualified for the quarters I think I may have been rested. But we needed a result. So I wanted to play and, also, I had to play, really. I was a senior player in the side. But without doubt I could still feel the pain. Running was awkward.

In a tournament like the World Cup you can't stop the clock. The games come one after the other, and you have to live with that. These competitions are intense affairs. It is all very exciting for a player, provided you stay fit of course. This is what you have worked so hard for, so you must take everything in – good and bad – and enjoy every moment because you never quite know if you will get another opportunity like it.

As a squad, we try to use our free time wisely when we are abroad. Relaxation is very important between matches during an international tournament like this, whether you're fit and well or carrying a niggle. We had a games room sorted out in each hotel we stayed in during the World Cup in Germany. We also had a poker table on hand, which was a big hit with some of the girls, especially Fara, Eni, Jill, Unitt and Raff (Claire Rafferty). Fara always had to be in charge. It was played more for fun than money; no cash was ever really gambled. I stayed away from playing on it; I just watched what was going on every now and then among the others.

We travelled with our own table tennis table too. We always try and get a table tennis competition going when we are on tour, and more often than not Casey wins it. She's quite nifty with the bat, actually. I have watched her game plan closely: she makes her opponent move from one side of the table to the other while she is in control of the game, laughing her head off. She is a good player. We also had a Wii and some board games in there.

One night Alex and I organized a team game involving all the England players plus some of the coaching staff. We got the idea from a lady who came and did the same thing at Boston Breakers with us. It concerns team bonding and it's based on a game show we had seen out in America. The game is called 'In it to Win it'. That summed up the England team's philosophy too.

It was good fun to do. The two of us researched different topics on the internet so that we could make up our own games. A good example is wrapping a pedometer to the front of a team-mate's head with medical tape and getting them to move their heads back and forth as quickly as possible to register the biggest number of steps for their team. It was hysterical to watch. I think Jill got a bit of whiplash from doing that – or so she told us! Another one involved working in pairs to move three Red Bull cans from a chair to make a tower with strands of spaghetti, only using your mouth. This took a few hours. There were lots of giggles and a lot of people looked pretty stupid doing that, as you can imagine. But activities like these are much needed in camp, particularly during a long tournament. It brings everyone together.

Jill has a real interest in the media – she writes a blog on her website and all sorts – and she was given a camcorder by the Football Association for FATV. It was her job to capture some behind-the-scenes footage. Jill really thrives on tasks like that. She is very creative and quite funny, so she filmed lots of good stuff on the bus and in training. One day it was so cold and wet on the training ground that Jill and her camcorder lifted the mood. There were also bits and bobs happening around the hotel that were covered by her along with some player interviews and insights. It all got good coverage on theFA.com and was very popular. I think it was a really good idea and a great way for fans to connect with the players and see a World Cup from our point of view.

But our focus in the lead-up to a game was on nothing but the game. We had finished the match against New Zealand with Jess and Kaz either side of Ellen up front, and that is how we started against Japan in our final group game in Augsburg on 5 July. Young Sophie also came in for Faye in defence, and Anita replaced Fara in midfield. Both Faye and Fara were rested as a precaution following their pre-tournament injuries. Eni and Yanks were both on the bench for this one.

We needed a draw to go through to the quarter-finals, although that would most likely mean we would face Germany. If we could beat Japan, we would most likely avoid them. But there was no way of knowing because we wouldn't know how things would fall until later that night after Germany had played France in Mönchengladbach.

Japan were noted for being a quality side, and with such technically gifted players the comparisons with Barcelona were not too wide of the mark. We approached the match against them knowing that we had to try and condense their midfield as much as we could. They were so good on the ball that they could pass it around us and play it around us if they chose to. So we needed to get tight to them and we needed to be physical around them.

In an inspired performance, we beat them 2–0. Ellen scored a terrific goal, superbly lobbing the Japanese goalkeeper Ayumi Kaihori from twenty-two yards with her first touch after a beautiful defence-splitting ball into her path from Kaz. It was one of the goals of the tournament.

Just before half-time, Ellen almost doubled our lead when

she acrobatically hit an overhead kick that was tipped on to the bar by Kaihori.

Yanks came on for Jess at half-time and secured our passage into the last eight with a lovely touch and neat finish following a nice pass down the left from Unitt.

We had scored two goals of the highest quality against a team ranked in the top four in the world. So we felt we now had nothing to fear going into the knockout stages. We had seen nothing to fear either. The days of fearing anybody in world football were behind us anyway.

I came off after an hour against Japan. I was still struggling with my ankle, and with our passage as good as secure, it was a relief to give it a rest for the last half an hour. Eni came on for me.

I suppose we rode our luck a little bit at times in the match, when you consider their supreme quality in the final third of the pitch, but our strategy was spot on and we pulled it off. We won the match with an impressive attack-minded performance. Our play was attractive to watch and we received praise again for the way we had gone out and played. It was as though the first match and a half of the tournament had never happened.

It was a comfortable win for us in the end. They showed some nice stuff, but Japan didn't really trouble us too much. So we won Group B, and Germany won Group A, after beating France 4–2 in a pulsating match later on that night. The quarter-final line-up would therefore pair us with France in Leverkusen while Germany would meet Japan in Wolfsburg.

That was the draw we'd wanted. We certainly didn't want to play Germany in Germany, that's for sure. Not yet anyway. We talked about it, of course, and we definitely wanted to avoid them if we could. But the way the matches were scheduled we couldn't control any aspect of that. Germany had more say in the matter than we did – so maybe they didn't want to play us either.

Having said that, I still felt we were closing the gap on Germany year on year. We had got close to them in the Euro 2009 final for an hour or so, and of course two years before that we'd held them to that goalless draw in the World Cup. So I no longer sensed any sort of fear factor about them. Not in the way we used to have. The days of them just having to turn up to get a result against whichever country they played were definitely over. They hadn't looked all that impressive in their first three games, either.

One player who was impressing was our new centre-forward. Ellen was fast becoming the star of the tournament. She had justified her position in our starting line-up. She is a very different type of player to Eni, which is always a good position for a squad to be in. They have different builds and different skills. They play in the same position, of course, but they bring different strengths and different talents to that role.

It is great for England to have options at international level. For instance, if we need some speed up front, we could play Eni; if we need somebody who can chase, run and hold the ball up, we could play Ellen. There's more to it than that, of course, but having choices certainly opens up more possibilities, more routes to success.

21

Penalty Shoot-Out Heartbreak

WE MOVED TO NORTH-WEST GERMANY AHEAD OF OUR WORLD Cup quarter-final match against France. Growing interest in us back home had led to the match being scheduled to be shown live on BBC Two. Our previous three games had been on the BBC's Red Button service with highlights being shown late at night on BBC Two. Press coverage had grown as well as we'd progressed in the competition, just like it had done in 2005, 2007 and 2009. We felt that we were where we wanted to be again – with the eyes of the nation on us.

Our last few matches against the French had been tight. But we still had this rotten record of not beating them in thirty-seven years. Although, personally, I never think that such statistics mean too much. They had been beaten by Germany, but they had had their goalkeeper Bérangère Sapowicz sent off in that match and so, down to ten players, it was hard to read too much into that result. They had playing for them ten squad members from the Olympique Lyonnais ladies team, the side that had won the Women's Champions League in 2010/11 – beating Arsenal Ladies on the way. And their 4–0 win over Canada was one of the most impressive performances in the group stage.

But the two teams were quite evenly matched. They stood at seven in the world rankings and we were tenth. We had similar levels of experience – they had reached the quarter-finals at Euro 2009. And we both had two players with over a hundred international caps – Yanks and me for us, Sonia Bompastor and Sandrine Soubeyrand for them. The danger player in their team looked like Marie-Laure Delie, who had twenty-three goals from twenty-three appearances for them, including two goals in the tournament so far.

All our big guns came back into the starting line-up – Faye, Fara and Yanks. Otherwise it was the team that had beaten Japan that stood for the national anthem at the BayArena Stadium in Leverkusen.

It was a red-hot atmosphere. The stadiums used in Germany were first class, and the BayArena was another example of that. The size of ground, the layout, the pitch, everything was just phenomenal, really. It was a great place to play a World Cup quarter-final. The tournament had been so well supported by the German public, with most of the venues close to capacity, and again the BayArena was no exception on this occasion.

Not for the first time, there was a large amount of support for the opposition in Leverkusen. Maybe that was because France is only across the border from Germany. Or maybe the home supporters were out in force to cheer against us again. We certainly didn't feel as though we were the most popular team in the tournament, for whatever reason. But this didn't really have an effect on us, either as individuals or collectively, as a team. We have had that a lot over the years. We're used to it now.

I was fit to play but my left ankle was still feeling sore. Given my age, the thought did flash through my mind, as I was out there on the pitch, that it might be my last match at a World Cup. If we lost, that was most likely going to be it for me. So I thought to myself: 'We'd better win this.' There was certainly no way I wasn't going to play in this one. Faye was passed fit to play and she replaced young Sophie Bradley, who had done nothing wrong against Japan, at the back.

In the opening seconds the ball broke to me and I quickly powered in a goal-bound effort that was turned around the post by the French defender Laura Georges. It was a bright start for us. But slowly France began to pile on a lot of pressure. Karen made good saves from Gaëtane Thiney and Louisa Nécib in the first half, and Camille Abily and Delie also went close.

We definitely knew we were in a match at half-time. Hope told us to be patient and to take our chance when it came to us.

On fifty-eight minutes, we did. Unitt hit a long ball forward from our own half and I combined with Yanks and then played the ball in to Jill, who was twenty-five yards from goal. A pass to Ellen looked the likeliest option, but, without breaking stride, Jill drifted between Laure Lepailleur and Sabrina Viguier and dinked it beautifully over the head of Céline Deville, France's third-choice goalkeeper, who was playing due to suspension and injury.

The goal came against the run of play. But the goal was

ours. We had the lead. All we had to do now was keep it and we would be in the Women's World Cup semi-finals.

The longer the game went on, the more pressure the French put on our goal. The pain in my ankle, too, was mounting as time passed. At one stage I remember looking up at the clock on the scoreboard – I think we were about seventy or seventy-five minutes into the game, and we had the lead – and I thought to myself: 'Just get through this.'

We were keeping them at bay. We were playing so well defensively that I thought they wouldn't score. Our backs were against the wall, admittedly, but I felt so confident in our back line and goalkeeper. But the clock seemed to be going very slowly and as a result our place in the semi-finals seemed so near yet so far away. The second half seemed to be lasting for ever.

With nine minutes left to play, Hope took our two full-backs off – Alex and Unitt – and brought on Steph Houghton and Claire Rafferty. These substitutions would be scrutinized afterwards in the media. My understanding is that, where Alex was concerned, there was a miscommuni-cation involving a number of players on and off the pitch.

Alex had been playing with an injury to her right ankle throughout the tournament. She made a strong challenge late on in the match and somebody asked her if she was all right. She motioned with her arms that she was. Somebody some-where read this wrongly and thought that she wanted to come off.

It is impossible to explain adequately the heat of the moment at a time like this. Split-second decisions can change games and nobody is necessarily to blame. We were playing in the World Cup quarter-finals and holding on for our dear lives to get into the semis for the first time in our country's history. When emotions are running high it's almost inevitable that somebody will be in danger of doing something that is going to be misinterpreted or misunderstood somewhere along the line. With us, it was this.

Alex was called over to the bench to be subbed. As she came off, she asked why she was being subbed; she said she was fine. But by that time the substitution had been made and she had been replaced.

We now had two young players at full-back who were making their World Cup debuts in the closing minutes of a quarter-final with us holding on to a slender lead. Had we held on it would never have been spoken about afterwards. Sadly, we didn't.

France kept pushing and the pressure kept mounting. Anita came on for Yanks to shore up the midfield and take the pressure off us a bit. The clock kept ticking, but it was still taking for ever.

My ankle was now feeling very sore. I was struggling to run. I hadn't realized the pain would get as bad as it did. It was literally at the moment of the third substitution that I felt it had become too painful to continue. But of course at that stage I had to carry on. The die had been cast. We had made all our substitutions.

We held out until three minutes from time, when we failed to clear one of the many attacks that were being thrown at our defence and Delie set up Elise Bussaglia, who curled the ball into the net from eighteen yards. It was immediate heartbreak for us.

As the French ran around, screaming their heads off in delight, it struck me there and then that I would now have to play on for another half an hour.

But first of all we had to get to extra-time. With their tails up, the French kept on peppering our goal until eventually, at last, the referee blew her whistle to signal the end of normal time.

I hobbled over to the bench to listen to the team talk. We were now a tired side carrying injuries. I couldn't walk properly. I had a lot of inflammation around my Achilles tendon. I couldn't even put my foot down to walk. I was in a bad way. Our inexperience going into extra-time in crucial positions at the back would later become a big talking point, even though none of the substitutes did anything wrong or anything to warrant that. They played well.

Essentially, given the state that I was in, we were down to ten players. I just hoped and prayed that we could get just one chance down their end and take advantage of it.

But the longer that extra period went on, the more the momentum of the French grew. They had that extra bit of confidence that we didn't have, probably from scoring right at the end of normal time, when they were on the verge of going out of the tournament. We were now hanging on. It was cruel. But that is how fortunes in football can flip so quickly.

Ellen had a chance for us in extra-time, but France dominated that half-hour. It got to the stage where I felt that if they should score again, we were out. I couldn't see us getting a goal. So, without thinking about it, I started to will the game to end. I wanted penalties.

I also knew that the more I ran, the more damage I was

doing to my ankle. In hindsight, I should have come off the pitch as soon as it tightened up. From that point on I couldn't actually physically push off it.

I didn't realize it at the time – I was so pumped up with the match and trying to get us into the semi-finals – but my World Cup was over. There was no way I was going to be able to play again for quite a while. But that thought never entered my head during the match. All I could think about was getting us through to the next game. It wasn't about whether I would be fit enough to play in it. It was all about getting us through, regardless of me.

Somehow I struggled through the 120 minutes. I had been in considerable pain for an hour. England managed to hold out for a 1–1 draw. That is really how it felt at the time. So now we had to face the dreaded penalty shoot-out.

I had been hoping for penalties. I thought it was the best chance we had of going through. I can't speak for my team-mates but I just felt that the French players had so much more belief in themselves and that the longer the game went on, the more likely it was that there'd be only one winner. So I felt relief when we got to penalties, to be honest. Penalties are a lottery, we all know that, but it was a chance I was very happy to take on that occasion.

Despite the ankle, I was more than happy to take a penalty. I felt that it was my responsibility as a senior player. I had never taken a penalty in a shoot-out for England before – we had only been in two shoot-outs in our history, and we had lost them both – but I felt confident about it. Even carrying an injury I felt that I would score.

When I got over to the touchline, having hobbled all the

way, the first thing I did was sit down so that I could rest my ankle. As has been well documented, we didn't have too many volunteers to take penalties after that match. Hope was stood there with a group of players around her and nobody was putting their hand up to take one. But, then, it's not a nice part of the game.

To make matters worse, there's not a lot of time between the final whistle and the first penalty. Hope needed to name her five penalty takers, but she didn't have five penalty takers.

She'd gathered the players around her and asked, 'Who wants to take a penalty?' There was complete silence. I think everybody was waiting for somebody else to speak. Nobody stepped up at all. Then young Claire popped up. 'I'll take one,' she said. She deserves so much credit for that.

Hope didn't stop to think about it. Claire was in. 'OK, what about somebody else?' was the next question to the team. I put my hand up. I was the team's penalty taker, along with Fara, and a senior player.

As I said, I was more than happy to take one. It was just that, with my injured ankle, I didn't want to let the team down. But I felt confident in myself that I wouldn't, and in the end I had no choice. I had to step up if nobody else was going to offer. Hope looked at me and said, 'You'll have the first one.'

But after I volunteered, it went silent again. Kaz eventually put her hand up next. Then, if I remember rightly, it was Casey, and then Faye.

France won the toss and decided to take the first kick. Abily tried to place it to Karen's right but our goalkeeper was equal to it and made a comfortable save. She smashed the ball down hard on the ground in celebration. It was the perfect start for us.

I was up next. It felt like a long way from the centre circle to the penalty spot. My Achilles tendon was red raw now. I was in a lot of pain. I usually place my penalties, but this time, due to where I was at with my ankle, I was angry and I decided to go for power. I just wanted to blast it and get it over and done with. I remember saying to myself, 'Put the ball down in a good spot. Focus on the frame of the goal. Keep your head over the ball. And don't put it over the bar.' I kept repeating that over and over again in my head.

I leathered it, and the ball flew into the top right-hand corner of the net. My reaction was pure emotion. I was just so pleased it had gone in. I gestured to the England fans in front of me in the stadium. It was a big release. I have been told that it reminded some people of Stuart Pearce's penalty at Wembley against Spain in Euro 96. I can understand why people make that comparison. The reaction was quite similar, I guess.

More importantly, my goal put us in a great position. Kaz and Casey put their kicks away too, and with France scoring both their penalties, it was 3–2 to us after three kicks each. France scored again, through Bompastor, to level at 3–3, but we still held the advantage.

Claire stepped up next and, sadly, placed her kick wide of the post. Eugénie Le Sommer, another substitute, then put France into the lead for the first time, and suddenly we needed to score with our last kick to force a sudden-death shoot-out. It was agonizing to watch this unfold from the centre circle.

It fell to Faye to take the fifth penalty for us. She had bravely battled through cramp in the latter stages of the match and volunteered to take a penalty because she thought she should do so, that it was her duty as team captain.

Faye stepped up to take her kick and struck the bar. She was devastated. We were all devastated. It was heartbreak again – but much, much worse this time. We were out of the 2011 Women's World Cup. We were unbeaten in the tournament but we were going home.

There were a lot of tears. Faye took it very badly, bless her. She felt that she had missed the penalty that knocked us out. That is all she could see at the time. We didn't see it that way at all. Faye had shown the courage to get up there and take a penalty. People should take their hats off to her for that. It isn't an easy thing to do, particularly when so much is riding on the result.

I would like to take this opportunity to say that we practised penalties after virtually every training session in Germany. I would also like to say this: you can practise penalties all day long and it makes no difference to what will happen on the day when it matters.

You can't prepare for the stadium, the crowd, the pressure. How can you plan for who is going to be on the pitch after ninety minutes, or who is going to be fit or injured? It's impossible. How can you re-create in training the pressure you feel when you walk up to the penalty spot at the end of a tense World Cup encounter? It's all about how the individual deals with everything on the day. You don't do that after a training session, when players are larking about and having a laugh with each other.

As the men's team have fallen at this hurdle so many times as well, a cry went out that something had to be done about it. But what can be done about it? Some people in the press said that we should have known our five penalty takers before the match. How can you do that if one, two or three of your five penalty takers are no longer playing?

The debate raged on. Should Hope have said to us 'One, two, three, four, five' or 'You, you, you, you and you'? But she couldn't have done that in the situation we were in.

I do know that in 1999, my coach at Boston Breakers, Tony DiCicco, who was then the coach of the USA team, picked his players for the penalty shoot-out in the World Cup final against China. He told them who was going to take each one. I know that Mia Hamm didn't want to take one. Tony was a big believer in putting your best five up there at all times. But Hope's beliefs are different to that. In Leverkusen, she asked us all – as individuals within a group – if we wanted to take a penalty or if we felt confident enough to take one. It's all down to the coach and how they manage their players. Tony was proved right, of course, in what he did then, but was that down to skill or was that down to luck? I still think penalties are a lottery.

A lot was made in the English press afterwards about penalty shoot-outs and the fact that England always seemed to exit World Cups and European Championships after losing them. The argument was that this was now as true of the women as it was of the men. Of course England's men's team have had a torrid time of it in the past, going out of the 1990 World Cup, the 1996 European Championship, the 1998 World Cup, the 2004 European Championship and the 2006 World Cup on penalties. That is quite a list. By contrast, England's women's team have gone out of tournaments at that stage against Sweden in the European Championship final in 1984, when the team was still not officially recognized by the Football Association, and against China in a competition that didn't really matter to us, the Algarve Cup in 2005. The defeat by France in the 2011 Women's World Cup was only the third occasion. It's hardly an epidemic. But I suppose people can draw parallels if they want to do so.

I was so upset when I was able to sit down and consider everything that had happened in our defeat by France. We had missed out on such a great opportunity. The tournament was there for the taking, really. Overall, I think we had the right players at the right age with the right experience playing in the right team. It was a good blend. It felt right to me.

To make matters worse, I had to suffer alone immediately afterwards. Or should I say that I had to suffer with French players to keep me company. I was selected to be drug-tested, so I was sat in this cold room with – of all people – the French goalkeeper. Laure Boulleau and Elise Bussaglia were there too.

All of this meant that I didn't meet up with my team-mates after the match. They all went back to the hotel, and some of them went straight to their rooms and packed up their stuff. When I got back, it was late. My dad had left our hotel by that time because he needed to get back to his hotel before they locked the doors! So I actually didn't speak to anybody until the next day.

A few of the players were down in the bar. Faye was there,

bawling her eyes out, bless her. I had come back to the hotel straight from drug testing and I felt sick. I was sick. I threw up when I got back to my room, probably due to the pure emotion of the evening. Not seeing my dad after the match didn't help either. So I couldn't go back down to join my team-mates, even if I had wanted to, in the circumstances. As it was, I didn't want to see anybody anyway. It was a weird experience to go through.

I went to bed. When I woke up the next morning I found that only half the squad was left in the hotel. There was an early flight back to the north of England for some of them that morning. The squad departed at different times.

Those of us who were left had red eyes. We were all very upset about going out of the tournament. We felt even worse when we heard about the result from the other quarter-final played the night before, in Wolfsburg: Japan had beaten Germany 1–0. Karina Maruyama scored the goal twelve minutes from the end of extra-time. So the winners of Group A and Group B were out and the runners-up of Group A and Group B were in the semi-finals. How does that work? The tournament was wide open. We felt quite deflated and flat when we heard about that.

Japan went on and won the 2011 Women's World Cup, which was terrific for them. They beat the USA in the final on penalties after twice coming from behind to force a 2–2 draw after extra-time. I felt really happy for Japan because the country had recently suffered a lot of disasters and tragedies due to a tsunami and an earthquake. It had been a terrible time there.

It was a fitting climax to a great tournament. The Japanese

captain Homare Sawa won the Golden Ball and the Golden Shoe too with five goals. She was later crowned FIFA World Player of the Year, denying Marta the top prize for the first time in six years.

Women's football had reached another new high: the total attendance figure for the 2011 Women's World Cup was recorded at a staggering 845,751 spectators – an average of 26,430 per match. Many millions more had watched live coverage across the globe on television.

But it was still frustrating for us to consider that we were the only team to beat Japan in the World Cup, just as we had been the only team not to have been beaten by the champions Germany in the previous World Cup. We had also been good enough to beat the USA a month or two before the tournament began, and although this was a friendly match, they had played a full-strength side against us and come for the win. The match was shown live in the States and it certainly mattered to them.

All this was genuine proof of the progress we had made year on year, and continue to make. It makes for positive reading. We have just got to go out there next time and beat these teams – the best in the world – when it matters. We have got to do it in the quarter-finals, the semi-finals and the finals of major international tournaments.

Nobody was better than us in Germany in the summer of 2011 – that is why nobody beat us. Yet we went out of the competition at the quarter-final stage. We didn't take our chance, and we have to live with that.

22

Hope

FOLLOWING OUR SAD AND SUDDEN EXIT FROM THE 2011 Women's World Cup, the focus of attention in the media soon shifted from England's persistent problems with penalty shoot-outs in international tournaments to some comments made after our spot-kick defeat by our esteemed coach, Hope Powell.

Two days after we had been knocked out in Leverkusen, Hope was quoted in some of our national newspapers referring to the lack of volunteers to take penalties in the shoot-out against France as 'cowardice'. She had not used that word to us in the changing room.

This prompted a lot of further comment in the media and a fair amount of upset in the camp at the time. Hope later said that her remarks had been blown out of all proportion.

Hope has now been in charge of the England women's team for fourteen successive seasons, deservedly so. Our performance in Germany, however disappointing it felt to us all at the time, put us sixth in FIFA's women's world rankings, behind the USA, Germany, Brazil, Japan and Sweden – the highest position we have ever held. That is one indication of what she has done for women's football in this country.

Two months after the end of the World Cup, at the first match of England's Euro 2013 qualifying campaign against Serbia in Belgrade, Hope set a new Football Association record, passing Sir Walter Winterbottom's run of 139 matches in charge of the England men's team (1946 to 1962). His record had stood for almost fifty years. Hope's tally, at the time of publication, is 150. She is also, of course, coach of Great Britain's women's team at the 2012 London Olympics.

Hope played sixty-six times for England and scored thirty-five goals as a player. She was in the side that lost to Sweden on penalties in the European Championship final in 1984 and she played in the 1995 World Cup finals. She was also in the team when I made my international debut at Roker Park, in Sunderland, later that year.

She was appointed as England's first full-time women's coach in the summer of 1998. She was the first woman to obtain UEFA's Pro Licence, the highest coaching qualification available in the game. And she now oversees the entire women's football set-up at the FA from Under-15 level. Looking after Great Britain's first ever appearance in the women's football tournament at the Olympic Games has become just another of her growing list of responsibilities within our growing game.

During her time as national coach, she has led England to two World Cups and three European Championships. Hopefully that number will soon rise to four with our qualification for the Euro 2013 finals in Sweden.

Her impact on all levels of the women's game in our

country has been massive. And, as I have previously stated, her impact on me personally has been massive too. I reckon she's 99 per cent of the reason why I was able to do what I have done in the game.

When I first started playing, England just had a senior women's team. So the fact that I was sixteen years old and playing well for Wembley Ladies meant I was put straight into the full national squad. That was achievable in the 1990s, because women's football wasn't as advanced as it is now. Our world ranking was a lot lower than it is now too. For a sixteen-year-old player to make that jump to full international level today – well, it just would not happen. Unless, of course, the player in question was absolutely phenomenal – a female version of Wayne Rooney, for instance. But I don't ever see that happening in the women's game because the players are now so much stronger mentally and physically; faster, fitter, more tactically aware.

The great thing about Hope having responsibilities at Under-15, Under-17, Under-19 and Under-23 levels plus the senior side is that players can now progress through the ranks. Each team plays the same formation as the senior team, which makes for really good strength in depth. I think that is brilliant because Hope knows the way she likes to work and she wants us all to play in that way. So she uses the 4–3–3 formation at all levels. All players coming through the system learn how to play like the senior team. This is her coaching philosophy, and it makes the transition from player to player and from team to team so much easier within the national set-up. Every time somebody steps up into a new age group, they know what is required of them. Once they get to the stage where they are close to making the senior side, the move up is simple because they have been playing that way for five or six years.

There have been dozens of examples of that during the last decade or so. But I never had that. It was like 'Bang, you're in the squad!' for me, and then 'Bang, you're in the team!' There's no comparison to what it was like when I was starting out.

Without a doubt, I do not believe that women's football could have progressed in our country in the way it has since those days without Hope at the helm. She is the reason why we have reached the quarter-finals of the last two World Cups and the final of the last European Championship, as well as rising to sixth in the world rankings. It is all down to Hope, to her hard work and her dedication to the task.

She started off in the England job with not a lot of experience. She was thrown into what was a new full-time position and she has developed the role according to how she sees the game and what needs to be done for us to fulfil her vision. She brought in Dawn Scott, our exercise scientist, who has played a crucial role in the development of our fitness. I think it wasn't really until the long build-up to Euro 2005 that all the players started getting on board properly and training every day as a professional would. They were working, they had a day job, but they still had to train. A programme was devised to help them do that – by themselves if need be. As a team, we had to work around the situation we found ourselves in. That was one of the frustrations I experienced when I returned home from playing professionally in the USA. Those days are in the past now.

Tactically, Hope has worked a lot with us defensively for a number of years now, because her vision was always that if we were not conceding goals, then we weren't losing games. It's a simple philosophy, really. I think that as a result we are now a very difficult side to beat. We didn't used to be, perhaps, but we definitely are now.

Getting to where we have got defensively was quite a long road and it was a bit boring at times for me, to be honest. I used to question it from time to time. 'Why are we doing this?' I would think to myself. But it has paid off. Our team shape is now right. We are now in motion, reaching levels we would never have got close to without Hope. We were some way off a top six world ranking before we had her, that's for sure. We were nowhere near that level.

Since Hope became the England women's coach, we have almost always played in a 4–3–3 formation with a back four, three in midfield – including one holding player and one attacking player, who sits at the tip of a triangle – and a front line of two wingers and a centre-forward. The three forwards all know that they also have a responsibility to defend. We all have a responsibility to defend. She has had to put a lot of hard work in over the years to get us all to play in that system, understand the reasons for that system and make us defensively sound enough to allow us to play in that system too, to use it to its full potential.

Very rarely have we changed from that formation over the years. In fact, I can't even count on one hand the number of occasions when we have done so. Even then it would have been due to us having a player sent off or something. It has always been 4–3–3 with Hope. That's the way she likes it.

With a holding midfielder, we are always protecting the back line. I have a free role to play when we are going forward. But it has always been drilled into me that I must do the right thing defensively. Matches at international tournaments are often decided by such small margins. If you make one mistake at international level, you can get punished for it and you find yourself letting the whole team down – letting the whole country down, really.

At club level it can be different, or at least it used to be when I was playing for Arsenal Ladies in our pomp. But we were so good we could get away with making the odd mistake here and there, though we seldom did. England have never been where Arsenal were in those days, of course. So we had to learn, concentrate and focus at all times, particularly at the back. This could be a bit of a drag for me as a result – an attacking player being asked to work on defending. All I wanted to do was get the ball forward, create goals, score goals and win games.

But I understood where Hope was coming from. She was making us as solid as possible at the back so that we could keep leads and win games. She knew that we had the flair players, the quality players, like Yanks and me. We were left to devise our own attacking options when we had the ball going forward. What we didn't have, as a team, was the ability to shut teams out. We have that now – from one to eleven.

Hope instilled in us the mantra that defence leads to attack. Once we get our shape right at the back and place people in certain positions to deal with certain situations, making sure that every angle and every gap is covered, we can think about going forward and attacking teams. It took a long time for us to take that on board. But gradually we did. We started losing fewer matches and winning more of them.

Defending remains Hope's main focus with us today: stopping other teams playing, winning the ball for ourselves, making space, and then going on the attack to score goals.

But, make no mistake, this has been the best, most consistent generation of women's footballers England has ever had. There are currently about five of us in the England squad with over a hundred international caps. There have been few changes to our line-up for almost a decade now. Hope saw that generation come through the ranks, and that is why so much was made of us reaching our potential in or around 2009.

Of course, some players, such as Katie Chapman, have moved on since, and in April 2012 Faye White announced her retirement from international football, with ninety caps to her name. She recently had keyhole surgery on both knees. She's due to be a mum for the first time later this year too. So it's the right decision. But we will miss her. England will miss her.

We are all getting older, of course, and we can't go on for ever. But the way that the systems are now set up, we don't need to. Look at the youngsters we unearthed at the 2011 Women's World Cup in Germany, players like Sophie Bradley and Ellen White. Both of them came straight into the England team on the biggest stage of them all and did a terrific job. I think we are in great hands, going forward.

Hope has introduced a lot of analytical stuff to our

regime, both collectively and individually. We never studied the opposition too much until she arrived. Now we do – footage of ourselves as well as other teams. We look at the England team performance, but we also look at our own individual performances. Hope has always been really big on that. She encourages us to be students of the game, sitting, watching and learning about ourselves. I might get asked: 'When you ran down the wing and crossed the ball, where else could you have put it? Was the final ball good enough?' We go over things in fine detail, and we improve as players as a result.

We actually grade ourselves. We used to get DVDs sent out to us, now we can view things on a special website. We watch our performances and then we have to put marks down on a spreadsheet with comments – effectively writing our own reports on how we think we did. We then send them back to Phil Worrall, our video analyst at the FA. If we have any questions we can discuss them with other team-mates on this site.

The idea behind this is that Hope can then get an understanding of how *we* think we have done on the pitch – what *we* think we are doing right and what *we* think we are doing wrong. Obviously she has her own opinions, and so do the coaching staff, but the players' take on things is a valuable perspective to have as well. That is how it works – collectively and individually. We have done a version of this for years. It works well and it pays dividends.

Phil is always on hand to clip things up during the first half of a match too, which is really useful at half-time. Hope may see something that she wants to discuss. We can now do that with video and talk about it properly during the break, with the aim of us going out in the second half and putting it right. The attention to detail is top notch.

Hope is an expert at not tweaking what doesn't need to be tweaked up front. I am lucky. She has always allowed me to go forward and attack in a way that comes naturally to me. I have my own natural 'savvy' to roam around the pitch. I can see chances, I can create chances, and I can take chances too. I am, pretty much, left to myself in the final third of the pitch, which is great. There is little that I am told to do. Of course, Hope may alter it a bit if there is a certain situation on the field and she wants certain players to support the play in whatever way. But, generally, if I am in a one-on-one situation, either on the wing or in the box, then she will always want me to show my skill and to be as creative as I can be, either by getting a shot in on goal or by finding somebody who is in a better position than me.

This works perfectly for me. It's how I like it. It gives me the freedom to do pretty much what I want to do in the final third. And I prosper in that position. Any attacking player will tell you that they just want to be allowed to play their game.

I would soon be told if I was doing something wrong, though. If I made a bad decision – trying to take on two or three players when there was a team-mate who was 'open', for instance – then I would expect her to address that with me. And she would. So there is a responsibility there. But, after so many matches under her, we know each other so well.

In my opinion, structurally, the whole FA set-up regarding

women's football is now very sound. That is down to Hope. Everything that is in place, she has helped to put into place. The big question people keep asking me is, 'How long will Hope go on for with England?' I can't answer that. They'll have to ask her. But I personally see her staying within the FA for some time to come, making sure that everything is ticking along nicely and going smoothly within the women's game. At forty-five she is still young for a coach. Sir Alex Ferguson is twenty-five years her senior and he hasn't quit his job yet. Her experience is now at a quite phenomenal level.

A few years ago, Hope was linked to the vacant manager's job at Grimsby Town. This was at a time when the club was still in the Football League. I don't know how serious the interest was, but the fact that she was linked with the club says so much about what she has already achieved in women's football.

Hope has overseen a massive change in our game in a relatively short space of time. If football is now the number one participated-in female sport in our country, as it has been for some time, she deserves credit for that. As I keep saying, the situation is unrecognizable from the one I found myself in at Watford when I first started to play the game.

With so many more girls playing football, the England players have become role models for them, which is fantastic. They really do look up to us because we play for England. They see us on television, in magazines and in newspapers. They don't just know our names, they know where we play and how we play. Recognition of this nature makes a big difference. It is now, perhaps, something that they want to achieve for themselves later on in their own lives – and something that they can see is achievable.

When I talk to these young girls or do a question-and-answer session at a school or for a team, they always want to know, 'How did you get to where you are? How much work did you have to put in? How did you get spotted?' I get asked the same sort of questions every time, wherever I go. That is what seems to be at the forefront of a lot of these young minds: 'How can I get to where you are?'

It is great for them to be able to ask these questions and receive some advice. I didn't have anything like that. I couldn't ask anybody, because nobody came to see me at my school. I didn't really know what to do or where to go. I had to struggle through, as we all did at that time. But now I can feed back the information they want to know and therefore help them achieve their goals. We can all help these youngsters develop and find a team to play in. On certain occasions I give them tips on some of the skills I use. All of it helps them, and helps the game in our country. I so longed to have this sort of input as a child, and I think that it's lovely that the children of today in England have that. That is the way it should be.

When I was growing up, my role model was male, Ian Wright. That's all I had. But today, a nine- or ten-year-old can watch women's football on the television – in a World Cup or whatever – and see us play in front of thousands of people. This inspires them, maybe to one day be like a Kelly Smith, a Karen Carney, an Alex Scott, a Faye White, an Ellen White or whoever. If a young female football fan can watch people like us playing football with the Three Lions on our shirts, they will inevitably look up to us. That is why television plays such a big role in the continued growth of the game. And that is why it's so important for England to do well.

Young girls can now reach out and touch the potential if they have the ambition, the drive and the right attributes. They can all strive for a higher standard. You can't put a price on that. If you don't see that, you don't really know about it. We are in a good place right now.

On a personal note, I want to say that the biggest thing Hope has ever done for me is being there for me. She cares about me more as a person than as a footballer. She said that to me at my lowest point. She also made me realize that she wouldn't leave me to struggle through my problems on my own. She wanted me to be healthy again. To get my mind right. To get my life right. She saw that as my priority. She didn't just care about the player in her team. Far from it. She cared more about me as a person than about my footballing ability, which is what I really appreciated at that time. Looking back, it was absolutely necessary for me.

There are so many people out there who just want to speak to you because of who you are or because of your status in the game or whatever. When that goes, so do they. Hope was never like that with me. At my lowest point, she was my strongest support.

Our friendship is now a very strong one. She just says it how it is and I give my opinions too. We respect each other so much due to the trust we have built up over the years. We are honest with each other and we can tell each other anything. That is a nice thing to have with someone, even more so when you're a footballer and that person is your national team coach.

That whole dark episode in my life is the main reason why the two of us get along so well today. I really appreciate having Hope in my life. She got me through. She didn't have to do that. She could have left me with my problems. She could have left me with my drinking. She didn't have to pick me up. But she saw that I had a serious problem and she was there for me. She told me what she was going to do to try and help me. She wanted me to know that she cared for me and that she was there. She respected me enough to remain in my life. I didn't make it easy for her – and that is an understatement. But she stayed strong for me throughout it all.

In fact I was a pain in the arse at times, I know that. I wasn't a very nice person to be around when I was drunk. Hope saw me in that situation with her own eyes. It was far from ideal, but maybe that is what had to happen. She knew that wasn't the proper me. She knew me well enough to appreciate that.

I had demons, and I didn't know how to cope with them. Hope knew that by getting me the right help I could start to beat them. That is why I have said she is 99 per cent responsible for where I am today. Without her, my story would have been very different. At the very least, I don't think I would have played football any more.

Hope told me that she would always be there to catch me if I fell. As a player, going through what I was going through at the time, those words meant the world to me. That is why she remains a true friend in my life and will always be so. What she has done for me means so much to me. Another approach from another person could easily have meant another ending. An ending I don't even want to think about.

and obviously they were also now dealing with theirs.

Then Aya Sameshina, Japan's left-back at the tournament and our team-mate at Boston, turned up with her Women's World Cup gold medal. That broke the ice somewhat. I felt very happy for her. The American girls were really humble too – but what a situation for us all to be in! It was awkward and nice at the same time. I saw the medal but I couldn't touch it. Aya hung it up in her locker. She was very proud of it. It was a case of 'what might have been' for the rest of us. I felt that very much.

The Women's Professional Soccer league had been stopped mid-season to allow us all to play in the World Cup. On our return, I was obviously out of action due to my ankle. It was now that I started to fully realize how much damage I had done by ignoring the pain for so long. But hindsight is a wonderful thing, and it takes no account of adrenalin, emotion or occasion.

Nevertheless, playing on in that match did hinder my recovery. I didn't play a full ninety minutes for Boston after the WPS league restarted. I managed just another forty-five minutes for them in all, which wasn't ideal. My end-of-season statistics showed ten games played and nine games started, largely due to the injury I'd picked up in Germany. I pushed it to the absolute limit in that game against France. It kept me out of football for three months.

I missed the beginning of England's Euro 2013 campaign too, which started with a very disappointing 2–2 draw – because we had led 2–0 – in Belgrade against lowly ranked Serbia. We let ourselves down in that one, and it may yet prove costly. I also missed the subsequent matches: a 4–0 win against Slovenia in Swindon and a goalless draw against Holland in Zwolle.

My international comeback eventually came at the end of November, at the Keepmoat Stadium in Doncaster, for the return fixture against Serbia. This time England won 2–0. I came on as a seventieth-minute substitute. It was good to be back on the field wearing an England shirt again but I still didn't feel fully match fit, so to get the last twenty minutes in that one was a bonus.

It was a comfortable win for us but it was a little annoying that we only got two goals. After the disappointing result in Belgrade, we had been left playing catch-up behind Holland in our group, and with only one team qualifying automatically for the finals it's crucial that we score as many goals as we possibly can against such teams. Four days after we drew with Serbia, Holland beat them 6–0 at home. We have since beaten Croatia by that very same scoreline. But we have made winning the group a lot harder for ourselves due to that slip-up in Belgrade.

Alex and I spent the rest of the year in early winter training at Arsenal. I would soon be back to full fitness. I was looking forward very much to my fourth season with Boston. It promised to be a good one. There were also some important Euro 2013 qualifiers coming up, and just around the corner there was the big one, the London Olympics.

But then, out of the blue, I received the devastating news that the 2012 WPS season had been suspended due to financial reasons. Suddenly I was without a club again. I received the news via an email. It was the second time that something like this had happened to me, the first being when the Women's United Soccer Association league folded in 2003 while I was at Philadelphia Charge. I couldn't believe it. It came as a total shock to me.

I didn't speak to anybody in America about it. I just had this email sitting there from my head coach telling me what had happened, apologizing for it and explaining that, in the circumstances, it was felt that the best option was to suspend the league.

I have always felt that if a professional women's football league is going to work anywhere in the world, it's going to be the USA. But once again that no longer looked like being the case – at least not at the moment anyway. Admittedly, the fervour around the women's game in the States had not been what it was in 1999 after the USA won the World Cup and it all went crazy over there, but it was still a very good product, with the best in the world playing out there.

I really couldn't understand it. All I knew was that I had to find another club. But what were my options? I had such a big year ahead of me, culminating with the Olympic Games, so it was very important that I made the right decision. There was a fair amount of worry and a bit of a stress involved in making that correct decision, I can tell you.

There was an offer for me from FFC Frankfurt, in Germany. Birgit Prinz, their star player for so many seasons, had just announced her retirement. But the offer was not straightforward. Due to the transfer window in Germany, I would not have been able to play for Frankfurt until after the Olympics – not a good fit for me, then. I needed to be playing on a regular basis to put myself in the best position possible to be selected for the Euro qualifiers and the GB team.

Alex and I had been training with Arsenal Ladies in the off-season, before planning to go back to America, so when the WPS was suddenly suspended, conversations naturally developed there, in our own backyard. We were there and we were easily accessible. We were training with the team, we knew the girls well, and we were comfortable with the whole set-up. We had both had very successful years with the club too. So it would be an easy transition for us both to make.

In hindsight, with the connection I'd enjoyed with Arsenal for so many years, from being a fan as a young girl to playing for them for a number of years and winning the whole lot with them, I suppose the Gunners were always going to be one of the favourites to sign me if I could sort something out with them. Geographically it's great for me too. I also fancied playing in the new Women's Super League in England, particularly after hearing so much about it. So I agreed a season-long deal and joined them for the third time in my career.

I was to wear the number 23 shirt this time round. The number 6 means a lot to me, given my success at Seton Hall; the number 8 shirt is the one I always wanted to wear at Arsenal for obvious reasons, and I did that; and the number 10 shirt is the one I wore for Boston and, more importantly, the one I still wear for England. That has everything to do with the position you play at international level, of course, but I do love that number. It's an attacking number. Pelé, Diego Maradona, Lionel Messi and Wayne Rooney all wore or wear number 10. Marta wears 10 too. I chose to wear number 23 at Arsenal because it was one of only a few numbers left.

My old boss, Vic Akers, played a big part in sorting out my move back to Arsenal for me. Although Laura Harvey is now the team coach, I didn't really have too much contact with her during that whole process. There are contrasts between the two of them. Laura has a different coaching style and a different philosophy to Vic, but it still feels like the old Arsenal. I still see Vic at training anyway. He's not really down there to watch our sessions, but he is still working at the training ground. He will come and watch us sometimes, and when he does he is always involved with all of the banter with the girls.

By the way, back in America, the WPS has now folded. Boston Breakers remain, for now, as a team. The club doesn't want to lose the franchise and the big hope over there is to get a professional league back up and running sometime. That is the hope, but of course we will have to wait and see if it happens. With the problems that have occurred over the years, I think it's understandable for me to feel that there may always be some kind of issue with women's football at the highest professional level. Let's just say that I don't think things will ever run smoothly. It's a shame, but that's the way it seems to be.

Whatever happens, I won't be over in America to see it. I have decided that my time in the States is over. I am going to be thirty-four years old in October 2012 and I plan to see my career out at Arsenal. I am content with that. My American journey has come to an end. I would have liked to have had another year out of it and to have seen out my contract with the Breakers, but I got to live in Boston for three years and I am grateful for that. I am also so glad that I went back out to the States and left there, in the end, with happy memories. I was quite fearful about going back in 2009 and having to face the demons I'd had when I was out there before.

For me to do all that had a lot to do with Alex being out there with me. She knew what I had been through and she was on hand to help me recognize a given situation if ever I began to slip into the wrong frame of mind. I also knew myself a lot better the second time round, and I knew all about the sort of support network I needed to have around me.

Thankfully, the second time around in America was nothing like the first time for me. It feels really good that I did go out there and that I saw it out. I ended my time there on a high. I am so pleased and so proud to have done that.

So, now I am an Arsenal player again. It is good to be back. How long it will last, who knows? I just want to enjoy the moment. I have certainly had thoughts about when would be a good time to end my playing career. It crossed my mind, briefly, immediately after the 2011 Women's World Cup. But there is always a low period after being knocked out of a tournament, so I don't dwell too much on that. London 2012 is obviously a big goal for me. Euro 2013 in Sweden would be a target too, should England qualify.

I honestly haven't thought about anything after that. I would love to say that I could go on to play in the 2015 World Cup in Canada as well, but that's a hard one for me to think about right now. I will be thirty-six years old by then, and as much as I would love to put myself forward for that, I appreciate that there are young players coming through who are champing at the bit to take my place. We'll have to wait and see. A lot depends on how my body feels – this season, next season, and so on.

When the day does come to hang up my boots, I'm not sure what I will do next. I don't know if coaching is for me. I have been told that I'm good at it. But finding the confidence to stand up in front of a group of people and coach them will not come easy.

Playing the game is what comes naturally to me. I have reached levels in my playing career where I knew I would be happy if I called it quits the next day. Coaching is an entirely different prospect. I would have to work at that a lot more. To be honest, I am a little bit scared that I wouldn't be good enough to do it, and that's where my lack of confidence kicks in again. But I guess it would be another challenge, and who is to say it won't happen? I have started my level two coaching, so it's definitely a possibility.

The other thing I would say is that I think there are many more opportunities for female coaches in America than in England, due to the college game and youth soccer. There are many more paid opportunities over there. In our country, I don't see an easy route I could take, other than perhaps being involved in the England set-up somewhere along the line. But until I stop playing it's hard to know how that could happen.

24

A Stupid Mistake

JUST BEFORE MY MOVE BACK TO ARSENAL LADIES WAS officially announced, I travelled to southern Europe with the England squad to play in the 2012 Cyprus Cup competition.

I like playing in the Cyprus Cup. We won it in 2009 and it has been a good preparation tournament for England for many years. It's always nice to get together as a squad, enjoy the sun during the late English winter and play against some good teams.

It was three months since I had made my England comeback in Doncaster and I was now fit and raring to go again. All my targets were in place for the months ahead – Arsenal, Euro 2013 qualifiers with England, Olympic Games with Great Britain. I started, and scored two goals – both penalties – in our opening match, a 3–1 win against Finland. These two strikes took my England goals tally up to forty-five. I was rested for the next match, against Switzerland, which we also won, 1–0.

I returned to the side when we played France in the semi-finals. It was our first meeting with them since the World Cup clash in Leverkusen. All their top players were in their line-up. They always are. The French always seem to play their strongest team, even at the Cyprus Cup, whereas we have been known sometimes to give our whole squad opportunities there.

It was my 111th appearance for my country and, sadly, it would be my last for a little while because I broke my left leg in the match after a late challenge from Elise Bussaglia. France went on to beat us 3–0 and lift the trophy, but that hardly mattered to me.

The tackle was late and, again, it was from behind. She caught me on my left leg and, again, I felt the pain right away. It was a direct blow, just above my ankle. She did say sorry afterwards, but it is hard to take when you know it was a late challenge. I still haven't seen the tackle, but there are players on my team who said it should have been a red card instead of a yellow.

The England physiotherapist initially thought I would be OK, that I just had bad bruising of the bone. I actually tried to warm up for our next match, the third-place play-off against Italy. But the ankle was quite sensitive to touch and it became obvious to me that there was no way I could play. I quickly pulled myself out of the warm-up and watched the game from the sidelines. We lost, 3–1. We flew home after the match.

The next few days were going to be very big for me. It was to be announced that Alex and I were re-signing for Arsenal after the cancellation of the WPS and there was a fair amount of WSL promotional work to do as well. But when I arrived at the training ground on my first day back, Vic saw me limping around and he wasn't happy. 'What's going on?'

he asked me. I told him I'd taken a knock from a late challenge against France. Vic didn't like the look of it and he took me off to the doctor at the training ground. The doctor pushed on the area where I was in pain and it felt quite tender. For peace of mind, he told me to have an X-ray. I got the X-ray done and it revealed that I had a fracture on the inside of the fibula. It is a rare break; apparently it usually only happens in children. But it had now happened to a thirty-three-year-old.

I was lucky, though. I felt relieved that we had nipped it in the bud early. If Vic hadn't taken an interest and I hadn't had the X-ray done and I had played on it, the damage would have been a lot worse. As it was, the doctor put me in a walking boot and told me that I would be back playing in six weeks, which was good to hear.

A few days later, Steph Houghton, Alex Scott, Kim Little and I were required to do some interviews and photographs on behalf of Arsenal Ladies at a film studio in London for ESPN television, to promote their coverage of the new WSL season. I had my walking boot on my left foot, but I took all the kit, boots and everything with me. I had my hair and make-up done and I got kitted up for the interviews and the pictures. I was upstairs, downstairs, all over the place. It was a pretty hectic schedule. But it was great to be involved, and quite exciting too.

We were then shown to another part of the studio where some action shots were to be taken. At this point my head was everywhere, with all the interviews and pictures and everything. I was also kitted up in my beloved Arsenal strip once again with my boots on, and that felt so good. So good that I completely forgot about my injury.

I started off by doing some headers, and then I was asked if I was OK to kick a ball. Without even thinking about it, I said yes. I think I was just so excited about being there and talking about the upcoming season, and being back at Arsenal. It sounds so stupid, looking back, but I just forgot that I had this injury, which of course was going to mean disaster for me.

The ball came to me, and I volleyed it first time with my left foot. I probably didn't volley it as well as I'd intended to because it hit the top of my foot. But immediately the discomfort I felt was severe. When I landed, I couldn't believe the pain I had in my ankle. I couldn't put any pressure on it at all. I certainly couldn't walk on it. So I just had to sit there, in pain again, shaking my head.

I guessed the pain would ease off. It didn't. I had to hop to the reception area and ask for some ice to calm it down. Everything now began to dawn on me. I started to feel sick inside and I started to fear that I had probably done something pretty bad.

I know my body, and this felt like I had made the injury worse. I had an appointment with the Arsenal physiotherapist later that day and I just told her everything. She was positive, which was good. She believed that I had irritated the original injury but nothing more. It sounded, at this stage, that I had had a lucky escape. She told me that the inflammation would start to ease within a week.

But I remained in a lot of discomfort for more than a week. I was on crutches. I rang Vic and told him what had happened at the ESPN shoot. He wasn't very happy with me.

I also felt that I needed another X-ray. So I had another one done. I asked the nurse if I could see the two X-rays together, and when she put them side by side I could tell immediately that the crack on the bone had developed into a big letter 'V'. The first X-ray showed little more than a slight crack in comparison.

This was very bad news. I immediately went back to the Arsenal training ground and saw the doctor. He wanted to get a second opinion because he was now unsure whether the bone would heal naturally by itself. So I went to see an ankle and foot surgeon. He studied the X-rays and advised me that if my aim was to get back to playing football as soon as possible – and it was – I should have surgery and have a plate put in. I said, 'OK, let's do it.' I had no choice. This year, 2012, could be the biggest year of my career. So I now have a three-inch plate in my left leg.

The prognosis was that, provided everything went according to plan with my recovery, I should be back in full training after a few months. That meant I would miss the first two months of the WSL, the FA Women's Cup and the Women's Champions League. This was a big blow, and incredibly frustrating: I had to miss out as the Gunners were dumped out of the latter competition, beaten 2–1 by FFC Frankfurt at Meadow Park and then 2–0 in the second leg; and just a couple of weeks later, in early May, Chelsea booted us out of the FA Cup, scoring two goals without reply. Only the week before we'd beaten them 3–1 in the WSL as well. Their goalkeeper Sarah Quantrill was in inspired form in that semi-final, denying Yanks, Alex and Jordan Nobbs a place on the scoresheet on a number of occasions. These were bitter pills to swallow, particularly in Europe, given the way I'd missed out on our last final appearance in that competition five years earlier by showing my middle finger to the crowd.

As far as England was concerned, the injury meant I wasn't selected for the two Euro 2013 qualifiers in mid-June, which was another big frustration for me. In the end, these matches against Holland and Slovenia just came too soon for me.

So, my next big target was the Olympics.

25

London 2012

WHEN I CONSIDERED MY IMMEDIATE FUTURE IN THE GAME, it seemed a realistic aim to be back playing for Arsenal before the WSL broke for six weeks at the beginning of July, and therefore in good time before Great Britain's women's team kicked off the Olympic Games in Cardiff, scheduled for Wednesday 25 July.

I accept it is touch and go. It will certainly be tight. But I think that if luck is on my side, it is achievable. If I can get a few games under my belt then everything becomes possible again. I just have to hope and pray that this is the case. But I admit: I don't do it easy, me!

I have beaten myself up enough about it all over the past few months, from forgetting that I was injured when I kicked that ball at the TV shoot to putting myself through all this agony again, and so on. I accept that I am the one who has put my chances of playing for Arsenal, England and Great Britain in jeopardy.

That is the order in which it all hit me. My initial thought was that I felt bad because I couldn't play for Arsenal. Then I started to think about England. Then I started to think about the Olympics. I only have myself to blame. I certainly can't blame anybody else. The fact is, I was stupid.

Thankfully my coping strategies are much stronger now than they were a few years ago. My personal journey has taught me how to accept whatever happens to me and understand what needs to happen for me to get back on track. I have set my targets and I am on schedule to achieve those targets. The rest of it I cannot control.

I am trying not to think too negatively about it all. I need to have a positive frame of mind and to send positive vibes out to my whole body that I am going to get there. I will certainly be doing everything possible to achieve that. That is the route I am going down. I don't even want to think about any disappointment or heartache. I won't allow myself to do that.

I am really looking forward to playing in the WSL. Reducing the number of teams in the top league from twelve down to eight – Arsenal, Birmingham, Bristol, Chelsea, Doncaster, Everton, Lincoln and Liverpool – has made it more elite. But it is still a semi-professional set-up. Most of the players still have to find part-time work elsewhere. None of the eight clubs are allowed to pay more than four of their players an annual salary of more than £20,000. This excludes the £16,000 per annum that the England international players receive under their central contracts from the Football Association.

Having said that, the first WSL season was successful, with decent media coverage too, and of course it was great that Arsenal won it.

The Arsenal side is a mix of youth and experience. It has

a lot of potential. We have still got some of the core players from our glory days – Faye White, Rachel Yankey and so on. I can now add Alex and me to that list too. That experience remains a big part of the Arsenal team; it's essential to have players who have gone through a lot and know how to win games. Our younger players will learn from us, and that will only help them and Arsenal going forward. I think that the mixture we have at the club at the moment is ideal. Looking ahead to the future, it could be great – again.

I haven't played in the WSL yet, so I can't comment too much about it. But I can see certain improvements in the league from the time when I used to play for Arsenal a few years ago, and certainly from my first time at the club. I am mainly talking about the standard of play, but to some extent also the attitude of the players involved.

Everybody is on their own individual training programme now, even if they are only training for a couple of nights per week with their club. At Arsenal, we still train together for just two nights a week, like we did when I was there before. But it does feel a much better set-up now all round, across the board.

Of course, Arsenal is a top club, so our facilities – everything from the kit upwards, really – have always been spot on. It's the other teams that have not been up to our standards. So the WSL is a long overdue step in the right direction for women's football in our country.

Sadly, that has not been reflected in the salaries for the players. It is not ideal money-wise for us, only enough for us to train on and to live on. I have to accept that I am not going to make a lot of money from women's football in

England. That has always been the case and, to be blunt about it, it is still no different. But it is better than it was.

Some of the non-league pitches that we have to play on are very poor. We are the elite players in our sport and we have to compete on hard and bobbly surfaces. This isn't good enough. We need better facilities to showcase our talent. Some of the changing rooms are small and dingy and that needs to change as well. It would be nice to think that the way forward could be for the WSL teams to have their own purpose-built stadiums with a 3,000 to 4,000 capacity.

I have noticed a shift in the national media coverage since Alex and I re-signed for Arsenal. Faye White and Ellen White featured in a piece on *Football Focus* with us, prior to the WSL starting up again. I was impressed with the comments made by Mark Lawrenson and Robbie Savage in the studio afterwards. They recognized the importance of the WSL and women's football at the Olympic Games and the opportunity for us to take the game on to another level on home soil should we be successful this summer. They mentioned my name too, which was nice.

Social media is also becoming a new way forward for women's football. Players can now reach out to fans without the need of newspapers, radio or television. The FA and the WSL have both recognized the growth in this area and they have tried to promote our game through it. Each of the eight WSL clubs now has two 'ambassadors' to promote the team and the sport through social media. Some players have their Twitter usernames on their sleeves to promote this initiative. My username is @kjs8eng.

ESPN show live coverage of WSL matches and they also

have a weekly highlights programme. This is healthy for the growth of our game. Any exposure is good, but professional, positive exposure is very good. As a player, it makes you feel like the WSL matters. Viewers can watch their team live or catch up with the highlights every week. This allows them to get an overview on which team is top and which team is bottom, and to see the best goals of the week and so on. They can now follow the league properly, as they would do in men's football.

It cannot be overstated how important television coverage is to the growth of our game. I mentioned earlier how some of us have become role models for young girls due to our performances for England at international tournaments that are being shown live on television. The same applies to the WSL. The greater audience, the greater impact.

However, a lot of people still say to me that they don't see enough women's football on television in the United Kingdom. They ask me why that is, and I am like, 'I don't know.' It seems to me that it has always been on the back burner rather than at the forefront of thinking in the world of television. Hopefully, that is slowly changing.

But when it comes to television, we have seen a big interest in the game followed by nothing a few times over the past decade or so. When England got to the final of Women's Euro 2009, for instance, we only got terrestrial coverage for our very last match, despite us doing well at the 2007 Women's World Cup two years earlier. So I can understand it when people say that they don't find it easy to follow what we are up to as a team sometimes, that they have to go searching for coverage of us here and there. On many occasions in the past they have been disappointed. On many occasions in the past, so have the players.

The BBC's coverage of women's football has been very good over the last decade. Gabby Logan really cares about the game, and having ex-professionals in the studio such as Martin Keown and, before that, Gavin Peacock has been very important. Sue Smith, who is still involved with England of course, has now become a name associated with television coverage too.

So it's excellent for women's football that the BBC are extensively screening the Olympic Games this summer. It's the biggest sporting event on earth, and 2012 is going to be the biggest Olympics yet. As British athletes, we are in a privileged position to represent our country at home. As footballers, both the men's and women's team are in a privileged position to be able to take part. It is many years since Great Britain has entered a men's team in the Olympics football tournament, and we have never entered a women's team.

It has been a long road for us to get to this stage. With England, Scotland, Wales and Northern Ireland all having separate football associations and competing as separate nations, in both FIFA and UEFA tournaments, there is no Great Britain team in the world of football. But, as hosts in 2012, Great Britain has received a special invitation to enter teams in both the men's and women's football events. We qualified, of course, for the 2008 Olympics in Beijing after finishing as one of the top European teams in the 2007 Women's World Cup. But, sadly, we weren't allowed to take part because GB competes in the Olympics, not England. So it's a real bonus for us that we now have this chance due to London staging the games.

I remember how ecstatic I felt when I thought that we were going to the 2008 Olympics. This was before the truth of the situation sank in. We were all buzzing, and then suddenly we weren't going. It was taken away from us and Sweden went to Beijing instead. I just wanted to bang my head against the wall in frustration. It was so disappointing at that time because we felt that we were there. It was a sad situation. Whatever the reasons, it's the athletes who lose out at times like that, and that feels wrong to me.

I always dreamed about playing in a Women's World Cup, because I could see that goal. But I never really fantasized about playing in the Olympics because we have never had a Great Britain women's football team. So it took a while for it all to sink in with me.

The Olympic Games women's football competition is the ultimate for the American players, even more so than the World Cup. That is how big they view the Olympics over there. It is the same across all sports. The Olympics is at the top of the ladder for any athlete. So, having lived in the States for so long, I heard about that a lot. To think that I now have an opportunity to take part myself is glorious.

It will seem a little strange for us to be wearing a Great Britain kit and not an England one. All of my international appearances have been with the Three Lions on the chest. I am now just eight caps behind Gill Coultard's women's record of 119 England caps. But I am still behind Yanks, and a few more of my team-mates have recently won their hundredth caps too, so setting records in that area isn't a priority for me. I don't think along those lines at all, actually.

I am, however, proud to be England's top goalscorer in women's football. And I am proud of each and every one of the forty-five goals I've notched up for my country. The two goals I scored against Japan in the 2007 World Cup are my favourites – just because they meant so much to me. Sir Bobby Charlton holds the record for the England men's team at forty-nine. But, again, I wouldn't hang on in there just to try and beat that. I just enjoy playing the game and doing what I do, and whatever happens, happens. I shall be content.

In agreement with the British Olympic Association, the (English) FA will select the GB teams. Hope Powell is the women's coach and Stuart Pearce is the men's coach. Apart from England, none of the other home football associations have been in favour of a Great Britain football team. Whether any players, male or female, from Scotland, Wales or Northern Ireland will be selected remains to be seen.

Either way, I think we have a good chance of doing well in the tournament, especially now that we know who we're facing. New Zealand in our opening game will no doubt be a tough proposition, but I think we'll get past them, and we should beat the Cameroon side as well, despite them being pretty much an unknown quantity. The England team has competed at the highest level in women's football over the past few years; we have held our own, and we should be confident of doing the same in a GB shirt. The big group game will be Brazil at Wembley – a mouth-watering prospect. I have never played against Brazil. They have truly amazing players in their ranks. If selected, it would be another dream come true for me to line up against those famous yellow shirts at Wembley.

All England's traditional big rivals will be there, with one exception – Germany. Due to their quarter-final defeat at the hands of Japan in the 2011 World Cup, the strongest team in our game over the past decade have not qualified to compete at London 2012. France and Sweden will take part. Both these countries reached the semi-finals in Germany last year.

I think it's a shame that Germany will not be here. They have always been there or thereabouts as a nation in women's football. They have been a consistent and dominant force in our sport for so long. They still are, make no mistake about that. I have always considered them to be the country to beat. They have always produced excellent players – big, strong competitors – and they continue to do so. Sometimes I wonder what they put in the water over there. Look at someone like Birgit Prinz in her prime! She has now retired, of course, but the success of the German women's team has always been about replacing one great player with another. They have a formidable production line. So I say again, it's a big loss for the competition. Then again, the competitive side of my nature has to admit that it does whet my appetite a little bit more. To lose one of the big nations before we even kick off in the summer is a big boost for all of us.

Without the Germans, I see the USA, Japan, Brazil, France and Sweden as our main rivals. These are five very strong, very capable teams. So going far in the competition is not going to be easy for us. But having strong home support behind us will help us enormously.

We should also not forget that in the 2011 World Cup we beat Japan, the winners of the tournament, and we led against France in the quarter-finals until a few minutes from time. We also beat the USA and Sweden in friendlies last year. So on our day we will fear nobody, and we shouldn't fear anybody either.

I expect both last year's World Cup finalists, Japan and the USA, to do well. I really rate Japan at the moment. The USA went over there recently and lost to them again, but the States always turn up for the big tournaments and they will be in the mix again. Brazil, just because they're Brazil, and for having Marta in their side, will be great to watch again and they have a big chance too.

I think France are the dark horses of the competition. I felt that we showed them too much respect in the Cyprus Cup earlier this year, but they are a very good side. A lot of their players are with Olympique Lyonnais, and, as we found with Arsenal a few years ago, that is a big plus. When players are together on a regular basis, playing at the highest level, it really does help and it can take a team to another level. Lyon currently rate as one of the best women's club teams in the world.

We have got to make sure that we get our mental attitude right. We need to use all our experiences in tournament football to Great Britain's advantage. We have got to go into the Olympics striving for gold. This is a once-in-a-lifetime opportunity for our nation. We know that. England got silver in Euro 2009 and we were bitterly disappointed with how everything ended up at the World Cup last year. So I think there will be that extra bit of hunger in the English players. I genuinely think that all of us have a good chance of standing on top of the podium in August.

It's a twelve-team competition so it will work in the same way as Euro 2009, with the top two teams and the two best third-placed teams qualifying for the quarter-finals from three groups of four.

We will play our first two group matches at the Millennium Stadium in Cardiff, and then move to Wembley Stadium for our final game before the knockout stages. That match against Brazil is on the evening of Tuesday 31 July, and I can't wait for it. Fingers crossed and all that. Old Trafford, home of Manchester United; St James' Park, home of Newcastle United; the Ricoh Arena, home of Coventry City; and Hampden Park in Glasgow will also host matches. These are big stadiums to play in, some of the very best in Great Britain.

But I would prefer it if all the matches were being played in and around London. That is how I would personally view the Olympics. London was awarded the Games, it is the host city, so I don't quite understand what those other cities have to do with London, to be honest. Obviously the idea is to spread the games around the country, so that's cool. Let's just wait and see if the attendances justify that decision. My personal opinion is that if the football was being held just in London, it would be better supported. It will certainly be a strange feeling to be competing in the London Olympics in a stadium in Cardiff. Having said that, I do see the bigger picture and it will be great to feel that we have the whole nation behind us.

Wembley, however, will host the final of the Olympic

women's football tournament on the evening of Thursday 9 August. That is the big one.

If I can just go back to when I was first starting out as a footballer, as a young girl, having to play in a boys' team just to get a game ... the thought then of representing my country in an Olympic football final at Wembley Stadium with the chance of winning a gold medal would have been a complete fantasy. There wasn't an Olympic football tournament for women for a start. But all these years later it is possible that it can now happen for me. It is so near that I can almost touch it.

As a fitting finale for a footballer, could there ever be anything better than winning a gold medal for Great Britain at the Olympic Games at Wembley Stadium? Whatever dreams that young girl in Garston had, she could never have made that one up.

Kelly Smith's England Career Statistics

Date	Home	Score	Away	Competition	Venue	Goals
01.11.95	England	1–1	Italy	Euro Qualifier	Sunderland	
19.11.95	England	5–0	Croatia	Euro Qualifier	Charlton	1
11.02.96	Portugal	0–5	England	Euro Qualifier	Benavente	
16.03.96	Italy	2–1	England	Euro Qualifier	Calabria	1
18.04.96	Croatia	0–2	England	Euro Qualifier	Osijek	1
19.05.96	England	3–0	Portugal	Euro Qualifier	Brentford	1
08.09.96	Spain	2–1	England	Euro Qual. (PO)	Montilla	
29.09.96	England	1–1	Spain	Euro Qual. (PO)	Tranmere	
27.02.97	England	4–6	Germany	Friendly	Preston	
09.03.97	England	6–0	Scotland	Friendly	Sheffield United	
23.04.97	Italy	2–0	England	Friendly	Turin	
09.05.97	USA	5–0	England	Friendly	San Jose	
11.05.97	USA	6–0	England	Friendly	Portland	
08.06.97	Norway	4–0	England	Friendly	Lillestrom	
08.03.98	England	0–1	Germany	WWC Qualifier	Millwall	
14.05.98	England	1–2	Norway	WWC Qualifier	Oldham	
23.05.98	Holland	2–1	England	WWC Qualifier	Waalwijk	
26.07.98	England	0–1	Sweden	Friendly	Dag & Red	
15.08.98	Norway	2–0	England	WWC Qualifier	Lillestrom	
20.02.00	England	2–0	Portugal	Euro Qualifier	Barnsley	
07.03.00	England	0–3	Norway	Euro Qualifier	Norwich	
04.06.00	Norway	8–0	England	Euro Qualifier	Moss	
30.10.00	Ukraine	1–2	England	Euro Qual. (PO)	Kiev	1

Date	Home	Score	Away	Competition	Venue	Goals
28.11.00	England	2–0	Ukraine	Euro Qual. (PO)	L. Orient	
22.03.01	England	4–2	Spain	Friendly	Luton	1
24.06.01	Russia	1–1	England	W. Euro 2001	Jena	
27.06.01	Sweden	4–0	England	W. Euro 2001	Jena	
30.06.01	Germany	3–0	England	W. Euro 2001	Jena	
23.08.01	England	0–3	Denmark	Friendly	Northampton	
27.09.01	Germany	3–1	England	WWC Qualifier	Kassel	
04.11.01	England	0–0	Holland	WWC Qualifier	Grimsby	
25.01.02	Sweden	5–0	England	Friendly	La Manga	
24.02.02	England	3–0	Portugal	WWC Qualifier	Portsmouth	2
23.03.02	Holland	1–4	England	WWC Qualifier	The Hague	1
03.09.03	England	1–0	Australia	Friendly	Burnley	
11.09.03	Germany	4–0	England	Friendly	Darmstadt	
21.10.03	Russia	2–2	England	Friendly	Moscow	
13.11.03	England	5–0	Scotland	Friendly	Preston	
19.02.04	England	2–0	Denmark	Friendly	Portsmouth	1
22.04.04	England	0–3	Nigeria	Friendly	Reading	
14.05.04	England	1–0	Iceland	Friendly	Peterborough	
06.05.05	England	1–0	Norway	Friendly	Barnsley	
26.05.05	England	4–1	Czech Rep.	Friendly	Walsall	1
05.06.05	England	3–2	Finland	W. Euro 2005	Man. City	
08.06.05	England	1–2	Denmark	W. Euro 2005	Blackburn	
11.06.05	England	0–1	Sweden	W. Euro 2005	Blackburn	
01.09.05	Austria	1–4	England	WWC Qualifier	Amstetten	1
27.10.05	Hungary	0–13	England	WWC Qualifier	Tapolca	3
17.11.05	Holland	0–1	England	WWC Qualifier	Zwolle	
09.02.06	Sweden	1–1	England	Friendly	Achna	
09.03.06	England	1–0	Iceland	Friendly	Norwich	
26.03.06	England	0–0	France	WWC Qualifier	Blackburn	
20.04.06	England	4–0	Austria	WWC Qualifier	Gillingham	
31.08.06	England	4–0	Holland	WWC Qualifier	Charlton	3
30.09.06	France	1–1	England	WWC Qualifier	Rennes	
25.10.06	Germany	5–1	England	Friendly	Aalen	
26.01.07	China	2–0	England	China Cup	Guangdong	
28.01.07	USA	1–1	England	China Cup	Guangdong	

Date	Home	Score	Away	Competition	Venue	Goals
30.01.07	Germany	0–0	England	China Cup	Guangdong	
08.03.07	England	6–0	Russia	Friendly	Milton Keynes	1
11.03.07	England	1–0	Scotland	Friendly	Wycombe	
14.03.07	England	0–1	Holland	Friendly	Swindon	
13.05.07	England	4–0	N. Ireland	Euro Qualifier	Gillingham	1
17.05.07	England	4–0	Iceland	Friendly	Southend	1
11.09.07	Japan	2–2	England	WWC 2007	Shanghai	2
14.09.07	Germany	0–0	England	WWC 2007	Shanghai	
17.09.07	Argentina	1–6	England	WWC 2007	Chengdu	2
22.09.07	USA	3–0	England	WWC 2007	Tianjin	
27.10.07	England	4–0	Belarus	Euro Qualifier	Walsall	1
25.11.07	England	1–0	Spain	Euro Qualifier	Shrewsbury	
12.02.08	Sweden	2–0	England	Friendly	Larnaca	
14.02.08	Norway	1–2	England	Friendly	Larnaca	1
06.03.08	N. Ireland	0–2	England	Euro Qualifier	Lurgan	
08.05.08	Belarus	1–6	England	Euro Qualifier	Minsk	
17.07.08	Germany	3–0	England	Friendly	Unterhaching	
28.09.08	Czech Rep.	1–5	England	Euro Qualifier	Prague	2
02.10.08	Spain	2–2	England	Euro Qualifier	Zamora	1
09.02.09	Finland	2–2	England	Friendly	Larnaca	1
11.02.09	Finland	1–4	England	Friendly	Larnaca	1
05.03.09	S. Africa	0–6	England	Cyprus Cup	Larnaca	1
07.03.09	France	2–2	England	Cyprus Cup	Larnaca	
12.03.09	Canada	1–3	England	Cyprus Cup	Larnaca	1
23.04.09	England	3–0	Norway	Friendly	Shrewsbury	
25.08.09	Italy	2–1	England	W. Euro 2009	Lahti	
28.08.09	Russia	2–3	England	W. Euro 2009	Helsinki	1
31.08.09	Sweden	1–1	England	W. Euro 2009	Turku	
03.09.09	Finland	2–3	England	W. Euro 2009	Turku	
06.09.09	Holland	1–2*	England	W. Euro 2009	Tampere	1
10.09.09	Germany	6–2	England	W. Euro 2009	Helsinki	1
01.03.10	Switzerland	2–2	England	Cyprus Cup	Larnaca	
03.03.10	Italy	2–3	England	Cyprus Cup	Larnaca	
01.04.10	England	1–0	Spain	WWC Qualifier	Millwall	

Date	Home	Score	Away	Competition	Venue	Goals
20.05.10	Malta	0–6	England	WWC Qualifier	Ta' Qali	1
19.06.10	Spain	2–2	England	WWC Qualifier	Aranda de D.	
21.08.10	Austria	0–4	England	WWC Qualifier	Krems	2
12.09.10	England	2–0	Switzerland	WWCQ (PO)	Shrewsbury	1
16.09.10	Switzerland	2–3	England	WWCQ (PO)	Wohlen	1
19.10.10	S. Korea	0–0	England	Peace Cup	Suwon	
21.10.10	N. Zealand	0–0	England	Peace Cup	Suwon	
02.03.11	Italy	2–0	England	Cyprus Cup	Larnaca	1
07.03.11	Canada	2–0	England	Cyprus Cup	Nicosia	
09.03.11	S. Korea	0–2	England	Cyprus Cup	Larnaca	
02.04.11	England	2–1	USA	Friendly	Leyton Orient	
17.05.11	England	2–0	Sweden	Friendly	Oxford	
27.06.11	Mexico	1–1	England	WWC 2011	Wolfsburg	
01.07.11	N. Zealand	1–2	England	WWC 2011	Dresden	
05.07.11	Japan	0–2	England	WWC 2011	Augsburg	
09.07.11	France	1–1**	England	WWC 2011	Leverkusen	
23.11.11	England	2–0	Serbia	Euro Qualifier	Doncaster	
28.02.12	Finland	1–3	England	Cyprus Cup	Larnaca	2
04.03.12	France	3–0	England	Cyprus Cup	Larnaca	

*AET
** England lost 4–3 on penalties
PO = play-off
WWC = Women's World Cup
W. Euro = Women's European Championship

Totals: Caps – 111   Goals – 45

Acknowledgements

To Mum and Dad: without your support, guidance and love I would not be where I am today or have achieved what I have. Thank you xx.

To Glen: thanks for being the best brother anyone can ask for.

To Alex: thanks for being there for me when times were hard, being patient and never giving up on me.

Also, thanks to: Beryl Smith, for supporting me, coming to all my England home games and for being there; Gavin Pugh, for travelling all over the world to watch me play – it means more than you'll ever know; Margaret Pearson, for following my career and taking me to football all those years ago when Dad couldn't make it; Lois Fidler, for helping me when I was struggling and always being there for me; Norman Burns, for being an amazing man, believing in me and making football fun; Peter Kay and James West at Sporting Chance clinic and Umbro, my boot sponsor.

In the USA, thanks to: Betty Ann Kempf, Robin Cunningham, Marie Wozniak, Charlie Naimo, Mark Krikorian, Tony Dicicco and Joe Cummings.

For *Footballer*, my thanks to: Lance Hardy, former women's football editor at BBC Sport, who worked on this project with me; Giles Elliott and all at Transworld, for publishing my story; Jonathan Harris, for securing the book deal; Lijana Sutich, for transcription of interviews; Daniel Balado-Lopez, copy editor; Glenn Lavery and David Barber at the Football Association for help with statistics.

And big thanks to: Hope Powell, for all the support and friendship you have given me and for helping me reach the highest levels on the playing field; Dr Pippa Bennett (aka Mama Doc), for looking after me for all these years on and off the field; Vic 'The Boss' Akers, for everything you have done for me; Arsenal FC, for leading the way in women's football and for allowing me to play for the best club team in England and our captain, Faye White, for being a true friend and room-mate on the national team for over a decade. We have had many a laugh and many a cry . . . Thank you!

Picture Acknowledgements

Every effort has been made to contact the copyright holders. We apologize for any omissions in this respect and will be pleased to make the appropriate acknowledgements in any future edition. All images have been supplied courtesy of the author unless otherwise stated.

Section one

Page 5: Kelly at Philadelphia Charge: © Sports Illustrated/ Getty Images; Kelly at Boston Breakers training: © The Boston Globe via Getty Images; page 7: scoring against Charlton Athletic: © Mike Egerton/EMPICS Sport/Press Association Images.

Section two

Page 9: playing at the European Championship 2005: © Matthew Ashton/EMPICS Sport/Press Association Images; pages 10–11: England training session: © Getty Images; celebrating a goal against Japan at the 2007 World Cup: © Eugene Hoshiko/AP/Press Association Images; pages 12–13:

celebrating a goal against Switzerland, playing against Sweden and the USA: all courtesy of the FA via Getty Images; scoring a penalty against France at the 2011 World Cup: © Frank Augstein/AP/Press Association Images; page 14: England team photo at the 2011 World Cup: © Federico Gambarini/DPA/Press Association Images; Kelly receiving her 100th Cap and Kelly with Hope Powell at training: both courtesy of the FA via Getty Images; page 16: at the draw for the London Olympics 2012: © Sean Dempsey/PA Wire/Press Association Images; promoting London 2012 outside Wembley Stadium: © Rebecca Naden/PA Wire/Press Association Images.

Index

Abily, Camille 225
Adams, Tony 12
Adriana 204
Akers, Vic 23, 24–5, 45–6, 99–101, 118, 119–20, 123–4, 165, 257, 261–2
Algarve Cup 103, 206
Aluko, Eniola 112, 126, 164, 179, 186, 187–8, 198, 205, 208, 212–13, 214, 222
Angerer, Nadine 198
Argentina
and Women's World Cup (2007) 138
Arsenal Ladies 23, 99, 115–24, 164, 242, 256, 256–7
2004/05 season 102
2006/07 season and trophies won 115–16
2011/12 season 264
attack-minded 122
domination of English football 119–22, 162
FA Women's Cup Final wins 119–20, 121
influence of Akers on success of 123–4
loss of players to America 164, 165
strength of team 122–3
win FA Women's Premier League (1996/7) 25
win FA Women's Premier League (2004/5) 102
win first WSL season (2011) 267–8
win UEFA Cup (2006/07) 115, 116–19

Arsenal (men's team) 12–13, 115
Asante, Anita 161, 164, 165–6, 167, 178, 193, 198, 208
Atlanta Beat 53, 63, 65
Austria
and 2007 World Cup qualification 126, 127

Bachmann, Ramona 205
Bardsley, Karen 164, 208
Barr, Amanda 74, 107
Bay Area CyberRays 53, 66
BBC 191, 196, 271
Beckham, David 57, 58, 172, 216
Behringer, Melanie 198, 200
Belarus 173–4
Bend It Like Beckham 71–2
Bennett, Pippa 93
Bermudez, Sonia 156, 204
Big East conference 38–9, 40
Bindon, Jenny 216
Bompastor, Sonia 156, 224
Boston 168
Boston Breakers 53, 161, 163, 166, 170–1, 252–3, 257
Bousefield, Dick 8, 9–10
Boxx, Shannon 139
Bracken, Kyran 147
Bradley, Sophie 208, 220, 225, 243
Brazil 273–4
Brooking, Sir Trevor 182
Brown, Rachel 97, 109, 125, 188, 205, 208

Burns, Jackie 15
Burns, Norman 15, 16, 21–2, 23
Bussaglia, Elise 227, 261
Byrne, Emma 101, 115, 118

Canning, Michelle 41
Carlisle, Duane 64
Carney, Karen (Kaz) 103, 107–8, 112,
    122, 134, 161, 164, 167, 174, 175,
    183–4, 193, 198, 200, 207, 211,
    214, 225, 230
Carolina Courage 53
Cassano, Christine 33, 34–5
Chapman, Herbert 24
Chapman, Katie 61, 98, 108, 112, 122,
    138, 165, 182, 186, 200, 206–7,
    243
Charlton, Sir Bobby 48, 273
Charlton Ladies 102, 119
    defeat by Arsenal Ladies in FA
        Women's Cup Final (2007) 121
Chastain, Brandi 49, 66
Chelsea Ladies 162, 264
Chicago Red Stars 164, 171
China Cup (2007) 130
Clarke, Jess 193, 206, 217
Clemence, Ray 15
Clemens, Mandy 55, 63
Coe, Lord Sebastian 3
Community Shield 115, 116
Copeland, Ted 21
Coultard, Gillian 21, 112, 272
Cristiane 156, 163
Crowson, Russ 12
Cyprus Cup
    (2009) 260
    (2011) 206
    (2012) 260–1
Czech Republic 174
    and Women's Euro 2007 qualification
        174–5

Daily Mail 94
Davis, Paul 12
Dawson, Matt 146
DeGale, James 147
Dein, David 117
Delie, Marie-Laure 224

Denmark
    and Women's Euro (2005) 108–9
Deville, Céline 225
Diacre, Corinne 74
DiCicco, Tony 49, 170, 233
Diguelman, Ludivine 129
Dixon, Lee 12
Doncaster Belles 21
Doskova, Katerina 174

Elizabeth II, Queen 149–50, 158
England women's football team
    and 4–3–3 formation 241–2
    analysis of games 243–4
    early struggle of on international stage
        49–50
    focus on defence by Powell 241–3
    impact of Powell on 184–5, 239–46
    improved performance of 62, 95
    maturing of 125
    refusal by FIFA to allow
        representation of GB in 2008
        Olympic Games 140, 271–2
    sixth in world ranking 237
    and training 96
    see also individual competitions
ESPN 269–70
Euro competition see Women's European
    Championship
Everton Ladies 162

FA Women's Cup Final
    (2002) 98
    (2006) 115, 119–20
    (2007) 121
    (2008) 120
FA Women's Premier League 17, 25, 38,
    102, 115
FA Women's Premier League Cup Final
    (2008) 121
Fair, Lorrie 55
Al-Fayed, Mohammed 60
Ferguson, Sir Alex 246
FFC Frankfurt 255
Fidler, Lois 3, 85–7, 93
Finland
    and Women's Euro (2005) 106–8, 109,
        113, 186

and Women's Euro (2009) 185–9
Fitschen, Doris 55, 64
Flack, Caroline 147
Fleeting, Julie 55, 115, 122
Fletcher, Jo 109
Football Association 16–17, 87, 93, 95, 114, 142, 160, 191
Football Focus 75, 269
Foran, Marybeth 34–5
Fox Soccer 171
France
  and Cyprus Cup (2012) 260–1
  and Olympic Games (2012) 275
  and Women's World Cup 2007 qualification 127–9
  and Women's World Cup (2011) 223–8
Francis Combe School 10
Frankham, Barry 9
Friday Night with Jonathan Ross 142–5
Fulham Ladies 60–1, 98

Gabbiadini, Melania 177
Garefrekes, Kerstin 137, 198, 199
Garston Boys Football Club 7–8, 9
Garvey, Debbie 15
Georges, Laura 225
Germany 62, 157, 274
  domination of women's football 76
  not playing in Olympics (2012) 274
  win Women's Euro (2005) 112
  win Women's Euro (2009) 195–202
  win Women's World Cup (2007) 132, 137–8, 140
  Women's Euro record 196
  and Women's World Cup (2011) 211, 221–2, 235
Gerrard, Steven 155
Giggs, Ryan 12–13
Gladiators 146–7
Gray, Ashley 94
Greater London League 16
Gregorius, Sarah 217
Grimsby Town 246
Grings, Inka 198, 201

Hamm, Mia 32, 48–9, 53, 233
Harvey, Laura 257

Haugenes, Margunn 61
Head, Graham 7–8
Healy, David 148
Henry, Thierry 58
Herdman, John 214
Herons FC 10
Holland
  and Women's Euro (2009) 191–5
Holmes, Kelly 146
Houghton, Steph 226, 262
Hungary
  and Women's World Cup 2007 qualification 126, 127

Italy 21, 22
  and Women's Euro (1997) 25–6
  and Women's Euro (2009) 177, 182

Japan 275
  and Women's World Cup (2007) 132–4
  win Women's World Cup (2011) 211, 214, 220–1, 235, 252
Jerray-Silver, Kim 61
Johansson, Lennart 114
Johnson, Lindsay 178, 186, 193
Jones, John 16, 22

Kaihori, Ayumi 220
Kaká 155
Kalmari, Laura 107, 186
Kay, Peter 92
Kelly Smith Money Box 65
Kempf, Betty Ann 19–20, 38, 41, 43–4, 46
Keown, Martin 24, 271
Klinsmann, Jürgen 48
Knudsen, Mariann 108
Krikorian, Mark 54, 64
Kulig, Kim 198, 201
Kurochkina, Olesya 178
Kutner, Steve 161, 163

Lattaf, Hoda 129
Laudehr, Simone 198
Lawrenson, Mark 269
Le Sommer, Eugénie 231
Lea Farm Junior School (Watford) 5, 7

Leeds United Ladies 119
  defeat by Arsenal Ladies in FA
    Women's Cup Final (2006)
    119–20
  defeat by Arsenal Ladies in FA
    Women's Cup Final (2008) 120
Lihong, Zhao 65
Lilly, Christine 139
Lindahl, Hedvig 110, 182
Lingor, Renate 137
Little, Kim 262
Ljungberg, Hanna 110
Logan, Gabby 271
Loughborough 3
Ludlow, Jayne 101, 115, 120

McDonald, Chris 28
McKee, Amy 33, 41
Major League Soccer 58, 172
Manchester United 13
Markgraf, Kate 43
Marta 118, 140, 156, 157, 158, 163,
    169, 236
Maruyama, Karina 235
Melis, Manon 194
Merson, Paul 12
Messi, Lionel 155
Mexico
  and Women's World Cup (2011)
    210–12
Mitts, Heather 55, 160, 161
Miyama, Aya 133, 135–6, 156, 211
Montoya, Albertin 156
Morace, Carolina 22, 26
Mowbray, Guy 129
Murphy, Danielle 97

Nagle, Stacey 41
National Collegiate Athletic Association 29
Nécib, Louisa 225
Neguel, Thérèse 215
Neid, Silvia 137
New England Revolution 172
New Jersey Lady Stallions 47
New Jersey Wildcats 1, 76–7
New York Power 53
New Zealand
  and Women's World Cup (2011) 211,
    213–17
Northern Ireland
  and Women's Euro (2009)
    qualification 173, 174
Norway 49, 60, 62
Notre Dame 39

Ocampo, Monica 211
O'Leary, David 12
Olympic Games
  (2008) 140
  (2012) 95, 222–7, 238, 266, 271
Olympique Lyonnais 223, 275
Owen, Mark 144

Panico, Patrizia 177
Pauw, Vera 193
Pavlou, Rachel 177
Peace Cup (2010) 205
Peacock, Gavin 112, 271
Pearce, Stuart 231, 273
Pedersen, Merete 109
Pelé 153–4
Pettersen, Marianne 61
Philadelphia Charge 53–4, 56–7, 63–5,
    70–1
Philadelphia Independence 171
Phillip, Mary 112, 129
Pichon, Marinette 64, 69–70, 74, 76–7,
    80–1
Pickering, Karen 147
Pieëte, Marlous 194
Pinner Park 15–16, 19
Pittsburgh 41
Powell, Hope 1, 22, 60, 62, 86, 93, 95,
    103, 113–14, 125–6, 173, 184–5,
    200, 212, 214, 230, 233, 237–50
Prinz, Birgit 76, 132, 137, 138, 155,
    156, 156–7, 158, 198, 199, 200,
    201, 211, 255, 274

Quantrill, Sarah 264
Question of Sport, A 145–6

Rafferty, Claire 226, 230, 231
Rantanen, Anna-Kaisa 107
Rasmussen, Johanna 109
Reckord, Meredith 33

referees 215
Rice, Pat 24
Riley, Paul 156
Robinson, Paul 13–14
Robson, Bobby 155
Rohlin, Charlotte 182
Ronaldo, Cristiano 155
Rooney, Wayne 215–16
Ross, Jonathan 143, 144–5
Russia
   and Women's Euro (2009) 178–80, 182

Sällström, Linda 188
Sameshina, Aya 253
San Diego Spirit 53, 56
Sanderson, Lianne 120, 164–5, 194
Sapowicz, Bérangère 223
Savage, Robbie 269
Sawa, Homare 236
Schelin, Lotta 182
Scott, Alex 112, 118, 123, 126, 161,
   164, 166–7, 186, 193, 208, 226–7,
   262
Scott, Dawn 240
Scott, Jill 138, 175, 178, 187, 194, 198,
   207, 208, 219, 225
Seton Hall Pirates 19–20, 26–44
Sinclair, Christine 163
Sissi 53–4
Sjölund, Annica 187
Sjöström, Anna 109
Sky Blue 165
Smisek, Sandra 137
Smith, Alan 12
Smith, Bernard (father) 5, 83–4, 153–4
Smith, Carol (mother) 5, 162
Smith, Glen (brother) 5, 11–12
Smith, Kelly
  Football Career
   breaking of leg and out of game
     (2012) 261–5, 266–7
   and coaching 259
   early comments on women's football
     in England 46, 96–7
   early Arsenal fan 12, 23
   Giggs as footballing role model 13
   injuries and out of the game during
     recovery 1–2, 63, 64, 65–9,

     70–1, 73, 77–8, 86, 94, 105,
     107, 126, 171, 216–17, 221,
     227, 228, 231, 253–4
   meeting of Pelé 153–4
   nominated for FIFA's World Player
     of the Year 152–5, 158
   offered assistant academy director
     job at Arsenal 100–1
   playing of football in early years
     and at school 6–12
   plays for Pinner Park 15–16, 19
   plays for Watford Ladies 14–15, 21,
     22
   plays for Wembley Ladies Reserves
     16
   scores first senior goal 21
   sendings off 216
   senior debut for Wembley Ladies
     21
   strengths and technical abilities 8,
     40, 64
  Arsenal Ladies 162, 169
   first FA Cup Final won (2006)
     119–20
   goals scored for 102, 120, 122
   initial signing for (1996) 23–5
   plays in number 8 shirt 101
   re-signs for after cancellation of
     WPS (2012) 256–7, 261
   re-signs for and first appearance
     (2005) 100, 102
   suspension and misses UEFA Cup
     final 116–18
  International Career 59, 74, 97
   first full England cap 21–2
   first goal scored for England 22
   first hat-trick scored 126
   first World Cup goal 134–5
   fitness programme 169
   goal celebration in 2007 World Cup
     134, 135, 136, 137
   goals scored for England 25, 60, 74,
     102, 126, 130, 138, 173, 179,
     194, 201, 204, 260, 273
   hair-pulling incident 110–11, 175–6
   hundredth cap 206
   influence and support of by Powell
     104, 239, 248–50

Smith, Kelly (*cont.*)
  injury during Women's World Cup
    (2011) 216–17, 221, 227, 228,
    231
  missing of Euro 2013 campaign
    matches due to ankle injury
    253–4
  plays for England whilst in America
    97–8
  return to England side after absence
    102–4
  statistics 279–83
  top goalscorer 273
  see also individual competitions
United States
  accolades won 39, 40–1, 43, 56
  assistant football coach at Seton
    Hall 46, 47–8
  broken leg caused by dirty tackle
    and slow recovery 1–2, 77–81
  departure from and return to
    England 83–4
  and folding of WUSA 75–6
  injuries suffered and out of the game
    during recovery 63, 64, 65–71,
    77–8, 86, 94, 171
  media attention and celebrity 40, 41–2
  named in the WUSA Global Eleven
    All Star Team 63
  plays for New Jersey Lady Stallions
    47
  plays for New Jersey Wildcats in W
    League 76–7
  retirement of number 6 shirt on
    departure from Seton Hall 41–2
  scholarship and playing for Seton
    Hall Pirates 19–20, 26–44
  second stint in, playing for Boston
    Breakers 160–4, 167–72, 253,
    258
  signs for Philadelphia Charge in new
    WUSA league and games played
    for 53–7, 63–5
  and suspension of WPS season
    (2012) 254–5
  training 64
  voted Star-Ledger Woman Athlete of
    the Week 38

Personal Life
  appearance on *A Question of Sport*
    145–6
  appearance on *Friday Night with
    Jonathan Ross* 142–5
  appearance on *Gladiators* 146–7
  awarded MBE and meeting of
    Queen 147–51, 158
  birth 5
  Daily Mail interview 94
  fearful of public speaking 43–4
  personal problems and recovery 4,
    80–94, 99, 150, 159, 249
  at school 10–11
  shyness and lack of confidence
    29–30, 30–1, 34, 43, 73, 91
  studies for BTEC National Diploma
    in Sports Science 18, 20, 26
Smith, Sue 112, 176, 271
social media 269
Sørensen, Cathrine Paaske 109
Soubeyrand, Sandrine 224
Spacey, Marieanne 22, 112
Spain 26, 174
  and Women's Euro 2007 qualification
    174
  and Women's Euro 2009 qualification
    175
  and Women's World Cup (2011) 204
Sporting Chance clinic (Liphook) 90–3,
    167
Sports Illustrated 54
Stone, Tom 65
Stoney, Casey 177, 178, 181, 208, 218
Sun Wen 53
Svensson, Victoria Sandell 182
Sweden 62
  and Women's Euro (2005) 109–11
  and Women's Euro (2009) 181–2
Switzerland
  and Women's World Cup 2011
    qualification 205

Take That 144
Terry, John 155
Thiney, Gaëtane 225
Torres, Fernando 154
Toseland, James 146

Tsybutovich, Ksenia 178
Tuttino, Alessia 177
Twitter 212–13, 269

UEFA 196
UEFA Cup (2006/07) 115, 116–19
Umbro 137
Umea 118
Undercoffer, Terry 19–20, 27
United States
  men's football 57–8
  women's football in *see* women's
    football (United States)
United States women's football team 275
  success of 58
  win Women's World Cup (1999) 48–9,
    52, 56
  and Women's World Cup (2007)
    139–40
  and Women's World Cup (2011) 235,
    252
Unitt, Rachel 61, 178, 181, 204, 208, 225

Valkonen, Sanna 107

W League 33, 76
Wahl, Grant 54
Walker, Karen 21, 22, 74, 112
Wambach, Abby 139, 156
Washington Freedom 53
Watford Football Festival 18–19
Watford Ladies 14–15
Webber, Saskia 55
Wembley Ladies 21
Wembley Ladies Reserves 16
Wenger, Arsène 24, 115
West Herts College (Watford) 18
West, James 92
Westwood, Emily 175
White, Ellen 206, 207, 208, 214, 220,
  222, 228, 243, 269
White, Faye 101, 108, 112, 116, 123,
  129, 137–8, 139, 157, 182, 186–7,
  190, 196, 198, 204, 207, 232, 234,
  243, 269
Williams, Fara 108, 112, 125, 126,
  138–9, 177, 186, 193, 200, 205,
  207, 218

Willow Foundation 146
Winterburn, Nigel 12
Women's Champions League (2010/11)
  223
Women's European Championship
  (Women's Euro)
  (1984) 196
  (1997) 25–6
  (2001) 60, 61–2
  (2005) (England) 1, 102–14, 126, 186,
    191
    attendances and television viewing
      figures 112
    Denmark group game 108–9
    Finland group game 106–8, 109,
      113, 186
    success of 105
    Sweden group game 109–11
    winning of by Germany 112
  (2009) (Finland) 95, 165, 173–202
    final against Germany 195–202
    Italy group game 177
    media interest and television
      coverage 191–2, 196, 197, 270
    qualification campaign 173–5
    quarter-final against Finland 185–9
    Russia group game 178–81
    semi-final against Holland 191–5
    Sweden group game 81–2
    Yankey's omission from squad
      176–7
  (2013) 238, 253–4
women's football (England) 46, 59
  brief period of professionalism 60–1
  creation of Women's Super League
    (WSL) 95, 163, 164, 256, 267,
    268–70
  growth and increased profile of 60,
    95, 114, 152, 160
  salaries for women footballers playing
    in WSL 268–9
  television coverage 191, 269–71
women's football (United States)
  creation of Women's United Soccer
    Association (WUSA) league 49,
    50–1, 52–3
  folding of WUSA (2003) 75–6, 255
  national camps 32–3

women's football (United States) (*cont.*)
  rise in popularity 48–9, 50
  setting up of Women's Professional
    Soccer (WPS) league 160–1,
    164–5
  suspension of WPS season (2012)
    254–5
  see also Smith, Kelly: United States
Women's Premier League *see* FA
  Women's Premier League
Women's Professional Soccer league
  (United States) *see* WPS
Women's Super League (England) *see*
  WSL
Women's United Soccer Association
  league (United States) *see* WUSA
Women's World Cup
  (1999) 32, 48–9, 49–50, 52, 56
  (2003) 74–5, 76
  (2007) (China) 95, 132–41, 157
    Argentina group match 138
    Germany group match 137–8, 157,
      183
    Japan group match 132–6
    preparation for 130–1
    qualification campaign 126–30, 193
    quarter-final against USA 139–40
  (2011) (Germany) 95, 113, 203–36
    attendances 236
    criticism of England's performance
      against Mexico 212
    Japan group match 220–1, 275
    Mexico group match 210–12
    New Zealand group match 213–17

    preparation for 206–7, 209–10
    qualification campaign 203–5
    quarter-final against France and
      penalty shoot-out 223–34, 251
    relaxation time 218–19
    squad for 207–9
    television and press coverage 223
    Twitter remarks against Aluko
      212–13
    winning of final by Japan against
      USA 252
Wood, Courtney 41
World Cup *see* Women's World Cup
Worrall, Phil 244
WPS (Women's Professional Soccer)
  league (United States) 160–1, 164–5,
  168–9, 170, 171, 184
  suspension and folding of (2012)
    254–5, 257
Wright, Ian 12, 24, 101, 147, 247
WSL (Women's Super League) (England)
  95, 163, 164, 256, 267, 268–70
WUSA (Women's United Soccer
  Association) league 2, 50–1, 52–3,
  168, 171
  folding of (2003) 75–6, 255
WUSA Global Eleven All Star Team 63

Xavi 155

Yankey, Rachel 60, 98, 108, 112, 122,
  176, 206, 207, 221

Zatopek, Emil 185

ABOUT THE AUTHOR

Kelly Smith was born on 29 October 1978. She played for Garston Boys Football Club before being prevented from playing in mixed teams, then for Watford Ladies, Pinner Park, Wembley Ladies and Arsenal Ladies. After being spotted by American scouts, she was offered a scholarship at Seton Hall University in New Jersey, where standout performances saw her number 6 shirt retired.

In 2001, Kelly became England's first ever women's professional footballer, and played for Philadelphia Charge in the WUSA before returning home to win every honour in the domestic game with Arsenal, including their sensational quadruple in 2007 when they became champions of Europe. Between 2005 and 2009, Kelly scored 100 goals in 112 games for the team she had always supported. After playing for Boston Breakers in the WPS, she returned to Arsenal in March 2012.

Kelly made her England debut just three days after her seventeenth birthday, and has gone on to score a record forty-five goals in more than a hundred appearances for her country. She helped England reach the final of the European Championships in 2009 and the quarterfinals of the World Cup in both 2007 and 2011, and was shortlisted for the

FIFA World Player of the Year four times. She was awarded an MBE in 2008.

Lance Hardy, who collaborated with Kelly Smith on this book, is an author, journalist and television producer who worked at BBC Sport for more than twenty years on programmes such as *Final Score, Football Focus* and *Match of the Day.* He also led coverage of two Women's World Cups, two Women's Euros and seven FA Women's Cup finals on BBC television. He received a special contribution to women's football award from the Football Association in 2008.

He has written two other books, including *Stokoe, Sunderland and '73,* shortlisted for Best Football Book at the 2010 British Sports Book Awards.